Processing Interclausal Relationships

Studies in the Production and Comprehension of Text

Processing Interclausal Relationships

Studies in the Production and Comprehension of Text

Edited by

Jean Costermans
Université Catholique de Louvain

Michel Fayol
Université de Bourgogne

LEA LAWRENCE ERLBAUM ASSOCIATES, PUBLISHERS
1997 Mahwah, New Jersey

Lawrence Erlbaum Associates, Inc., Publishers
10 Industrial Avenue
Mahwah, New Jersey 07430-2262

Cover design by Kristin L. Alfano

Library of Congress Cataloging-in-Publication data

Processing interclausal relationships: Studies in the production and comprehension
of text / J. Costermans & M. Fayol, eds.
p. cm.
Includes bibliographical references and indexes.
ISBN 0-8058-1846-4 (alk. paper). — ISBN 0-8058-1847-2 (pbk. alk. paper)
1. Grammar. Comparative and general—Clauses. 2. Grammar. Comparative
and general—Connectives. 3. Discourse analysis. 4. Comprehension. I. Costermans, J. (Jean) II. Fayol, Michel.
1947- .
P297. P76   1996   96-16776
415—dc20   CIP

Books published by Lawrence Erlbaum Associates are printed on acid-free paper, and
their bindings are chosen for strength and durability.

Printed in the United States of America
10 9 8 7 6 5 4 3 2 1

Contents

Preface

Since the mid-1980s, more and more linguistic and psycholinguistic research has been devoted to the study of discourse and written texts. A number of these deal with the markers that underline the connections and the breaks between clauses and sentences and with the use of these markers in the production and comprehension of oral and written material, by adults and by children.

It seemed to us that sufficient data of an interesting nature has been gathered, on both sides of the Atlantic Ocean, to justify the idea of bringing together some of the major observations and the main theoretical views in the field. The idea was not to publish original data for the exclusive attention of specialists, but rather to present an overview of observations and perspectives to bring this research to the attention of a wide range of linguists, psychologists, and speech therapists.

In the production of text or discourse, whether it is of a narrative, descriptive, or argumentative nature, one has to cope with several universal constraints. On the one hand, when the author introduces pieces of information that are new or supposedly new to the addressee, he or she has to ensure the continuity of the stream of discourse, that is to say, bring together these new pieces of information with the ones already known or given. The connection between old and new information is achieved through the use of linguistic markers varying from one language to another, but also from one developmental level to another. These markers are concerned with referencing processes and with the linking of predicates. They either work within the clauses (like word order) or between clauses (e.g., indefinite vs. definite determinants, anaphora, imperfective vs. perfective forms of the verb).

On the other hand, the linearity that characterizes oral as well as written language forces us to juxtapose information that is not necessarily closely linked in the multidimensional representation of the situation of reference (i.e., the mental model). In oral speech, the variations in the strength of these links may be translated by some modulations in the duration of pauses between linguistic segments of varied span (e.g., words, sentences, episodes). They may also be shown by the use of connectives that indicate the strength of the links between states or events described in adjacent segments and provide some information about their nature. Similar variations are observed in written language by the use of connectives as well as by the use of a specific paradigm, namely, punctuation. Connectives and punctuation marks simultaneously signal the boundaries of information blocks and their integration into hierarchically organized structures. Again, the differences between languages and the specificities of the various developmental levels must be considered.

vii

For realizing the referential and predicative continuity–discontinuity marking, as well as the segmentation–integration of the information flow, people need to make use of some system of markers that are more or less complex and, consequently, are more or less easy to acquire. They must perceive the corresponding notional distinctions, which are culturally bounded and may depend on specific areas of knowledge. They have to link the markers with what they are referring to in accordance with the specificity of each language, and take into account that these links may be dependent on the fields of knowledge and on the pragmatic conditions of the speech or text production.

After considering some aspects of the production processes, let us now devote some attention to comprehension. The comprehension of text or discourse may be viewed as the reconstruction of a mental model that wanders as little as possible from the one that the author had in mind. It bears on the addressee's previous conceptual and linguistic knowledge, on the procedures to which he or she resorts, and on the attentional resources at his or her disposal at the different processing stages. In this perspective, the markers of interclausal relations play a fundamental role. First, they demarcate linguistic segments of variable span, from clause to paragraph, at least. Second, they trigger some processes activating certain links with previous knowledge. Third, they induce a focalization of attention by inhibiting certain dimensions in favor of others (e.g., inhibiting some features of the surface form of an item in favor of its meaning). Finally, they contribute to the elaboration of a mental model by facilitating the conceptual setup between the states and events to which they refer.

The efficiency of the processing of the interclausal markers depends on their availability for the addressee, but also on the activation of the associated procedures and on the action of these procedures on the representations. The success of the comprehension process also requires the previous knowledge to be sufficient to allow the elaboration of the different representational levels and also demands relevant procedures to be activated. It finally assumes that attentional resources be sufficient so that the different treatments can go through without one of them being adversely affected.

In the chapters gathered in this book, these various facets are taken into account. The volume presents contributions from researchers mainly interested in adult language and others mainly concerned with developmental aspects. Some contributors deal mainly with production, and others deal with comprehension. Some work on oral discourse, and others are mainly concerned with written texts. To preserve overall coherence, however, the contributors were given four recommendations:

• The first recommendation concerned the level of linguistic analysis and asked the contributors to put the main emphasis on the clause level or, more in particular, on the relationships between clauses, even if this should not discard some interesting considerations about the way of linking sentences or even paragraphs.

• The second recommendation was to put special emphasis on the linguistic markers (such as connectives, markers of segmentation, and punctuation). The book should not primarily be devoted to discourse or text structure, but to how linguistic devices are used to process, signal, and detect that structure, as many authors do not seem to pay enough attention to the nature, function, and use of such devices.

• The third recommendation was to write the chapters so as to offer an overview of a given field of research. Although reporting current research is clearly desirable, much attention should be devoted to put this work in perspective, both with respect to the author's own research programs and with respect to the entire field.

• Finally, a fourth recommendation was especially addressed to contributors in the developmental field. They were asked to pay attention to the fact that an account of the acquisition of some language functions throughout childhood would be coherent with the present context only as far as it could be exploited to derive general principles of interclause relations that might be masked by the exclusive examination of adult evidence.

The 13 chapters gathered in this volume are divided into four parts. Part I presents two contributions very well suited to open the field by covering the use of a large range of linguistic markers that maintain discourse and text cohesion in adults and in children. Part II gathers five contributions on connectives, some of the main devices that secure the cohesion of discourse. Part III, in contrast, assembles three chapters devoted to some linguistic tools that allow for the expression of discontinuity, in particular, the punctuation marks and also some lexico–syntactic devices that hold similar functions in oral discourse. Finally, the three chapters of Part IV widen the subject beyond the cohesion–segmentation dichotomy and insert the problem into the broader field of text and discourse structuring.

No book, even dealing with as limited a field as the interclausal relations, could pretend to be exhaustive. It is obvious that the current volume does not escape form this rule. Two major themes remain unquestioned: the difficulties encountered during the production and the comprehension of cohesive devices, and the children's comprehension of such cohesive devices. Other aspects are barely mentioned; for example, the differential treatment of the diverse punctuation marks in comprehension, the individual variations in the implementation of different types of markers, or finally, and probably one of the most difficult questions to envisage, the problem of the relationships between the use of markers in production and their role in comprehension.

It goes without saying that these themes should be the concern of empirical and theoretical work in the coming years. The conceptions developed in the chapters of this book, the methods used, and the results described aim to provide the researchers with material for reconsidering many questions and for elaborating new research programs. In that perspective, this work has to be conceived as a step toward the scientific study of the comprehension and the production of interclausal markers. Our wish is that it would lead other researchers to develop this field of investigation.

ACKNOWLEDGMENT

We thank Dr. Yves Bestgen for his very efficient collaboration in preparing the present publication.

— Jean Costermans
— Michel Fayol

Part I

PROCESSING INTERCLAUSAL RELATIONSHIPS:
A MANY-SIDED TOPIC

Part I gathers two chapters, which, due to the complementarity of the topics encountered, give a general overview of the questions considered in this book and the way one can deal with them. Indeed, chapter 1 deals with comprehension by the adult and focuses on the linguistic cues and the previously acquired knowledge used by the subjects to elaborate a mental representation. In contrast, chapter 2 considers the children's oral production of narratives. Here, the authors evoke the relationships between the story plots and the cohesive devices, but also the constraints affecting the performance.

In chapter 1, Gernsbacher summarizes her model of the general processes implied in text comprehension: the Structure Building Framework. According to this model, comprehension aims at the elaboration of a coherent representation. This elaboration takes place by the setting up of foundations, followed by the development of the mental structures through mapping of the new information with the previous items. Depending on the coherence of the incoming information with the previously established items, either there is a follow up on the building of the ongoing structure or a new structure is initiated. The problem is to determine how the addressee knows whether a new piece of information can and must be put in relation with the one just processed. Two parameters determine the pairing: first, the previous knowledge of the world, which allows the interpretation of what remains implicit, and, second, some linguistic cues that operate as pairing instructions. A series of empirical data is reported illustrating how these two parameters intervene during the elaboration of different types of coherence: referential, temporal, situational, causal, and structural.

In chapter 2, Shapiro and Hudson develop a functional approach to the production of narratives by children. They wonder why canonical narratives are produced at a later stage of development. To account for the difficulties encountered, they consider that children are confronted with two tasks requir-

1

ing simultaneous treatment: to elaborate a coherent frame and to set up markers ensuring cohesion (e.g., use of subordinate clauses, pronouns, and conjunctions). This hypothesis predicts that, when the task demands become too important to manage both tasks, performance degrades. It also predicts that an alleviation of one of the tasks would lead to an improvement in the text quality. This hypothesis is tested in two experiments during which help is provided: for example, pictures facilitate the production management. The data confirms that this help induces a complexification of the story plots as well as a diversification and an increase in the use of cohesive devices. The authors conclude that the use of interclausal devices vary with the complexity of the frames and with the task demands.

 Chapter 1

Coherence Cues Mapping During Comprehension

Morton Ann Gernsbacher
University of Wisconsin-Madison

Language can be viewed as a specialized skill involving language-specific processes and language-specific mechanisms. Another position views language as drawing on general, cognitive processes and mechanisms—processes and mechanisms that underlie nonlinguistic tasks as well. Such a commonality might arise because language comprehension evolved from nonlinguistic cognitive skills (Bates, 1979; Lieberman, 1984), or because the mind is based on a common architecture, such as a connectionist architecture (Rumelhart & McClelland, 1986).

In my research, I have adopted the view that many of the processes and mechanisms involved in language comprehension are general cognitive processes and mechanisms. I have proposed a simple framework, the Structure Building Framework, that identifies a few of those general cognitive processes and mechanisms (Gernsbacher, 1991a, 1996, in press). According to the Structure Building Framework, the goal of comprehension is to build coherent mental representations or *structures*. At least three component processes are involved. First, comprehenders lay foundations for their mental structures. Next, comprehenders develop mental structures by mapping on new information when that information coheres or relates to previous information. However, when the incoming information is less coherent or related, comprehenders employ a different process: They shift and build a new substructure. Thus, most representations comprise several branching substructures.

The building blocks of these mental structures are memory nodes. Memory nodes are activated by incoming stimuli. Initial activation forms the foundation of mental structures. Once memory nodes are activated, they transmit processing signals to enhance (increase) or suppress (decrease or dampen) other nodes' activation. Thus, once memory nodes are activated, two mechanisms control their level of activation: suppression and enhancement. Memory nodes are enhanced

3

when the information they represent is necessary for further structure building; they are suppressed when the information they represent is no longer necessary. Previously, I have empirically explored the three processes involved in structure building: (a) laying a foundation (Carreiras, Gernsbacher, & Villa, 1995; Gernsbacher & Hargreaves, 1988, 1992; Gernsbacher, Hargreaves, & Beeman, 1989); (b) mapping information onto a foundation (Carreiras & Gernsbacher, 1992; Deaton & Gernsbacher, in press; Gernsbacher, 1991b; Gernsbacher, Goldsmith, & Robertson, 1992; Gernsbacher & Robertson, 1992, 1996b; Haenggi, Gernsbacher, & Bolliger, 1993; Haenggi, Kintsch, & Gernsbacher, 1995; Oakhill, Garnham, Gernsbacher, & Cain, 1992); and (c) shifting to build new substructures (Foertsch & Gernsbacher, 1994; Gernsbacher, 1985; Gernsbacher, Varner, & Faust, 1990).

I have also explored the two mechanisms that control these structure-building processes: suppression and enhancement (Faust & Gernsbacher, 1996; Gernsbacher, 1989, 1993; Gernsbacher & Faust, 1991a, 1991b, 1994; Gernsbacher & Jescheniak, 1995; Gernsbacher & Robertson, 1995; Gernsbacher & Shroyer, 1989). I have found that these general cognitive processes and mechanisms underlie many comprehension phenomena. I have also found that differences in the efficiency of these processes and mechanisms underlie differences in adult comprehension skill (Gernsbacher, 1993; Gernsbacher & Faust, 1991a, 1994; Gernsbacher & Robertson, 1995; Gernsbacher, Varner, & Faust, 1990) and adult written composition skill (Traxler & Gernsbacher, 1992, 1993, 1995).

This chapter focuses on one of the central processes of structure building involved in text and discourse comprehension—the cognitive process of mapping. According to the Structure Building Framework, once comprehenders have laid a foundation for their mental structures, they develop those structures using the cognitive process of mapping. I envision the cognitive process of mapping as similar to creating an object out of papier-mâché. Each strip of papier-mâché is attached to the developing object, augmenting it. Appendages can be built, layer by layer. Comprehenders build mental structures in a similar way. Each piece of incoming information can be mapped onto a developing structure to augment it, and new substructures (like appendages) are built in the same way.

What guides this mapping process? In this chapter, I suggest that comprehenders interpret various cues that the incoming information coheres with the previously comprehended information. Comprehenders interpret these cues as signals or *instructions* to map the incoming information onto the structure or substructure that they are currently developing. Comprehenders learn the cues of coherence through their experience with the world and their experience with language (Gernsbacher & Givón, 1995).

Some coherence cues are explicitly provided in the text or discourse; for instance, anaphoric pronouns such as *she* and the definite article *the* are provided in the text or discourse. Yet, even for coherence cues that are explicitly provided in the text or discourse, comprehenders must acquire knowledge of these cues to interpret them as signals of coherence. Other coherence cues are more implicit; they are not explicitly provided by the text or discourse, but they arise through what some researchers call *inferential processing*. To interpret these cues, comprehenders also rely on previously acquired knowledge; however, this knowledge is knowledge of the events and relations in the world. Thus, coherence cues lie along a continuum, ranging from cues that are provided explicitly in the text or discourse to cues that are only implicitly suggested by the text or discourse.

Applicable to the entire continuum of coherence cues is the proposal that interpreting coherence cues is knowledge-based, be it the knowledge of the roles that different linguistic devices play (e.g., that the pronoun *she* refers to an animate female) or the knowledge that different descriptions of real-world situations imply. In contrast to other models of text and discourse comprehension, the Structure Building Framework does not distinguish between the type of knowledge that comprehenders have acquired about language nor the type of knowledge that comprehenders have acquired about the real world that language describes. Thus, according to the Structure Building Framework, comprehenders use their previously acquired knowledge to interpret cues of coherence, and they use these coherence cues as signals to map the incoming information onto the structure or substructure that they are currently developing. In this way, coherence cues the process of mapping during comprehension.

But what is coherence? Dictionaries define coherence as consistency, continuity, or coordination. In text and discourse, I have identified five types of coherence: *referential coherence*, which is consistency in *who* or *what* is being discussed; *temporal coherence*, which is consistency in *when* the events that are being discussed occur; *locational coherence*, which is consistency in *where* these events occur; *causal coherence*, which is consistency in *why* these events occur; and *structural coherence*, which is consistency in the *form* in which events are described in the text or discourse. These five types are not independent; coherent information in text and discourse is typically characterized by all five—and sometimes more. According to the Structure Building Framework, each of these types of coherence should be cued by either implicit or explicit signals, and comprehenders' interpretation of the cues that signal each of these types of coherence should promote the cognitive process of mapping. The experiments I review in this chapter support these predictions. I begin by reviewing research that supports the prediction that comprehenders interpret cues that signal referential coherence as signals for mapping.

REFERENTIAL COHERENCE

Two utterances are considered referentially coherent if they refer to the same people, places, or things. So, one way to signal referential coherence is simply to repeat a word or phrase, for instance, the repeated word, *beer*, in the following two sentences: *We got some beer out of the trunk. The beer was warm.* These two sentences seem referentially coherent because they refer to the same concept: *the beer from the trunk, which was* (unfortunately) *warm.* However, simply repeating a word does not ensure referential coherence; the word must refer to the same concept. These two sentences both contain the word *beer*, *We got some beer out of the trunk. John was especially fond of beer*; yet, the beer referred to in the second sentence is not necessarily the same as the beer introduced in the first sentence.

According to the Structure Building Framework, comprehenders interpret coherence cues as signals to map the incoming information onto the structure or substructure that they are currently developing. If comprehenders interpret repeated reference as a signal of referential coherence, then comprehenders should map sentences that contain repeated references onto their representation of sentences that contain previous references. And indeed, the sentence, *The beer was warm*, is read considerably faster when it follows the sentence, *We got some beer out of the trunk*, than when it follows the sentence, *We checked the picnic supplies* (Haviland & Clark, 1974), suggesting that comprehenders interpret repeated reference as a signal of referential coherence.

Referential coherence is also signaled in English by the definite article, *the*. Consider the following two sentences: *A psycholinguist was writing a chapter. The psycholinguist was trying to think of examples.* The use of the definite article, *the*, in the second sentence suggests that the psycholinguist who was writing a chapter was also the psycholinguist who was trying to think of examples. In contrast, consider the following two sentences: *A scholar was reading a chapter about coherence. A scholar could think only about how hungry he was.* In these two sentences, it is unclear whether the scholar who was reading a chapter was also the scholar who was getting hungry. However, if the definite article, *the*, replaces the indefinite article, *a*, in the second sentence, *A scholar was reading a chapter about coherence. The scholar could think only about how hungry he was*, this unfortunate situation is more apparent. Indeed, the definite article, *the*, can signal co-reference even when the noun it modifies is only a synonym of the previously mentioned noun, for instance, *A scholar was reading a chapter about coherence. The litterateur put down the book and went to the kitchen to fix dinner.* These examples illustrate how the English definite article, *the*, can signal co-reference.

According to the Structure Building Framework, comprehenders interpret coherence cues as signals to map the incoming information onto the structure or substructure that they are currently developing. If comprehenders interpret the English definite article, *the*, as a signal of referential coherence, then comprehenders should map sentences that contain the definite article, *the*, onto their developing representations. A pioneering experiment by de Villiers (1974) suggested that comprehenders do interpret the definite article, *the*, as a cue for mapping. In de Villiers' experiments, two groups of subjects heard the same set of 17 sentences. For one group, all the sentences occurred with only indefinite articles; for example, *A store contained a row of cages. A man bought a dog. A child wanted an animal. A father drove to his house. A cottage stood near a park.* For the other group of subjects, the same sentences occurred, but in this condition the indefinite articles were replaced with definite articles; for example, *The man bought the dog. The child wanted the animal. The father drove to his house.* When the sentences were presented with indefinite articles, subjects were more likely to interpret them as independent sentences that referred to multiple people and unconnected events. In contrast, when the sentences were presented with definite articles, subjects were more likely to interpret them as forming a coherent narrative in which the same persons and events were referred to repeatedly. *The man bought a dog at the store. He drove home and gave the dog to his son, who was delighted.*

Recently, Robertson and I (Gernsbacher & Robertson, 1996) conducted two experiments to demonstrate that the phenomenon originally observed by de Villiers generalized to more than one set of experimental sentences. More importantly, the goal was also to demonstrate that comprehenders interpret the definite article, *the*, as a cue of referential coherence while they are building their mental structures. Ten different sets of sentences were constructed. Each set contained 14, 15, 16, or 17 sentences. These sentences were presented to two different subject groups. One group of subjects read all the sentences with indefinite articles, and the other group of subjects read the sentences with definite articles.

For example, one group of subjects read: *Some siblings were happy to be together. A road was icy and slick. A family stopped to rest. A cafe was almost deserted. A waitress took an order. A driver left to get gas. A man slipped and fell in a parking lot. A sister watched through a window. A gas station was nearby. An attendant rushed out of a building. A stranger helped a brother. A man walked slowly. A group stayed for a night. A trip was postponed.* The other group of subjects read: *The siblings were happy to be together. The road was icy and slick. The family stopped to rest. The cafe was almost deserted. The waitress took the order. The driver left to get gas. The man slipped and fell in the parking lot. The sister watched through the window. The gas station was nearby. The attendant rushed out of the building. The stranger helped the brother. The man walked slowly. The group stayed for the night. The trip was postponed.*

The length of time subjects needed to read each sentence was measured. If the definite article, *the*, is interpreted as a cue for mapping, then subjects who read the sentences with the definite articles should have read those sentences more rapidly than subjects who read the sentences with indefinite articles, which is exactly what was observed (i.e., a 23% benefit in average sentence reading time). Furthermore, the subjects who read the sentences with the definite articles recalled those sentences in a more integrative way, often combining two or more sentences into one, and they were more likely to use pronouns. These results suggest that subjects who read the sentences with the definite articles were more likely to map the sentences of each set together. In our second experiment, we tested this hypothesis more directly.

We again presented 10 sets of sentences to two groups of subjects. We again manipulated whether the sentences were presented with definite versus indefinite articles, and we again measured subjects' reading times to the sentences. However, in lieu of asking subjects to recall what they remembered after reading each set of sentences, McKoon and Ratcliff's (1980) priming-in-item verification task was used: Each time subjects read two sets of sentences, they performed a timed recognition task. Thirty-two test sentences were presented; half were old and half were new. Unknown to the subjects, the test list was arranged in such a way that each "old" sentence was preceded in the test list by either an "old" sentence that was from the same set of sentences or an "old" sentence that was from a different set. For example, for half the subjects, the sentence *The sister watched through the window* was preceded in the test by the sentence *The man slipped and fell in the parking lot.* These two sentences are from the same original set. For the other half of the subjects, the same sentence was preceded in the test list by a sentence from a different set. We predicted that subjects who read the sentences with the definite articles would be more likely to map the sentences of each set together. If so, then they should recognize an "old" sentence more rapidly when it was preceded by a sentence from the same set of sentences than when it was preceded by a sentence from a different set of sentences. And indeed, that is what we found.

Another potential cue of referential coherence in English is pronominal anaphora. For example, in the sentence *The aunt ate the pie, and she was senile*, the pronoun *she* in the second clause indicates that the two clauses refer to the same person; the person who was senile was the same as the person who ate the pie. In contrast, the sentence *The aunt ate the pie, and Alice was senile* suggests two different referents; the person who was senile was probably not the same as the person who ate the pie (unless the pie-eating, senile aunt is named Alice). Thus, when the second clause contains a pronoun, these two clauses are more referentially coherent.

According to the Structure Building Framework, comprehenders interpret coherence cues as signals to map the incoming information onto the structure or substructure that they are currently developing. If comprehenders interpret pronominal anaphora as a cue for referential coherence, then comprehenders should map clauses containing pronouns onto their mental structures that represent the referents of those sentences. And, indeed, comprehenders remember more sentences in their entirety when the second clause contains a pronoun, as in *The aunt ate the pie, and she was senile*, than when the second clause introduces a new referent, as in *The aunt ate the pie, and Alice was senile*. Comprehenders also recall more words of the sentences when the second clause contains a pronoun (Foertsch & Gernsbacher, 1994; Lesgold, 1972). Both results suggest that comprehenders interpret pronominal anaphora as a signal for mapping.

Comprehenders' interpretation of anaphora as a cue for referential coherence and therefore as a signal for mapping is knowledge-driven. In Gernsbacher (1991b), I demonstrated that this knowledge extends beyond simply knowing that the pronoun *she* most likely refers to a singular female. I discovered that after subjects read the sentence *I need a plate*, they more rapidly read the sentence *Where do you keep them?* than the sentence *Where do you keep it?* In contrast, after subjects read the sentence *I need an iron*, they more rapidly read the sentence *Where do you keep it?* than the sentence *Where do you keep them?* Thus, comprehenders' knowledge that plates usually come in sets, whereas irons do not, and that if a person has a plate, he is likely to have at least a few, whereas if a person has an iron, he is likely to have only one, guides comprehenders' interpretation of pronouns. Note that in these instances the anaphor (e.g., *them*) can mismatch its literal antecedent in number (e.g., *a plate*); the crucial match is between the number of the conceptual referent (e.g., *plates in general*). These sentences illustrate a phenomenon I call *conceptual anaphora*.

In Gernsbacher (1991b), I identified three categories of conceptual referents (i.e., referents that might literally be singular but are more easily referred to with plural pronouns than singular pronouns). These conceptual referents included (a) frequently or multiply occurring items and events (e.g., *a plate, a birthday, an exam*) as opposed to infrequently or singularly occurring items and events (e.g., *an iron, a 40th birthday, a final exam*); (b) generic items (e.g., *a Sony walkman, a pet, a vacation*) as opposed to specific tokens (e.g., *my roommate's Sony walkman, my childhood pet, the vacation I took last winter*); and (c) collective sets (e.g., *the team, the phone company, the class*) as opposed to individual entities (e.g., *the players on the team, the people who work at the phone company, the students in the class).* My European collaborators and I also demonstrated that conceptual anaphora are just as natural in British English and Spanish as they are in American English. Indeed, the phenomenon commutes to the verb in pro-drop languages, such as Spanish (Carreiras & Gernsbacher, 1992; Oakhill et al., 1992). Thus, interpreting anaphora as a cue for referential coherence is knowledge-based.

Referential coherence is crucial, but consistently referring to a previously mentioned concept does not guarantee that communication will be lucid. Consider the following passage, from Johnson-Laird (1983): *"My daughter works in a library in London. London is the home of a good museum of natural history. The museum is organized on the basis of cladistic theory. This theory concerns the classification of living things. Living things evolved from inanimate matter"* (p. 379). Each sentence in this passage consistently refers to a concept that was introduced in its preceding sentence. However, the passage seems disjointed. There must be other sources of coherence.

TEMPORAL COHERENCE

We communicate about actions, ideas, and events that occur, have occurred, or will occur during a certain time frame. Temporally coherent events occur during the *same* time frame. One simple cue of temporal coherence is consistency in the tense or aspect of the verbs within the sentences of a text or discourse. For example, these sentences share a common tense and aspect: *The siblings were happy to be together. The road was icy and slick. The family stopped to rest. The cafe was almost deserted. The waitress took the order. The driver left to get gas.* In contrast, these sentences differ in their tense and aspect: *The siblings are happy to be together. The road will be icy and slick. The family used to stop to rest. The cafe was almost deserted. The waitress had been taking the order. The driver will leave to get gas.* The first set of sentences seems more temporally coherent than does the second set.

Temporal coherence can also be cued by adverbial phrases. For example, if I were describing the events that occurred while I was running a marathon, I might say: *I arrived at the start line at 7:45 a.m. The marathon was scheduled to begin at 8:00. As I nervously awaited the start, I talked with the other runners. I also stretched a bit and tried very hard to relax. At 8 o'clock sharp the starter fired his pistol.* If I continued my narrative by saying *Half an hour later it began to rain,* the adverbial phrase, *half an hour later,* establishes the time that it began to rain at 8:30, a time during which I most likely was still running in the marathon. Thus, the sentence, *Half an hour later it began to rain,* coheres with the previous sentences. In contrast, if I continued my narrative by saying *Three days later it began to rain*, the adverbial phrase, *three days later*, suggests that the event (the rain) occurred while I was not still running the marathon (as even I do not run that slowly). Rather the adverbial phrase, *three days later*, suggests that I am now describing an event (the rain) that occurred during a different time frame. Thus, the sentence, *Three days later it began to rain*, is less temporally coherent with the previous sentences.

According to the Structure Building Framework, comprehenders interpret coherence cues as signals to map the incoming information onto the structure or substructure that they are currently developing. If comprehenders interpret adverbial phrases as cues for temporal coherence, then comprehenders should be more inclined to map sentences onto their developing mental structures when those sentences contain temporal adverbs that cohere with the previously suggested time frame than when those sentences contain temporal adverbs that do not cohere with the previously suggested time frame. Anderson, Garrod, and Sanford (1983) demonstrated that comprehenders do use their previously acquired knowledge of the typical duration of events to interpret cues of temporal coherence.

Anderson et al. (1983) collected subjects' estimates of the typical time frames for 20 common events. For example, the typical time frame for changing a baby is 30 seconds to 15 minutes, the typical time frame for eating a meal in a restaurant is 30 minutes to 3 hours, the typical time frame for attending a party is 1 hour to 5 hours, and the typical time frame for taking a vacation is 3 days to 4 weeks. After collecting these estimates of the typical time frames for common events, Anderson et al. (1983) presented narratives that were titled to indicate a particular event, for example, "Eating a Meal at a Restaurant." Following a sentence such as *John sat down at the restaurant table*, subjects read a sentence that began with an adverbial phrase that indicated a time period within the typical duration of the titled event, *Five minutes later, a waiter approached*, or subjects read a sentence that began with an adverbial phrase that indicated a time period that was beyond the typical duration of the titled event, *Five hours later, a waiter approached*. Anderson et al. (1983) observed that sentences were read considerably more rapidly when they began with adverbial phrases that indicated a time period within the typical time frame of the titled event (e.g., *five minutes later*, for the restaurant narrative) than sentences that began with adverbial phrases that indicated a time period outside the typical time frame of the titled event (e.g., *five hours later*). These data suggest that comprehenders use their previously acquired knowledge of the typical duration of events to interpret cues of temporal coherence, and that comprehenders use cues of temporal coherence, such as adverbial phrases, as signals to map the incoming information onto the structure or substructure that they are currently developing.

LOCATIONAL COHERENCE

Another type of coherence in text and discourse is locational coherence. The actions, ideas, and events about which we communicate typically occur, have occurred, or will occur at a certain location. Locationally coherent events occur at the *same* place. For example, if I were describing an impromptu meeting I had with a colleague, I might say: *Pat and I were standing in the hallway near my office. We were enthusiastically discussing a new set of data.* I might continue my description with a sentence such as, In *a nearby office, people had difficulty concentrating.* The adverbial phrase, *in a nearby office*, maintains the location established in the first two sentences. It signals that the sentence coheres with my two previous sentences. In contrast, if I would have said, In *a nearby town, people had difficulty concentrating,* the adverbial phrase, *in a nearby town*, changes the location of my narrative (and requires a new explanation as even I do not talk that loudly). Because the adverbial phrase, *in a nearby office*, maintains the previously established location, whereas the adverbial phrase, *in a nearby town*, changes the previously established location, the sentence containing the adverbial phrase, *in a nearby office*, is more locationally coherent.

A more subtle cue of locational coherence is consistency in narrative point of view. The narrative point of view is where the narrator would be located (if he or she were physically present) with relation to the other referents. For example, the verb, *came*, in the clause, *John came into the living room*, implies that the narrator is located inside the living room. In contrast, the verb, *went*, in the clause, *John went into the living room*, implies that the narrator is located outside the living room. According to the Structure Building Framework, comprehenders interpret coherence cues as signals to map the incoming information onto the structure or substructure that they are currently developing. If comprehenders interpret narrative point of view as a cue for locational coherence, then comprehenders should be more likely to map sentences onto their mental structures when those sentences contain verbs that preserve a previously established narrative point of view than when those sentences contain verbs that alter a previously established narrative point of view.

Black, Turner, and Bower (1979) demonstrated that comprehenders do interpret narrative point of view as a cue for mapping. After reading the sentence, *Bill was sitting in the living room reading the evening paper*, which establishes the narrative point of view inside the living room, subjects read the sentence, *Before Bill had finished the paper, John came into the room*, more rapidly than they read the sentence, *Before Bill had finished the paper, John went into the room*.

Recently, Dieter Haenggi, Caroline Bolliger, and I (Haenggi et al., 1993) demonstrated comprehenders can infer the location of a protagonist in a narrative, and comprehenders use that inferred knowledge as a cue for mapping.

The subjects in our experiments read narratives that only implied a protagonist's location; the narratives never explicitly stated the protagonist's location. For example, the following narrative implied a jogger's location on a jogging course: *Carol enjoyed jogging to keep in shape, but lately she hadn't been able to jog very much because she'd been so busy. On Sunday, she decided to try to jog around a new 5-mile course. It was a loop course, meaning that it was one big circle. She hoped she'd be able to make it the whole 5 miles around the course. After she had jogged 1 mile, she still felt okay. But after she had jogged 2 miles, she wished she was in better shape. Still, she thought she could make it all the way around the 5-mile loop. After Carol finished the third mile, her legs really began to ache. And after she had jogged 4¾ miles she was truly exhausted.*

After reading each narrative, subjects read a sentence that was either congruent with the protagonist's implied location or a sentence that was incongruent with the protagonist's implied location. For example, this sentence is congruent with Carol, the jogger's, location: *Although she was so close to where she wanted to finish, she had to walk the rest of the way.* In contrast, this sentence is incongruent with Carol, the jogger's, location: *Although she was so far away from where she wanted to finish, she had to walk the rest of the way.*

These same two sentences were incongruent versus congruent for a different narrative, which was the following: *Julie loved to cycle and today she decided to bike along a nearby river. Along the river was a great 25-mile bike path. The entire 25-mile path was well-paved and conveniently marked off after every 5 miles. After Julie had ridden 5 miles, the path got steeper and she needed to pedal harder. After riding 10 miles, Julie felt the path flatten. She even passed a few other bikers. But after riding 15 miles, Julie heard the chain on her bike snap. She got off of her bike and inspected the chain.* Thus, for this narrative, the sentence, *Although she was so close to where she wanted to finish, she had to walk the rest of the way* is incongruent, whereas the sentence, *Although she was so far away from where she wanted to finish, she had to walk the rest of the way* is congruent. We found that sentences that were congruent with the implied location of the protagonist were read almost twice as fast as sentences that were incongruent with the implied location of the protagonist. These data suggest that comprehenders use their previously acquired knowledge of the spatial relations in the world to interpret cues of locational coherence, and comprehenders map locationally coherent information onto the structure or substructure that they are currently developing.

CAUSAL COHERENCE

I have suggested that coherent text and discourse is characterized by referential coherence (i.e., the same persons, places, or things are referred to), temporal coherence (i.e., the time frame stays the same), and locational coherence (i.e., the location stays the same). But referential, temporal, and locational coherence are not the only types of coherence.

Consider the following set of sentences: *Brian punched George; George called the doctor; The doctor arrived.* Now, consider the following set of sentences: Brian punched George; George liked the doctor; The doctor arrived. The two sets of sentences are equal in their referential coherence as both sets repeat a reference to *George* and to *the doctor.* The two sets of sentences are equal in their temporal coherence. And the two sets are equal in their locational coherence. Nevertheless, the first set of sentences seems more coherent than the second. Because only the verbs in the middle sentences distinguish these two sets of sentences, it must be something about *George calling the doctor* versus *George liking the doctor* that makes the first set more coherent. *George calling the doctor* is a more likely cause for why *The doctor arrived* than is *George liking the doctor.* These sentences demonstrate the role of causal coherence—consistency in why events or actions occurred. The more causally coherent two sentences are, the more likely the action described by the first sentence caused the action described by the second sentence.

According to the Structure Building Framework, comprehenders interpret coherence cues as signals to map the incoming information onto the structure or substructure that they are currently developing. If comprehenders interpret causal consequences as a cue for coherence, then comprehenders should be more likely to map sentences onto their mental structures when those sentences describe a causally logical outcome than when those sentences do not describe a causally logical outcome. Haberlandt and Bihgman (1978) provided data that support this prediction. Subjects read sentences like *The doctor arrived* more rapidly when they followed sentences like *George called the doctor* than when they followed sentences like *George liked the doctor.*

Comprehenders interpret and use even finer gradations of causal coherence as a cue for mapping. Consider the following four context sentences: *(a) Joey went to a neighbor's house to play. (b) Joey's mother became furiously angry with him. (c) Racing down the hill, Joey fell off his bike. (d) Joey's big brother punched him again and again.* Now, consider the following consequence sentence: *The next day, Joey's body was covered in bruises.* The four context sentences vary in how likely they are to cause that consequence. The most likely cause is that *Joey's big brother punched him again and again,* and the least likely cause is that *Joey went to a neighbor's house to play.* Keenan, Baillet, and Brown (1984) observed that the more likely the context sentences was to cause the consequence, the faster the consequence sentences was read. The data, therefore, demonstrate that comprehenders interpret causal coherence as a cue for mapping.

Recently, Jennifer Deaton and I (Deaton & Gernsbacher, in press) demonstrated that comprehenders interpret the conjunction, *because*, as a cue for mapping. In three experiments, we demonstrated that two-clause sentences that described moderately causal events were read more rapidly when the two clauses were conjoined by *because* (*Susan called the doctor for help* because *the baby cried in his playpen*) than when they were conjoined by *and* (*Susan called the doctor for help and the baby cried in his playpen*), *then* (*Susan called the doctor for help then the baby cried in his playpen*), or *after* (*Susan called the doctor for help after the baby cried in his playpen*). In addition, when the clauses were conjoined by *because*, subjects recalled the second clauses more frequently when prompted with the first clauses. In two further experiments, we demonstrated that the facilitative effect of *because* depends on the clauses' causal relatedness. Unrelated clauses were read least rapidly and recalled least frequently, regardless of their conjunctions; as the clauses' causal relatedness increased, the second clauses of sentences conjoined by *because* were read more rapidly and recalled more frequently. We concluded that comprehenders use the conjunction, *because*, and their knowledge about causality as cues for mapping.

My colleagues and I have demonstrated that comprehenders use their knowledge about the emotional consequences of events as a cue for mapping. Subjects in our experiments read stories that explicitly stated only concrete actions but implied emotional consequences. For example, one narrative stated that the protagonist stole money from a store where his best friend worked and later learned that his friend had been fired. Following each narrative, subjects read a target sentence that contained an emotion word, which either matched the emotional state implied by the narrative (*guilt*) or mismatched that emotional state. In Gernsbacher, Goldsmith, and Robertson (1992), the nature of the mismatch was manipulated. Across three experiments, subjects read target sentences that contained matching emotion words at approximately the same rate; in contrast, and, as predicted, the more disparate the mismatching emotion words were to the implied emotional states, the more slowly subjects read the target sentences containing those mismatching emotion words. When the mismatching emotion words were the same affective valence as the implied emotions (*guilt* vs. *shyness*), subjects read the target sentences slowly; when the mismatching emotion words were the opposite affective valence of the implied emotions (*guilt* vs. *hope*), subjects read the target sentences even more slowly; and when the mismatching emotion words were the converses of the implied emotions (*guilt* vs. *pride*), subjects read the target sentences most slowly (40% more slowly than they read target sentences containing matching emotion words).

To demonstrate that the stories—without the target sentences—were indeed powerful sources of knowledge activation, subjects in Gernsbacher (1994)

simply pronounced the matching versus mismatching emotion words immediately after reading the stories (and did not read the target sentences). Mismatching emotion words were pronounced more slowly. In Gernsbacher and
Robertson (1992), we manipulated the number of emotional stories that our
subjects read. We predicted that subjects' knowledge of emotional states would
be more activated when they read more emotion stories, and, indeed, that is
what we observed. All these experiments demonstrated that comprehenders
activate knowledge about fictional characters' emotional states, and comprehenders use that activated knowledge about emotional consequences as a cue
for mapping during comprehension.

STRUCTURAL COHERENCE

The final type of coherence that I shall discuss is structural coherence. Writing
specialists stress the importance of parallel structure. For instance, Strunk and
White (1972) urged writers to "express coordinate ideas in similar form.
Expressions [that are] similar in content and function [should] be outwardly
similar" (p. 20). Strunk and White further proposed that "likeness of form
enables the reader to recognize more readily the likeness of content and
function" (p. 20). Thus, comprehenders might interpret likeness of form, or
what I refer to here as *structural coherence*, as a cue for mapping.

Recently, Robertson and I demonstrated that comprehenders do indeed use
the syntactic and conceptual form of a preceding sentence as a cue for mapping
(Gernsbacher & Robertson, 1996b). Subjects read pairs of sentences. In our
first experiment, subjects made grammaticality judgments to both members of
each pair; in our second, third, and fourth experiments, subjects simply read
the first member of each pair and made a grammaticality judgment to only the
second member of the pair (our second experiment replicated our first experiment with only this procedural change). Example experimental sentence pairs
are shown in Table 1.1.

As these examples in Table 1.1 illustrate, the first sentence in our experimental sentence pairs contained either an unambiguous gerundive nominal
(*washing clothes*) or an unambiguous plural noun phrase (*whining students*). The
second sentence of our experimental sentence pairs contained a head noun
phrase that, in isolation, would be ambiguous (*visiting relatives*; Tyler & Marslen-
Wilson, 1977). In our first and second experiments, we found that subjects
decided 16% more rapidly and 19% more accurately that the second sentence
of each pair was grammatical when it matched the first sentence (as the first
two example sentence pairs do). In our third experiment, we replicated this

Table 1.1

Example Stimuli for Structural Coherence Experiment

Experiments 1 and 2	Experiment 3	Experiment 4
Washing dishes is a drag.	Washing dishes is often a drag.	Washing dishes can be a drag.
Visiting relatives is, too.	Visiting relatives is often a drag, too.	Visiting relatives is often a drag, too.
Whining students are a drag.	Whining students are often a drag.	Whining students can be a drag.
Visiting relatives are, too.	Visiting relatives are often a drag, too.	Visiting relatives are often a drag, too.
Washing dishes is a drag.	Washing dishes is often a drag.	Washing dishes can be a drag.
Visiting relatives are, too.	Visiting relatives are often a drag, too.	Visiting relatives are often a drag, too.
Whining students are a drag.	Whining students are often a drag.	Whining students can be a drag.
Visiting relatives is, too.	Visiting relatives is often a drag, too.	Visiting relatives is often a drag, too.

effect, despite the fact that the second sentence was less syntactically dependent on the first sentence (because the elliptical verb phrase was replaced by a full verb phrase). In our fourth experiment, we also replicated this benefit, despite the fact that the verb in the first sentence was a modal, not marked for number. This last experimental result suggests that the conceptual form of the first sentence, in addition to its syntactic form, facilitated subjects' ability to comprehend (and map) the second sentence.

CONCLUSIONS

From the experiments I have reviewed in this chapter, I draw the following conclusions. Referential coherence facilitates mapping. Sentences that refer to previously mentioned concepts are more likely to be mapped onto developing structures. Cues to referential coherence are repeated words, pronouns, and the definite article, *the*. Temporal coherence facilitates mapping. Sentences that maintain a previously established time frame are more likely to be mapped onto developing structures. Cues to temporal coherence are adverbial phrases such as *At 10:15* or *Five hours later* as well as the tense and aspect of verbs. Locational coherence facilitates mapping. Sentences that maintain a previously established location are more likely to be mapped onto developing structures. Causal coherence facilitates mapping. Sentences that are logical consequences of a previously mentioned action are more likely to be mapped onto developing structures. One powerful cue to causal coherence is the conjunction, *because*.

Structural coherence facilitates mapping. Sentences that maintain the syntactic or conceptual form of a previous sentence are more likely to be mapped onto developing structures.

The experiments that I have reviewed in this chapter support the Structure Building Framework's proposal that comprehenders develop mental structures by mapping. According to the Structure Building Framework, once comprehenders have laid a foundation for their mental structures, they develop those structures using the cognitive process of mapping. Incoming information that coheres with or relates to previously comprehended information is mapped onto the developing structure or substructure.

Comprehenders use various cues of coherence; these cues are learned through experience with the world and experience with language. For example, comprehenders familiar with English pronouns have learned that *she* (typically) refers to a female; comprehenders familiar with English articles have learned that *the* typically precedes a definite concept (a concept that has been mentioned before, is in the deictic environment (e.g., *Just put the papers on the desk*), is part of a shared culture (e.g., *the sun, the President*), or is a component of a previously mentioned entity (e.g., *I'm reading a chapter about mapping. The ideas are terrific*). Comprehenders familiar with the meanings of the terms *scientist, man,* and *woman* have learned that the two expressions, *the man* and *the woman*, probably do not refer to the same entity, whereas the two expressions, *the scientist* and *the man*, can refer to the same entity, as can, *the scientist* and *the woman* (although mapping the latter two expressions is a bit harder, an unfortunate circumstance that we have begun to investigate empirically). Comprehenders familiar with the event described by the clause, *Susan's baby was sick*, have learned that the event described by the clause, *Susan phoned the doctor*, is a likely consequence. Thus, comprehenders' knowledge gained through their experience with events, entities, and relations in the world, as well as their knowledge of the language used to communicate about those events, entities, and relations, enables comprehenders to interpret cues that signal coherence.

Interpreting coherence cues can feel relatively unconscious or relatively deliberate. The Structure Building Framework allows for activation that occurs relatively "passively" and activation that occurs relatively "strategically." The crucial issue is that information—knowledge of various sorts—is activated during comprehension; indeed comprehension *is* a quintessential act of using and acquiring knowledge.

According to the Structure Building Framework, the building blocks of mental structures are memory nodes. Memory nodes represent previously stored information in a distributed fashion, such that a pattern of memory node activation can represent the meaning of a word, the meaning of a phrase, the meaning of a sentence, or the meaning of a passage (Hinton, McClelland, & Rumelhart, 1986). When memory nodes are activated, the information they represent becomes available for comprehension. This information might be knowledge that was acquired years earlier when the comprehender mastered the English pronoun system, knowledge that was acquired moments earlier when the comprehender read that a particular *cat is on a* (particular) *mat*, or knowledge that was acquired whenever that allows the comprehender to interpret the expression *the cat is on the mat* as a situation in which the cat is lying (as opposed to other positions) on a mat.

Although other models of language comprehension assume that previously acquired "real-world" knowledge is represented in a different "store" than is the knowledge used to comprehend language, the Structure Building Framework does not make this distinction. And although other models of language comprehension assume that the knowledge gained from reading or listening to a particular sentence, discourse, or text (what is sometimes referred to as a "text base") is represented separately from the knowledge used to comprehend that sentence, text, or discourse, the Structure Building Framework does not make that distinction (just as many models of memory find the distinction between episodic and semantic memory to be unnecessary, cf. Hintzman, 1984; McKoon, Ratcliff, & Dell, 1986). Thus, all aspects of comprehenders' interpretation of coherence are knowledge-based, and comprehenders' knowledge of coherence cues facilitates their cognitive process of mapping during comprehension.

ACKNOWLEDGMENTS

Much of the research reviewed in this chapter was supported by grants from the National Institutes of Health (R01 NS 29926 and K04 NS01376) and the Army Research Institute (DASW0194-K-0004).

REFERENCES

Anderson, A., Garrod, S. C., & Sanford, A. J. (1983). The accessibility of pronominal antecedents as a function of episode shifts in narrative text. *Quarterly Journal of Experimental Psychology*, 35A, 427–440.

Bates, E. (1979). *The emergence of symbols*. New York: Academic Press.

Black, J. B., Turner, T. J., & Bower, G. H. (1979). Point of view in narrative comprehension, memory, and production. *Journal of Verbal Learning and Verbal Behavior*, 18, 187–198.

Carreiras, M., & Gernsbacher, M. A. (1992). Comprehending conceptual anaphors in Spanish. *Language and Cognitive Processes*, 7, 281–299.

Carreiras, M., Gernsbacher, M. A., & Villa, V. (1995). The advantage of first mention in Spanish. *Psychonomic Bulletin and Review*, 2, 124–129.

Deaton, J. A., & Gernsbacher, M. A. (in press). Causal conjunctions and implicit causality cue mapping in sentence comprehension. *Journal of Memory and Language*.

de Villiers, P. A. (1974). Imagery and theme in recall of connected discourse. *Journal of Experimental Psychology, 103*, 263–268.

Faust, M. E., & Gernsbacher, M. A. (1996). Cerebral mechanisms for suppression of inappropriate information during sentence comprehension. *Brain and Language, 53*, 234–259.

Foertsch, J., & Gernsbacher, M. A. (1994). In search of complete comprehension: Getting "minimalists" to work. *Discourse Processes, 18*, 271–296.

Gernsbacher, M. A. (1985). Surface information loss in comprehension. *Cognitive Psychology, 17*, 324–363.

Gernsbacher, M. A. (1989). Mechanisms that improve referential access. *Cognition, 32*, 99–156.

Gernsbacher, M. A. (1991a). Cognitive processes and mechanisms in language comprehension: The structure building framework. In G. H. Bower (Ed.), *The psychology of learning and motivation* (pp. 217–263). New York: Academic Press.

Gernsbacher, M. A. (1991b). Comprehending conceptual anaphors. *Language and Cognitive Processes, 6*, 81–105.

Gernsbacher, M. A. (1993). Less skilled readers have less efficient suppression mechanisms. *Psychological Science, 4*, 294–298.

Gernsbacher, M. A. (1994). Activating knowledge of fictional characters' emotional states. In C. A. Weaver, S. Mannes, & C. R. Fletcher (Eds.), Discourse comprehension: Essays in honor of Walter Kintsch (pp. 141–155). Hillsdale, NJ: Lawrence Erlbaum Associates.

Gernsbacher, M. A. (1996). General cognitive processes and mechanisms in text comprehension. In B. J. Britton & A. Graesser (Eds.), *Models of text and discourse understanding*. Hillsdale, NJ: Lawrence Erlbaum Associates.

Gernsbacher, M. A., & Faust, M. (1991a). The mechanism of suppression: A component of general comprehension skill. *Journal of Experimental Psychology: Learning, Memory and Cognition, 17*, 245–262.

Gernsbacher, M. A., & Faust, M. (1991b). The role of suppression in sentence comprehension. In G. B. Simpson (Ed.) *Understanding word and sentence* (pp. 97–128). Amsterdam: North Holland.

Gernsbacher, M. A., & Faust, M. (1994). Skilled suppression. In F. N. Dempster, & C. N. Brainerd (Eds.), New perspectives on interference and inhibition in cognition (pp. 295–327). San Diego, CA: Academic Press.

Gernsbacher, M. A., & Givón, T. (Eds.). (1995). *Coherence in spontaneous text*. Philadelphia, PA: John Benjamins.

Gernsbacher, M. A., Goldsmith, H. H., & Robertson, R. R. W. (1992). Do readers mentally represent characters' emotional states? *Cognition and Emotion, 6*, 89–111.

Gernsbacher, M. A., & Hargreaves, D. (1988). Accessing sentence participants: The advantage of first mention. *Journal of Memory and Language, 27*, 699–717.

Gernsbacher, M. A., & Hargreaves, D. (1992). The privilege of primacy: Experimental data and cognitive explanations. In D. L. Payne (Ed.) *Pragmatics of word order flexibility* (pp. 83–116). Philadelphia: John Benjamins.

Gernsbacher, M. A., Hargreaves, D., & Beeman, M. (1989). Building and accessing clausal representations: The advantage of first mention versus the advantage of clause recency. *Journal of Memory and Language, 28*, 735–755.

Gernsbacher, M. A., & Jescheniak, J. D. (1995). Cataphoric devices in spoken discourse. *Cognitive Psychology, 29*, 24–58.

Gernsbacher, M. A., & Robertson, R. R. W. (1992). Knowledge activation versus sentence mapping when representing fictional characters' emotional states. *Language and Cognitive Processes, 7*, 353–371.

Gernsbacher, M. A., & Robertson, R. R. W. (1995). Reading skill and suppression revisited. *Psychological Science, 6*, 165–169.

Gernsbacher, M.A., & Robertson, R. R. W. (1996a). *The definite article 'the' facilitates mapping in story comprehension*. Manuscript submitted for publication.

Gernsbacher, M.A., & Robertson, R. R. W., (1996b). *Parallel form affects sentence comprehension.* Manuscript submitted for publication.

Gernsbacher, M. A., & Shroyer, S. (1989). The cataphoric use of the indefinite *this* in spoken narratives. *Memory & Cognition, 17,* 536–540.

Gernsbacher, M. A., Varner, K. R., & Faust, M. (1990). Investigating differences in general comprehension skill. *Journal of Experimental Psychology: Learning, Memory, and Cognition, 16,* 430–445.

Haberlandt, K., & Bingham, G. (1978). Verbs contribute to the coherence of brief narratives: Reading related and unrelated sentence triples. *Journal of Verbal Learning and Verbal Behavior, 17,* 419–425.

Haenggi, D., Gernsbacher, M. A., & Bolliger, C. M. (1993). Individual differences in situation-based inferencing during narrative text comprehension. In H. van Oostendorp & R. A. Zwaan (Eds.), *Naturalistic text comprehension* (pp. 79–96). Norwood, NJ: Ablex.

Haenggi, D., Kintsch, W., & Gernsbacher, M. A. (1995). Spatial situation models and text comprehension. *Discourse Processes, 19,* 173–199.

Haviland, S. E., & Clark, H. H. (1974). What's new? Acquiring new information as a process in comprehension. *Journal of Verbal Learning and Verbal Behavior, 13,* 512–521.

Hinton, G. E., McClelland, J. L., & Rumelhart, D. E. (1986). Distributed representations. In D. E. Rumelhart & J. L. McClelland (Eds.), *Parallel distributed processing* (pp. 77–109). Cambridge, MA: MIT Press.

Hintzman, D. L. (1984). Episodic versus semantic memory: A distinction whose time has come—and gone? *The Brain and Behavioral Sciences, 7,* 240–241.

Johnson-Laird, P. N. (1983). *Mental models.* Cambridge, MA: Harvard University Press.

Keenan, J. M., Baillet, S. D., & Brown, P. (1984). The effects of causal cohesion on comprehension and memory. *Journal of Verbal Learning and Verbal Behavior, 23,* 115–126.

Lesgold, A. M. (1972). Pronominalizations: A device for unifying sentences in memory. *Journal of Verbal Learning and Verbal Behavior, 11,* 316–323.

Lieberman, P. (1984). *The biology and evolution of language.* Cambridge, MA: Harvard University Press.

McKoon, G., & Ratcliff, R. (1980). Priming in item recognition: The organization of propositions in memory for text. *Journal of Verbal Learning and Verbal Behavior, 19,* 369–386.

McKoon, G., Ratcliff, R., & Dell, G. S. (1986). A critical evaluation of the semantic-episodic distinction. *Journal of Experimental Psychology: Learning, Memory, & Cognition, 12,* 1173–1190.

Oakhill, J., Garnham, A., Gernsbacher, M. A., & Cain, K. (1992). How natural are conceptual anaphors? *Language and Cognitive Processes, 7,* 257–280.

Rumelhart, D. E., & McClelland, J. L. (1986). *Parallel distributed processing. Explorations in the microstructure of cognition. Vol. 1: Foundations.* Cambridge, MA: MIT Press.

Strunk, W. J., & White, E. B. (1972). *The elements of style.* New York: Macmillan.

Traxler, M. J., & Gernsbacher, M. A. (1992). Improving written communication through minimal feedback. *Language and Cognitive Processes, 7,* 1–22.

Traxler, M. J., & Gernsbacher, M. A. (1993). Improving written communication through perspective taking. *Language and Cognitive Processes, 8,* 311–334.

Traxler, M. J., & Gernsbacher, M. A. (1995). Improving coherence in written communication. In M. A. Gernsbacher & T. Givón (Eds.), *Coherence in spontaneous text* (pp. 216–237). Philadelphia, PA: John Benjamins.

Tyler, L. K., & Marslen-Wilson, W. D. (1977). The on-line effects of semantic context on syntactic processing. *Journal of Verbal Learning and Verbal Behavior, 16,* 683–692.

Chapter 2

Coherence and Cohesion in Children's Stories

Lauren R. Shapiro
University of North Carolina at Chapel Hill

Judith A. Hudson
Rutgers, The State University of New Jersey

For the past 2 decades, psychologists have examined developmental differences in children's ability to produce structurally coherent and linguistically cohesive stories. To construct a story, the child must first acquire and subsequently coordinate and use various types of knowledge, such as knowledge about events to construct the content, knowledge about genre structure to create coherence, and knowledge about linguistic devices to weave cohesion. Thus, narrative production is viewed as a cognitive and linguistic task that draws on one's knowledge and memory for personal experiences and for fictional tales. This research focuses on how children acquire and translate different strands of knowledge into a narrative form. That is, how they get from "knowing" to "telling" (White, 1980). In this chapter, the development in children's ability to create coherent and cohesive narratives is examined, and the relationship between coherence and cohesion is explored using data from two studies.

DEFINING COHERENCE AND COHESION

Narrative coherence and cohesion, although related, can be theoretically distinguished (Karmiloff-Smith, 1980). To make a story coherent, the child uses story schema to structure the content into a culturally defined sequence that includes a formal beginning, setting and background orientation to introduce characters, internal responses (e.g., thoughts and feelings), a problem and resolution (i.e., the plot), and an ending. Story cohesion is established by employing linguistic reference devices, such as pronominalization, temporal and causal connectives, and subordinate clauses, which tie a span of sentences together to form a whole. It is possible to produce a narrative that has coherent content but lacks linguistic cohesiveness. Alternatively, text can be cohesive, but not coherent when structural components are omitted or incorrectly sequenced. Young children, in particular, have difficulty in producing narratives that are both coherent and cohesive (Applebee, 1978). Because structural coherence may influence linguistic cohesion (Hudson & Shapiro, 1991; Shapiro, 1990), it is important first to consider coherence and cohesion separately to better understand their role in narrative development.

Different types of narrative organization have been identified that describe development in storytelling (Applebee, 1978; Botvin & Sutton-Smith, 1977; Gruendel, 1980; Stein, 1988; Stein & Glenn, 1982). Several researchers (Applebee, 1978; Botvin & Sutton-Smith, 1977; Gruendel, 1980) have found that tales produced by 2- to 5-year-olds lack some of the basic constituent units of a story; the overall frameworks of these narratives more closely resemble either descriptions of settings and/or a loosely associated series of acts (i.e., act lists) or chronologically sequenced script accounts of incidents based on their knowledge of the world vis-à-vis personal and vicarious experiences. Gruendel (1980) asked children ages 4, 6, and 8 years to tell her "make believe" stories about four familiar events (planting a garden, building a campfire, making cookies, and a birthday party). Most of the narratives generated by her 4-year-olds (92%) were descriptions of real-world occurrences organized in the form of script reports (67%) or anecdotes based on their real-life personal experiences (30%). These findings indicate that young children may rely more on their event schemas (i.e., knowledge of event structure) than their story schemas (i.e., episodic structure) to accomplish the storytelling task.

In contrast, by age 6 there is an increased propensity for children to create complex plots (i.e., provide a problem-resolution structure) and a corresponding proficiency at connecting essential story elements together into a goal-directed, logical, and coherent whole. Both Botvin & Sutton-Smith's (1977) and Stein's (Stein, 1988; Stein & Glenn, 1982; Stein, Glenn, & Jarcho, 1982) research on narration indicated that although 5- and 6-year-old children are beginning to incorporate goals into their chronologically sequenced tales, it is not until children are age 7 or 8 that tangible efforts are first made to conform their reports, albeit not successfully, to the episodic structure (i.e., causally related, goal-based, problem-resolution episodes with reference to characters' internal states), resulting in 'transitional' narratives. Finally, the ability to produce traditional stories with sophisticated plots embedded into multiple episodes is mastered between ages 9 to 12 (Hudson & Shapiro, 1991; Leondar,

1977; Mandler, 1983, 1984). Similar development in narrative organization was found by Gruendel (1980). Between ages 6 and 8, the greatest progress was made in creating transitional (i.e., accounts containing incomplete plots) and traditional tales (from 38% to 50%), with a significant decline in the production of script and personal narratives in lieu of fictionalized stories.

Why is the ability to create traditional stories such a late development? Let's consider three possible explanations—variations in children's cognitive abilities, differences in their conceptualization of the task, and disparate effects of the topic on storytelling performance. It is interesting that preschoolers are able to use story schemas to comprehend and recall narratives (Botvin & Sutton-Smith, 1977; Mandler, 1983, 1984), but seem unable to use them to guide production (Botvin & Sutton-Smith, 1977; Gruendel, 1980; Mandler & Johnson, 1977; Nelson & Gruendel, 1986; Stein & Glenn, 1979). This suggests that story schemas for children under age 6 may merely not be under operational control (Mandler & DeForest, 1979; Seidman, Nelson, & Gruendel, 1986), may be less accessible than event schemas (Gruendel, 1980; Hudson & Shapiro, 1991; Shapiro, 1990), or may still be developing (Poulsen, Kintsch, Kintsch, & Premack, 1979; Pradl, 1979). Thus, preschoolers may be cognizant of the specific episodic components in stories, but have difficulty coordinating and integrating various strands of knowledge (i.e., information about events, stories, and linguistic devices) into the appropriate genre structure because of memory limitations (Hudson & Shapiro, 1991).

The simpler stories invented by young children in which a character obtains his or her objective without mishap may also be motivated by their desire to have events end in a positive fashion (Stein, 1988; Sutton-Smith, 1975). This approach, which corresponds to a broader concept of a story, detrimentally affects the complexity and causal structure of the parable by reducing the need for a second episode in which obstructions to goals are eliminated. In contrast, older children's preference to narrate tales with at least one barrier that prevents the protagonist from achieving his or her aims precipitates an additional, causally related episode in which the character removes the complication and attempts to obtain his or her objective anew. Story researchers suggest that the latter, which includes conflicts among protagonists that cause an affective response in the audience, is more representative of traditional stories (Brewer & Lichtenstein, 1981; Quasthoff & Nikolaus, 1981; Stein, 1988; Stein & Policastro, 1984).

We suggest that the topic of the narrative also plays an important role in children's competence in creating coherent tales (Hudson & Shapiro, 1991). Children's familiarity with certain event topics (e.g., a birthday party) may facilitate the production of script narratives (cf., Hudson & Nelson, 1984). In addition, some topics (e.g., building a campfire) may be less conducive to a story production task than others (also see Stein, 1988). We found that children produced better stories for causally structured events, such as accidents or injuries requiring medical intervention. Greater coherence may have been achieved because children's knowledge base for this event was accessible and organized in a form that was congruent with creating this type of narrative genre (i.e., less translation from knowing to telling was required to convert information into a fully plotted tale). Similarly, Stein (1988) indicates that even kindergarten children, under certain conditions and with the appropriate topic, can generate goal-based, plotted stories. Now consider story cohesiveness, that is, the degree to which children are able to utilize linguistic devices to make their narratives wholistic and comprehensible. There are several ways in which children can tie a story together across clauses, including the employment of subordinate clauses, conjunctives, and pronouns. Research generally indicates that children's ability to use these cohesive devices appropriately during narrative production increases with age (Bloom, Lahey, Hood, Lifter, & Fiess, 1980; French & Nelson, 1985; Hudson & Shapiro, 1991; Peterson & McCabe, 1991). However, there are specific developmental trends associated with each technique. In our research, we have focused on *subordinate clauses, interclausal connectives*, and *pronominal reference strategies*.

Subordinate clauses provide cohesion in a narrative by embedding related clauses into a single statement (e.g., "I go to bed when I am tired."). The degree to which children use subordinate clauses in a narrative is also a measure of the overall linguistic complexity (Halliday & Hasan, 1976). Interclausal connectives join adjacent clauses in a narrative at the sentence level. Conjunctives indicate whether the semantic relationship between the adjacent and preceding clauses is independent (e.g., additive, or continuative), sequential (e.g., temporal), or dependent (e.g., adversative/causal). At each point along the story frame, the narrator must select the most appropriate connective to adequately reflect the narrative component being related. Because the story unfolds over time, temporal connectives are used to recapitulate events that follow each other chronologically in the real world. In contrast, causal connectives are needed when the storyteller is describing goal-directed actions or the characters' thoughts and emotional reactions to the plot, whereas adversative and additive connectives are used to provide setting and background information when introducing the characters. However, additive conjunctives, particularly "and" which is used at all ages, are more commonly used to mark the simple co-existence of two independent activities or for relating internal states (e.g., characters' emotional responses). Elementary school children, unlike preschoolers, rely on more sophisticated linguistic devices, such as subordinate clauses linked together by prepositions, supplemented by a wide range of connectives, particularly temporal and causal conjunctions (Bennett-Kastor, 1986; Bloom, et. al., 1980; Hudson & Shapiro, 1991; John-Steiner & Panofsky, 1987; Scott, 1984; Peterson & McCabe, 1983; Stenning & Mitchell, 1985).

In contrast to connectives, pronouns create cohesive bonds at the narrative level by using specific markers to refer back to the same entity. That is, the narrator employs pronouns as a way of discussing the same characters who have been mentioned earlier in the story. Although young children understand pronouns, they often have difficulty applying them appropriately in an extended narrative (Warden, 1976). Preschoolers often use a pronominal form (e.g., "she") to talk about more than one previously introduced referent, thereby making both the relationship between earlier and later text elements unclear and the referent ambiguous to the audience (Bartlett, 1984; Menig-Peterson & McCabe, 1978; Pratt & MacKenzie-Keating, 1985).

Karmiloff-Smith (1980, 1986) and Bamberg (1986) identified predominant strategies for switching and maintaining pronominal reference which may vary with age. Very young children (about 3- to 5-years-old) may produce syntactically correct text, but utilize relatively unsophisticated techniques for organizing their discourse into an overall narrative. They are more likely than their older peers to employ a nominal strategy in which the proform (e.g., "the boy") rather than a pronoun is used or an undifferentiated strategy in which the application of pronouns is locally determined (e.g., refer to a girl in a picture as "she"). As children (ages 5 to 8 years) become more capable of monitoring the flow of connected utterances, they begin using a "thematic subject" pronominal strategy for organizing the narrative. This strategy, in which only the protagonist is identified and referred to with pronouns, is considered more advanced than the nominal and undifferentiated strategies because pronominalization is consistent throughout the narrative. During middle childhood (between 8- to 12-years-old), children learn to apply pronouns flexibly, which allows them to organize their narrative into a single unit through the use of a full anaphoric strategy. Unlike the "thematic subject" strategy, pronoun usage is not tied to one character. The full anaphoric strategy, the most sophisticated of the strategies, reserves nominal forms for reference switching and pronominal forms for reference maintenance.

Thus, with increasing age, children's tales become both more coherent and more cohesive. However, significant variations have been observed in both the structural and linguistic integrity depending on the context and difficulty level of the narration chore at hand. In general, children's stories are better when related spontaneously in conversations than when they are elicited under experimental conditions (Hudson & Shapiro, 1991). In comparison to recapitulating an interesting, novel experience to a friend, fulfilling an investigator's request to produce a fictional tale about a topic which the narrator has not selected is a considerably more laborious assignment. Research shows that once children master the framework requirements of a given genre, they are able to use more polished and diversified techniques for achieving cohesion, such as causal connectives (Hudson & Shapiro, 1991; Kernan, 1977; Peterson & McCabe, 1991). In contrast, when they are still in the process of learning how to compose a more elaborate narrative, children's competence in employing sophisticated linguistic devices is impaired. We propose that during narration, children are faced with two tasks that require simultaneous processing: producing a structurally coherent story and constructing a semantically cohesive one. The degree of effort children devote to one job will limit the amount of cognitive energy they will have available to accomplish the other.

Two major predictions arise from this proposal. First, children should be able to employ more sophisticated cohesive devices when the task is made easier by providing external aids during narration, such as pictures, or a relevant experience that could be used as the basis for a plot—the hallmark of coherent stories. Research shows that children's discourse is more complex when the topics they are discussing or the pictures or photographs of the events they are viewing are familiar and meaningful to them or have been personally experienced (Cazden, 1970; Labov, 1972; Peterson & McCabe, 1983). Second, although age differences in performance are expected for measures of both coherence and cohesion, within each age group children who are able to narrate more complex stories should also be able to employ more sophisticated cohesive devices than those producing structurally simpler narratives. We expect this pattern because more complex narrative structures often consist of multiple episodes involving a core of protagonists that require the use of causal connectives and advanced pronominalization to trace the characters' movements throughout the story. Moreover, although older children have more developed narration skills and broader bases of experience, reducing the task demands through our experimental manipulations should facilitate even young children's storytelling.

In the next sections, we present the results of two investigations that examined children's ability to produce stories containing all of the necessary components organized into complex episodes and to employ prepositions, connectives, and pronouns to make their narratives wholistic. We demonstrate how the use of cohesive devices is determined, in part, by the overall narrative structure. That is, by varying the situational demands, we have created more and less difficult storytelling tasks for children. This allows us to examine whether or not children who are able to produce tales with more complicated overall organizations can also narrate linguistically more refined text.

STUDY 1: CHILDREN'S PICTURE-ELICITED STORIES: EFFECTS OF PREVIEWING & TYPE OF EVENT SEQUENCE

Recently, researchers have selected an alternate method for obtaining stories, specifically the use of pictures, that can minimize in part the cognitive effort required in narration (Bamberg, 1986, 1987; Karmiloff-Smith, 1986; Pratt & MacKenzie-Keating, 1985; Stenning & Mitchell, 1985). Bamberg (1986) indicates that because children are familiar with this form of storytelling, they are able to employ previously established linguistic skills. Thus, by reducing the task demands during narration, researchers should obtain a better indication of children's ability to communicate effectively (i.e., tell a coherent and cohesive parable).

We used picture-booklets that either contained problem-resolution or mundane action sequences to elicit stories from preschool and first grade children. We predicted that children who had difficulty narrating fully plotted narratives might be able to do so if shown picture sequences of familiar events that included a problem-resolution sequence. Thus, one of our goals was to examine age differences in coherence and cohesion for tales narrated in situations of reduced task demands. In particular, we wanted to investigate the benefits, if any, of previewing the action sequence and providing plots on storytelling ability. We also wanted to obtain further support for the contention that children who have mastered story coherence are more proficient at creating cohesion.

Method

In this study (Shapiro & Hudson, 1991), 48 preschoolers (M age = 4 ; 6 years) and 48 first graders (M age = 6; 8 years)[1] were asked to construct make-believe stories using two original, bound picture-booklets each consisting of six clearly interpretable black-and-white pictures without text. These booklets were assembled to create a *problem* version (i.e., containing a problem-resolution sequence embedded into the event) and an *event-based* version (i.e., typical, but uneventful occurrence) of actions comprising two events—going on a trip to the beach and of baking cookies. For the problem version picture-booklets, we showed beach scenes in which a little boy's sand castles get washed away by waves and subsequently rebuilt by his father and him, whereas the baking scenes depicted a batch of cookies getting burned, prompting a mother and daughter to go to the bakery to buy "replacement" cookies. For the event-based version

---

[1]Three children were dropped from the study and replaced; one preschooler was unable to tell a story and two first-graders' stories were not recorded because of equipment failure.

picture booklets, we showed a family going to the beach, building sand castles, and swimming in the beach scenes, and portrayed a mother-daughter dyad making dough, baking, and eating cookies in the baking scenes. The picture sequences in both events were arranged so that the child character would most likely be identified as the "protagonist" (i.e., activity was centered around this individual). A sample sequence of each version is shown in Fig. 2.1.

The interview began with the experimenter showing children a sample picture booklet before presenting booklets to them of each event sequence (trip and baking) with the order counterbalanced. Half of the children in each grade were randomly assigned to the preview condition and the other half to the standard condition. Only the children in the preview condition were allowed to see the picture sequence in the booklets prior to story production. They were told: "First, look at each of these pictures, and I'll turn the pages so that I can see them too." Stories were elicited by the experimenter saying: "Now, tell me a make-believe story using the pictures in this booklet." In each condition, half the children were shown the problem versions of the picture-booklets and the remaining children were shown the event-based versions. The children's narratives were audio-taped and transcribed for analysis. At the end of the study, each child received a copy of both picture booklets with their make-believe narratives written in by the experimenter. Examples of children's stories are shown in Appendix A.

Overall Story Coherence

To measure story coherence, we focused on children's ability to incorporate important episodic components into their stories. Episodic components, which include goals, internal responses, obstacles, and repairs, are considered essential for plot development, but they must be inferred from the pictures based on schematic knowledge about stories. Goals were defined as statements about the character's purpose, plans, or intentions (e.g., "He wanted to go swimming"). Internal responses refer to the characters' thoughts and emotions (e.g., "She was sad") and responses by the character to the attainment or nonattainment of the goal (e.g., "Then she was happy," "She was proud of herself"). Obstacles are events that interrupt action and include an unexpected result or problem (e.g., "The cookies got burned" or "They forgot their towel at the beach"), whereas Repairs are attempts by the characters to rectify obstacles (e.g., "So they went to the store to buy new cookies" or "They returned to the beach for their towel"). Goals, which are often considered part of internal responses, were coded as a separate category to allow us to directly examine children's ability to incorporate event objectives into their stories. Obstacles and repairs were coded separately,

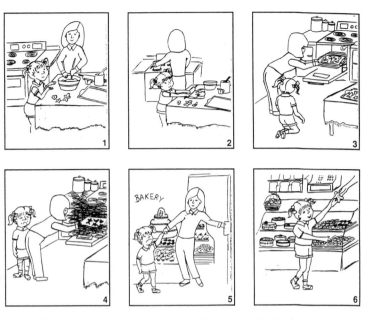

FIG. 2.1 A. Picture sequences of the problem version: Cookie baking.

FIG. 2.1 B. Picture sequences of the event based version: Trip to the beach.

but were combined into a unit measure because the inclusion of a repair depended on prior mention of an obstacle. Children were only credited for obstacles and repairs when they made explicit reference to the problem and how the repair addresses that problem, rather than merely describing the pictures (e.g., "Now it's all smoky," and "She brings her to the cake store").

To capture the degree to which children's stories embodied episodic components, each story was categorized into one of four levels of overall narrative organization. *Act List* Narratives (Level 1) simply consisted of a set of actions and/or background information juxtaposed in a seemingly random fashion (see Example 1 in Appendix A). *Chronologically Sequenced* Narratives (Level 2) were recapitulations of the event as it unfolds in the real-world and also incorporated one episodic component into the tale (see Example 2). *Transitional* Narratives (Level 3) contained two episodic components either organized into partially developed plots that artificially alters the event structure (see Example 3) or fails to provide "closure" to the plot (see Example 4). *Traditional* Narratives (Level 4) were fully developed problem-resolution episodes that included all three episodic components (see Examples 5 and 6).

Each story was assigned a score from 1–4 corresponding to the overall narrative level. Analyses were performed on each child's level of narrative organization averaged across both stories. Stories had a higher overall narrative organization when told by first graders (M = 2.88) rather than by preschoolers (M = 2.46) and when produced with the problem (M = 3.29) rather than with the event-based versions (M = 2.04). Thus, first graders were better at structuring information about characters' goals and the plot into a more complex story than preschoolers. However, the problem versions allowed children to develop the plot, to describe characters, to refer to characters' feelings and thoughts, and to organize their narratives into more coherent stories than those produced with the event-based pictures. Even preschoolers were able to incorporate these important components when the picture sequence contained the type of structure characteristic of stories. Indeed, the mean overall level of narrative organization for preschoolers was 3.03 with the problem versions as compared to a mean overall level of 1.89 with the event-based versions. This version difference was somewhat more pronounced for the first graders (M = 3.56 and M = 2.19 for problem and event-based versions, respectively).

Cohesive Reference Devices

Three types of cohesive reference devices were coded: subordinate clauses, conjunctions, and pronoun strategies.

Linguistic complexity. A subordinate index was devised by dividing the number of subordinate clauses by the total number of clauses as an index of overall language complexity in the story (Halliday & Hasan, 1976; Harrell, 1957). Overall, stories by first graders contained a higher level of linguistic complexity (M = .17) than stories by preschoolers (M = .11).

Interclausal connectives. Four types of conjunctions were coded: (a) *additive* conjunction (e.g., *and*), (b) *continuative* conjunction (e.g., *now*), (c) *temporal* conjunction (e.g., *then, and then, next, first, before*), and (d) *adversative* (e.g., *but, except, sometimes, usually, or*) and *causal* conjunction (e.g., *because, so, if*). For each type of connective, we calculated a proportion by dividing the mean number of each type of connective by the total number of connectives used for each story. Both additive and continuative connectives serve to relate independent propositions, whereas temporal connectives function to link propositions sequentially and adversative/causal connectives join dependent propositions.

Children generally used additive connectives (M = .51) more than temporal connectives (M = .26) which were employed more than both continuative (M = .13) and adversative/causal (M = .11) connectives. First graders utilized temporal conjunctions more than preschoolers (M = .34 vs. M = .19) who used more continuative connectives (M = .19 vs. M = .08). As shown in Fig. 2.2,

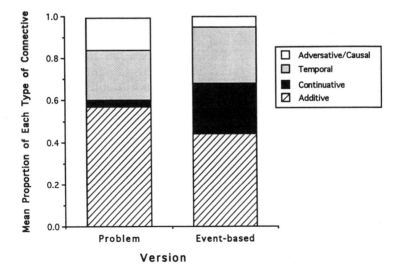

FIG. 2.2. Mean Proportion of Each Type of Connective By Version, Study 1.

continuative connectives were engaged more with the event-based version, whereas additive and adversative/causal connectives were applied more with the problem version. Children demonstrated sensitivity for the relationship between the types of categories included in their stories and the type of conjunctive needed to join them. This point is exemplified by the latter finding in which causal connectives were more often selected to structure goal-based stories.

Pronoun Strategies. Pronominal reference strategies indicate a co-referential relationship between particular nominal expressions and consecutive pronouns (Karmiloff-Smith, 1980; Bamberg, 1986). We coded each narrative as using one of five techniques. A *confused* (undifferentiated) strategy was indicated when the child's use of specific pronouns (e.g., *he, she*) was locally determined (i.e., based on the picture), thereby making the referent ambiguous when same gender characters were present. In a *general* strategy, the child sometimes introduced characters with nominal references (e.g., *a girl*), but predominantly used "general" pronouns for groups (e.g., *they*) rather than individuals (e.g., *she*) as a means for switching and maintaining reference. A *thematic subject* strategy was indicated when children reserved pronouns *he* or *she* for referring to the character identified as the protagonist of the story (usually the child character), whereas other characters were referred to by nominal forms or "general" pronouns. A *full anaphoric* strategy was indicated when children used nominals to introduce characters and switch reference, whereas pronouns were employed to maintain reference. A *nominal* strategy was indicated when the child avoided using pronouns and only employed nominal forms for switching and maintaining reference. Strategy use was coded as *indeterminable* when the type of strategy used could not be clearly classified because subjects seemed to employ more than one strategy, that is, their use of pronouns and nominals to switch or maintain reference was inconsistent.

For each story, a score of 1 for present or 0 for absent was assigned to each of the six types of pronoun strategies yielding six dichotomous variables indicating the mean proportion of children who employed that particular technique across events. The confused pronoun strategy was identified more in stories by preschoolers ($M = .18$) than by first graders ($M = .04$). The thematic subject strategy was used more in the problem version ($M = .60$) than in the event-based version ($M = .39$), whereas the general strategy was employed more with the event-based ($M = .29$) than with the problem versions ($M = .11$).

In summary, although first graders were better at creating linguistically more complex, temporally organized stories, even preschoolers were able to employ sophisticated cohesive reference devices, such as adversative/causal conjunctions and a thematic subject pronoun strategy, when the picture sequences were congruent with a well-formed story (i.e., problem version).

Effect of Story Coherence on Cohesion

An analysis was conducted to directly test the contention that structural coherence affects linguistic cohesion. We expected that as children mastered the ability to construct coherent narratives, they would become adept at making their stories more cohesive by utilizing sophisticated linguistic devices. To test this concept, analyses were performed on each child's level of narrative organization averaged across both stories. Because the mean levels of overall narrative organization ranged from 1 to 4 with increments of one-half, story levels were recoded for this analysis. Stories coded as Level 1 contained only stories at Level 1, Level 2 stories contained stories at Levels 1.5 and 2, Level 3 stories contained stories at Levels 2.5 and 3, and Level 4 stories contained stories at Levels 3.5 and 4. This coding system provided that the average story level was reflective of the level of at least one of the stories. Level 1 stories were dropped due to low production ($N = 2$); thus analyses were performed using stories at Levels 2 ($N = 35$), 3 ($N = 25$), and 4 ($N = 32$).

Figure 2.3 displays the mean proportion of cohesive devices used at each overall level of narrative organization. As shown in Figure 3, stories at Levels 3 ($M = .08$) and 4 ($M = .09$) contained more complex language as indicated by the subordinate index than stories at Level 2 ($M = .05$). Not surprisingly, stories

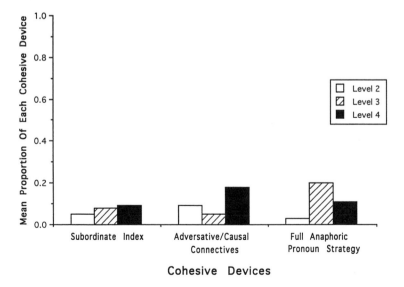

FIG. 2.3.   Mean Proportion of Cohesive Devices at Each Level of Narrative Organization, Study 1.

at Level 4 contained more adversative/causal conjunctions (M = .18) than stories classified at Levels 2 (M = .09) or 3 (M = .05). Stories at Level 3 employed a full anaphoric strategy (M = .20) more than stories at Levels 2 (M = .03)and 4 (M = .11), although Level 4 stories used this strategy more than those at Level 2. These findings generally support the idea that children's competence in employing each of the three linguistic tools effectively is dependent on the level of narrative organization that they have mastered. With each successive level of narrative complexity, there was an increase in the number of embedded clauses produced. Interestingly, children who constructed incomplete plotted accounts rarely used sophisticated conjunctives, yet they were able to employ an advanced pronominalization strategy. In contrast, children who created fully plotted stories had some difficulty in using pronouns flexibly to refer to characters, but were able to link the complex episodes with adversative/causal connectives.

This study showed that event complexity affected both the coherence and the cohesiveness of children's tales. Although first graders generally produced structurally elaborate and linguistically more cohesive stories than preschoolers, children at both ages produced more refined story plots when shown a picture sequence depicting a problem-resolution sequence. Thus, preschool children who have difficulty in telling plotted stories and in using more advanced conjunctions and pronoun strategies were able to do both if given the support of viewing pictures of familiar events already sequenced like a story. Finally, we showed that, regardless of age, children basically included more subordinate clauses, used more clausal conjunctives, and a more complex pronoun strategy when narrating more coherent stories.

STUDY 2: CHILDREN'S STORIES: EFFECTS OF EXPERIENCE AND PHOTOGRAPHS

In this study, we once again varied the task demands in narrating stories by manipulating children's experience with the event that served as the topic and by modulating the amount of support provided during narration. As in Study 1, we wanted to discover if these modifications would affect the level of narrative coherence children were able to achieve and the degree to which their use of cohesive devices was affected by the level of narrative coherence manifested in the story.

Children's familiarity with the event was influenced by allowing some of them to participate in an actual baking episode. Moreover, the cooking project included the type of problem (burning the cookies) and resolution (using a timer when baking the second batch) sequence that is typical of a traditional story.

Additional support was provided to some of the children who were also given photographs that depicted the cookie making process to view during the narrative production task.

We predicted that actually baking cookies prior to narrating would make this experience more salient to the children. Thus, the task of constructing a fictionalized tale should be considerably less difficult because children could draw on their own memory of this recent experience to use for a plot. In addition, viewing photographs of a real-world event during storytelling could also improve children's narrative production as found in Study 1. However, any improvement due to viewing the photographs should be more apparent for children who had not engaged in a baking project. For children who had participated in the activity, viewing photographs may not be necessary to produce a coherent story.

Method

Study 2 (Shapiro, 1994) involved 48 kindergarten (M age = 5; 8 years.) and 50 third grade (M age = 8; 6 years) children in a story production task.[2] One week prior to storytelling, about half of the children (N = 46) partook in a cookie baking activity (experience group) and the remainder (N = 52) did not (control group). For the cooking episode, groups of four children helped to make the batter and to shape the dough into cookies. The action sequence in the baking activity contained an obstacle to goal achievement involving a batch of cookies getting scorched which is resolved by employing a timer to prevent the next batch from burning. Children could subsequently draw on this experience and incorporate it into a narrative plot. The cooking itself was actually staged; the oven was never turned on and instead pre-made "good" and "burned" batches of cookies were substituted for the raw dough. Children decorated the second set of cookies with icing and sprinkles and then were allowed to eat one of their two cookies before returning to the classroom.

For half of the children in each group, the experimenter showed children a series of photographs one at a time that depicted a group of preschoolers participating in a baking experience identical to the one we provided. The experimenter instructed the children to look at the pictures by saying, "Here are pictures of a group of children baking cookies just like we did last week. Let's look at each photo, ok." These children were then told that they could use the depictions during the storytelling task (*photograph* condition), whereas the remaining children (determined by random assignment) were asked to

---

[2]One kindergartner was replaced for failure to respond to the request of telling a story.

produce stories without photographs (*standard* condition). The experimenter instructed children in both conditions, "Tell me a make-believe story about children who made cookies." The productions were audio-taped for subsequent transcription and children received a copy of their narratives. Examples of narratives are shown in Appendix B.

Overall Story Coherence

A modified version of coding schemes independently developed by Hudson & Nelson (1984), Peterson & McCabe (1983), and Stein (1988) was devised to classify event narratives (see Shapiro, 1990). Each child's story was classified at one of five increasingly more complex levels of overall narrative organization—*Impoverished, Act List, Chronologically sequenced, Transitional,* and *Traditional.* For each narrative, a 1 or 0 indicating presence or absence was assigned to each of the 5 levels of narrative organization and then a proportion was made by dividing the number of children who created each type of narrative by the total number of narratives. Table 2.1 shows the mean proportion of children's stories categorized at each narrative level by grade, condition, and group.

The first three types of narrative organizations are believed to be constructed more from event schemas than story schemas (Shapiro, 1990). *Impoverished* Narratives include one act, usually the most salient, in the event (see Example 1 in Appendix B). As shown in Table 2.1, very few children constructed this type of story. *Act List* Narratives consist of a set of behaviors that do not reflect an actual event sequence, but rather can be best described as an unorganized list of acts (Example 2). This type of narrative was told more by kindergartners (M = .16) than third graders (M = .00). *Chronologically sequenced* Narratives

TABLE 2.1
Study 2: Mean Proportion of Children Who Created Each Type
of Narrative Organization by Condition and Grade

		Level of Overall Narrative Organization				
Condition	Grade	Impoverished	Act List	Chronologically Sequenced	Transitional	Traditional
Standard						
	Kindergartners	.00	.09	.00	.46	.46
	Third Graders	.00	.00	.00	.08	.92
Photo						
	Kindergartners	.09	.09	.27	.18	.36
	Third Graders	.00	.00	.08	.50	.42

provide an explicit temporally sequenced episode that closely adheres to the order of the event as it unfolds in the real world (Example 3). Tales at this level were told more by kindergartners than by third graders (M = .26 vs. M = .08), by children in the control group rather than in the experience group (M = .28 vs. M = .07), and by those who viewed photographs than by those who didn't (M = .25 vs. M = .09).

The final two levels are considered to be more explicitly derived from story schemas. *Transitional* Narratives contain partially developed plots, often based on personal or vicarious anecdotes (i.e., borrowed from others' experiences) or on various media resources (e.g., movies and books), that demonstrate children have some knowledge about story structure. One of the two variations of this level is when children artificially alter the organization of the event by changing or violating an act, object, or outcome (Example 4). In the other type, the narrator only partially develops plots around an obstacle or "high point," but ends the story without removing the obstruction to the goal (Example 5). Older children constructed more transitional narratives than did younger children in the photograph condition (M =.58 vs. M =. 20), but this age difference was absent in the standard condition (M =.17 vs. M =.32). *Traditional* Narratives include a fully developed plot organized as one or more complete episodes (Example 6). Traditional Narratives were told more by third graders than by kindergartners (M = .54 vs. M = .29), by children in the experience group rather than in the control group (M = .54 vs. M = .30), and by those given the standard, instead of the photograph, condition of storytelling (M = .60 vs. M = .24).

Cohesive Reference Devices

Linguistic Complexity. Analyses of the subordinate index showed that narratives contained more complex language when produced in the standard (M = .19) than in the photo condition (M = .13) and when told by third graders (M = .20) rather than by kindergartners (M = .12).

Interclausal Connectives Only three of the four conjunctions used in Study 1 were examined here; continuative conjunctions were omitted because they were never employed. In general, children used additive connectives (M = .52) more than both temporal (M = .28) and adversative/causal connectives (M = .17) which also differed from each other. As shown in Figure 2.4, a higher proportion of additive (M =.57 vs. M =.46) and adversative/causal connectives (M =.22 vs. M =.12) were used in standard than in photo-elicited stories. In contrast, stories constructed in the photo condition contained proportionally

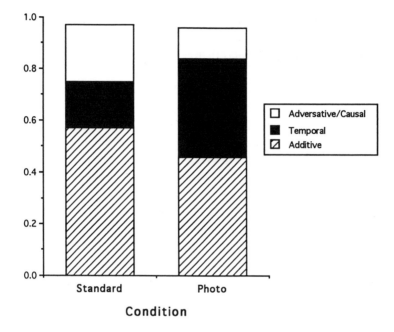

FIG. 2.4. Mean Proportion of Each Type of Connective By Version, Study 2.

more temporal connectives (M =.38 vs. M =.18) than those created in the standard condition.

Pronoun Strategies. A comparison of stories by children in the experience group indicated that the *General Pronoun Strategy* was used more by kindergartners (M = .45) than by third graders (M = .13). This strategy, although also employed by third graders, was utilized more by the control group than by the experience group (M =.58 vs. M =. 13). Children in the experience group (M = .33) used a *Full Anaphoric Pronoun Strategy* more often than those in the control group (M = .15). In addition, third graders (M = .31) tended to utilize this strategy more than kindergartners (M = .16). The *Confused Strategy* was also identified more in stories by third graders (M =.13) than by kindergartners (M = .02) and by children in the experience group (M =.12) more than in the control group (M = .02). Although this finding was surprising, the proportion of stories identified as employing a confused strategy was low. This anomaly was interpreted as an indication that children were having difficulty keeping track of their characters linguistically as the complexity level of the narrative increased. That is, the more advanced stories were longer and involved several characters requiring greater cognitive effort to keep track of them.

Effect of Story Coherence on Cohesion

This analysis, as in Study 1, examined the claim that the structural organization of the narrative influences children's use of cohesive devices. The Impoverished ($N = 2$) and Act List ($N = 8$) level narratives were dropped due to low production. Therefore, the comparison was conducted with the remaining sample of 18 Chronologically sequenced, 31 Transitional, and 40 Traditional stories.

As shown in Fig. 2.5, children produced more polished linguistic devices in traditional ($M = .29$) and transitional narratives ($M = .22$) than chronologically sequenced narratives ($M = .14$), as measured by the subordinate index. A higher proportion of adversative/causally linked propositions were found in traditional stories ($M = .28$) than in either transitional ($M = .13$) or chronologically sequenced ($M = .07$) tales. The trend for use of a full anaphoric pronoun strategy showed that this technique was employed more in traditional ($M = .35$) level narratives than in transitional ($M = .26$) and chronologically sequenced ($M = .06$) narratives. These findings lend further support to the conviction that more advanced cohesive devices are used in narratives in which the structural complexity has been mastered.

As in Study 1, we found that varying the task demands affected the sophistication level of coherence and cohesion found in children's stories. Children generally produced more structurally and linguistically refined tales if they could draw on a real-world experience for the narration task. However, showing

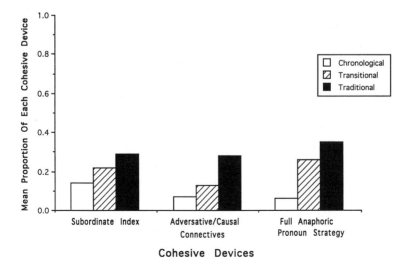

FIG. 2.5. Mean Proportion of Cohesive Devices at Each Level of Narrative Organization, Study 2.

children photographs of the same event was not as effective an aid for improving storytelling as providing a baking event. For some measures, it appeared that viewing photographs actually reduced children's narrative performance. Finally, our findings suggest that that children's use of cohesive markers was strongly influenced by the level of narrative coherence they displayed, independent of their age.

THE RELATIONSHIP BETWEEN COHERENCE AND COHESION IN NARRATIVE DEVELOPMENT

The theme of this chapter has been to examine the relationship between narrative coherence and narrative cohesion. The studies we presented provide support for the notion that these ways of looking at stories are very much related in development. We have shown not only that children's use of interclausal linguistic devices varies with the level of story complexity displayed in their tales, but that both vary with the demands of the narrative task. This latter point is important for understanding how narrative skills develop in young children.

Our research suggests that storytelling abilities in children vary considerably depending on the context and nature of the narrative task in which they are involved. When producing tales based on recent, real-world experiences (Study 2) or based on picture sequences depicting familiar events (Study 1), children from 4- to 8- years-old generally perform better when they are asked to construct make-believe stories with some support. Past research has also shown that children's ability to recount generalized script reports and specific anecdotes of personal episodes may be more developed than their ability to create fictional-ized accounts (Hudson & Shapiro, 1991). However, in more naturalistic con-texts, young children often display more advanced narration skills than those observed in more experimental contexts (Peterson & McCabe, 1983).

These findings indicate that we need to be especially sensitive to the task demands involved in assessing children's ability to use a variety of linguistic organizers when producing stories. The level of narrative skill that children demonstrate can be increased or decreased by providing them with more or less difficult tasks. Moreover, the structure of the story that they are telling (i.e., the degree of causal complexity) will affect the types of interclausal devices they employ, independent of their general ability to use these markers.

In line with Vygotsky's (1933/1935) notion of the *zone of proximal develop-ment*, we need to be aware of the narrative skills that children have already mastered, as well as those that they may display under different supportive contexts. Providing real-world experience and props, such as picture booklets, may be viewed as forms of internal and external aids that allow children to construct more complex stories and use more advanced linguistic devices. Other techniques, such as co-constructing narratives with others or narrating stories within a conversational format, may also help to determine children's use of various tools to create wholistic text within the "zone of proximal development" (Hickmann, 1985; Peterson & McCabe, 1994).

Thus, children's employment of interclausal connectives and pronouns can be seen as embedded in the overall task of telling a coherent story. How successful they are at producing a well-formed tale may vary with their familiarity with the topic of their narrative and the kinds of supports that are available during production. With age, children are better able to use more refined techniques for creating cohesion in a variety of task circumstances, however, young children may first display more sophisticated forms only under less demanding conditions.

APPENDIX A

Study 1:
Examples of Overall Level of Narrative Organization

1. *What she doing?* She's putting that thing in the bag. He was bringing that because that was in the bag already. And he was getting ready for him to put that in the car. And she was getting ready to put that in the car too. And they were going all the way to another street. He was taking a bath. And his mommy taking a bath for her. And he had a pair of shorts on. And he was going to paint. That's the daddy. But they were going somewhere because they were going to the store. (Level 1: Act List Narrative)

2. There was a mother and a little girl and it was Christmas. And they were making Christmas cookies for the old people that doesn't go out. They go shopping to get stuff, but they don't make food, except for the meals. *That's what I did for this Christmas at church.* And then the cookie batter is all ready. So the little girl used the rolling pin to punch the batter out so they could punch cookies down. While she was doing that, the mom was making the stove hot to bake the cookies. And then when the cookies were all ready, they put them on a pan. And they were all ready to put it in the oven. And then they finally put it in the oven. And the light flashed. And then very soon the cookies were all ready. And then they sat down and tested a few of them. And then they were sending them all out. (Level 2: Chronologically Sequenced Narrative)

3. Once upon a time when the mother, the father, and the little kid . . . and they were going on a picnic to the beach. They pack their things going to the

beach. And then they were on their way and they were nearly there. And they were all ready. And they were getting packed. And the mom was worried because the dad put the umbrella in without closing it. Ha. Ha. It's not closed. And then they saw a boat turn over. Ha. Ha. And then the mommy and the boy were out swimming and then the boy nearly drowned. And then when they got back to the beach, his father and him started making a big sand castle with buckets on the outside so no one could get in the sand castle. And then they finished the picnic so they were going home. And then on the way home they saw a seagull. (Level 3: Transitional Narrative)

   4. They're making the dough to make cookies. And the little sister can't wait 'til they're done. Now the mother is getting the stove ready and the sister is rolling out the dough to put the shapes on. Now they put the shapes on and they take the shapes out of the dough. And the stove is ready to put the cookies in. And now the cookies are done. And the little girl wants to eat them. But first they have to cool off. And now they're done. And the little girl is jumping up and down cause she's happy. And now they're eating the cookies. (Level 3: Transitional Narrative)

   5. Once there was an old man and an old woman and a little kid. They were going to the beach. Then when they got at the beach, the mother and father got out. When the mother and father got out, the little boy was lonely. The little boy was at the beach. He made a lot of sand castles. And a big wave came up and washed them away. Then when his little sand castles get all washed away, he was all sad. Then when he asked his mother and father, his sand castles all washed away . . . *He should make them further with wet sand cause that's what we did, we did that* . . . and then it breaked. They made another sand castle that was farther. (Level 4: Traditional Narratives)

   6. Once upon a time, there was a little girl. And her mother passed away a few years ago. And her mother left her in charge. And one day when they were baking cookies, the little sister was helping. And then she started to roll and roll, until it was really flat. And then the sister put the cookies in the oven cause the little sister wanted to learn how to bake cookies. So the older sister was trying to teach her. And then the older sister made a mistake. And she already put them in for a minute, then she read on the box for 4 minutes. And then she put it in for 4 minutes. And then it came out for 5 minutes. So then all the cookies were burnt and the little sister started to cry. And then the sister said, "I have an idea. Maybe we can go to the bakery and buy some cookies." So they went to the bakery and bought some cookies. The little sister wanted some gingerbread men. So she got some gingerbread men. And she looked at all the cakes and cupcakes and she wanted some of them too. But the sister said, "We came here for cookies." (Level 4: Traditional Narrative)

APPENDIX B

Study 2:
Examples of Overall Level of Narrative Organization

1. You bake them. (Impoverished Narrative)
2. We ate. We sat down. We baked. And we rolled it. (Act List Narrative)
3. First they took the dough and they rolled it out. And then they put it on the pan. Then she put it in the oven. Then they put the stuff on. Then they eat one. (Chronologically Sequenced Narrative)
4. Once these children were making cookies. And they didn't know how to make them. So they went and gathered some stuff. They thought first they could use the grass as the flour. And then they could use the flower petals as the sugar. And they didn't know how to make them, so they just added anything they could. And after they made them, the oven exploded and they had a mess! And then their mother came in and grounded them. And they tasted the cookies and they said, "Yuck!" And the mother said, "That's why you have to clean the cookies up a few weeks ago." (Transitional Narrative)
5. One day two kids were making cookies and one of them fell inside the dough. And he got mixed up in the dough. And his mom turned the beaters on and he grabbed one of the beaters. And he was going around and around and he got dizzy. And then his mom turned off the beaters and put them in the sink to dry and turned on the water. And he went swimming and he got pulled down the drain! (Transitional Narrative)
6. There was a boy and it was his mom's birthday. He needed to make cookies for her. So he asked some friends to come over that night to help him bake the cookies. He asked a girl named Michelle, a boy named Steven, and another boy named Michael. They first took the dough and they rolled it out and put heart shaped cookie cutters in them. And then they put them in the oven for 5 minutes. And then they came out and they were burnt! They had to start all over again. Then when they finished them, they put icing on them and chocolate chips. Then they put them on a tray and gave them to their mom. The mom took a bite out of the cookies and she liked them a lot.

ACKNOWLEDGMENT

Lauren R. Shapiro was supported by a postdoctoral fellowship from the Carolina Consortium on Human Development.

REFERENCES

Applebee, A. N. (1978). The child's concept of story: Ages two to seventeen. Chicago: The University of Chicago Press.

Bamberg, M. (1986). A functional approach to the acquisition of anaphoric relationships. Linguistics, 24, 227–284.

Bamberg, M. (1987). The acquisition of narratives: Learning to use language. Berlin: Mouton de Gruyter.

Bartlett, E. J. (1984). Anaphoric reference in written narrative of good and poor elementary school writers. Journal of Verbal Learning and Verbal Behavior, 23, 540–552.

Bennett-Kastor, T. L. (1986). Cohesion and predication in child narratives. Journal of Child Language, 13, 353–370.

Bloom, L., Lahey, M., Hood, L., Lifter, K., & Fiess, K. (1980). Complex sentences: Acquisition of syntactic connectives and the semantic relations they encode. Journal of Child Language, 7, 235–261.

Botvin, G., & Sutton-Smith, B. (1977). The development of complexity in children's fantasy narratives. Developmental Psychology, 13, 377–388.

Brewer, W. F., & Lichtenstein, E.H. (1981). Event schemas, story schemas, and story grammars. In J. Long & A. Braddeley (Eds.), Attention and performance IX (pp. 363–379). Hillsdale, NJ: Lawrence Erlbaum Associates.

Cazden, C. B. (1970). The neglected situation in child language research and education. In F. Williams (Ed.), Language and poverty: Perspectives on a theme (pp. 81–101). Chicago: Markham Publishing Co.

French, L. A., & Nelson, K. (1985). Young children's understanding of relational terms: Some ifs, ors, and buts. NY: Springer-Verlag.

Gruendel, J. (1980). Scripts and stories: A study of children's event narratives. Unpublished doctoral dissertation, Yale University, New Haven, CT.

Halliday, M. A. K., & Hasan, R. (1976). Cohesion in English. London: Longmans.

Harrell, L. E., Jr. (1957). A comparison of the development of oral and written language in school-aged children. Monographs of the Society for Research in Child Development, 22 (3, Serial No. 66).

Hickmann, M. (1985). The implications of discourse skills in Vygotsky's developmental theory. In J. V. Wertsch (Ed.), Culture, communication, and cognition: Vygotskian perspective (pp. 236–251). Cambridge, England: Cambridge University Press.

Hudson, J. A., & Nelson, K. (1984). Differentiation and development in children's event narratives. Papers and Reports on Child Development Research, 23, 50–57.

Hudson, J. A., & Shapiro, L.R. (1991). Children's scripts, stories, and personal narratives. In A. McCabe & C. Peterson (Eds.), Developing narrative structure (pp. 89–136). Hillsdale, NJ: Lawrence Erlbaum Associates.

John-Steiner, V., & Panofsky, C. (1987, April). The development of cohesion in children's retold narratives. Paper presented at the meetings of the Society for Research in Child Development, Baltimore, MD.

Karmiloff-Smith, A. (1980). Psychological processes underlying pronominalization and non-pronominalization in children's connected discourse. In J. Kreiman & E. Ojedo (Eds.), Papers from the parasession on pronouns and anaphora (pp. 231–250). Chicago: Chicago Linguistics Society.

Karmiloff-Smith, A. (1986). Some fundamental aspects of language development after age 5. In P. Fletcher & M. Garman (Eds.), Language acquisition (pp. 455–474). New York: Cambridge University Press.

Kernan, K. T. (1977). Semantic and expressive elaboration in children's narratives. In S. Ervin-Tripp & C. Mitchell-Kernan (Eds.), Child discourse (pp. 91–102). New York: Academic Press, Inc.

Labov, W. (1972). Language in the inner city. Philadelphia, PA: University of Pennsylvania Press.

Leondar, B. (1977). Hatching plots: Genesis of storymaking. In D. Perkins & B. Leondar (Eds.), *The arts and cognition* (pp. 172–191). Baltimore: John Hopkins University Press.

Mandler, J. M. (1983). Representation. In J.H. Flavell & E.M.Markman (Eds.), *Handbook of child psychology: Vol. 3. cognitive development* (pp. 420–494). New York: John Wiley and Sons.

Mandler, J. M. (1984). *Stories, scripts, and scenes*. Hillsdale, NJ: Lawrence Erlbaum Associates.

Mandler, J. M., & De Forest, M. (1979). Is there more than one way to recall a story? *Child Development, 50,* 886–889.

Mandler, J. M., & Johnson, N. S. (1977). Remembrance of things parsed: Story structure and recall. *Cognitive Psychology, 9,* 111–151.

Menig-Peterson, C., & McCabe, A. (1978). Children's orientation of a listener to the context of their narratives. *Developmental Psychology, 14,* 582–592.

Nelson, K., & Gruendel, J. M. (1986). Children's scripts. In K. Nelson, (Ed.), *Event knowledge: Structure and function in development* (pp. 21–46). Hillsdale, NJ: Lawrence Erlbaum Associates.

Peterson, C., & McCabe, A. (1983). *Developmental psycholinguistics: Three ways of looking at a child's narrative*. New York: Plenum Press.

Peterson, C., & McCabe, A. (1991). Linking children's connective use and narrative macrostructure. In A. McCabe & C. Peterson (Eds.), *Developing narrative structure* (pp.29–53). Hillsdale, NJ: Lawrence Erlbaum Associates.

Peterson, C., & McCabe, A. (1994). A social interactionist account of developing decontextualized narrative skill. *Developmental Psychology, 30,* 937–948.

Poulsen, D., Kintsch, E., Kintsch, W., & Premack, D. (1979). Children's comprehension and memory for stories. *Journal of Experimental Child Psychology, 28,* 379–403.

Pradl, G. M. (1979). Learning how to begin and end a story. *Language Arts, 56,* 21–25.

Pratt, M., & MacKenzie-Keating, S. (1985). Organizing stories: The effects of development and task difficulty on referential cohesion in narrative. *Developmental Psychology, 21,* 350–356.

Quasthoff, U. M., & Nikolaus, K. (1981, Sept.). *What makes a good story?* Paper presented at the International Symposium on Text Processing, Fribourg, Switzerland.

Scott, C. (1984). Adverbial connectivity in conversations of children 6 to 12. *Journal of Child Language, 11,* 423–432.

Seidman, S., Nelson, K., & Gruendel, J. (1986). Make-believe scripts: The transformation of ERS in fantasy. In K. Nelson (Ed.), *Event knowledge: Structure and function in development* (pp. 231–247). Hillsdale, NJ: Lawrence Erlbaum Associates.

Shapiro, L. R. (1990). *Developmental differences in children's ability to produce structurally coherent and linguistically cohesive personal narratives and stories.* Unpublished doctoral dissertation, Rutgers, New Brunswick, NJ.

Shapiro, L. R. (1994, April). *Children's ability to produce coherent and cohesive stories: Photographs are no substitute for experience.* Paper presented at the Conference on Human Development, Pittsburgh, PA.

Shapiro, L. R., & Hudson, J. A. (1991). Tell me a make-believe story: Coherence and cohesion in young children's picture-elicited narratives. *Developmental Psychology, 27,* 960–974.

Stein, N. L. (1988). The development of children's storytelling skill. In M.B. Franklin & S. Barten (Eds.), *Child language: A book of readings* (pp. 282–297). New York: Oxford University Press.

Stein, N. L., & Glenn, C. G. (1979). An analysis of story comprehension in elementary-school children. In R.O. Freedle (Ed.), *New directions in discourse processing* (pp. 53–120). Norwood, NJ: Ablex Publishing Corp.

Stein, N. L., & Glenn, C. G. (1982). Children's concept of time: The development of story schema. In W.J. Friedman (Ed.), *The developmental psychology of time* (pp. 255–281). New York: Academic Press.

Stein, N. L., Glenn, C., & Jarcho, H. (1982). *Children's stories: A method for describing the structural complexity and thematic content generated stories.* Unpublished manuscript, University of Chicago.

Stein, N. L., & Policastro, M. (1984). The concept of a story: A comparison between children's and teachers' perspectives. In H. Mandl, N.L. Stein, & T. Trabasso (Eds.), Learning and comprehension of text (pp. 113–155). Hillsdale, NJ: Lawrence Erlbaum Associates.

Stenning, K., & Mitchell, L. (1985). Learning how to tell a good story: The development of content and language in children's telling of one tale. *Discourse Processes, 8,* 261–279.

Sutton-Smith, B. (1975). The importance of the storytaker: An investigation of the imaginative life. *The Urban Review, 8,* 82–95.

Vygotsky, L. S. (1935). Dinamika umstvennogo razvitija shkol'nika v svjazi s obucheniem. In L.S. Vygotsky (Ed.), *Umstvennoe razvitie detej v processe obuchenija* (pp. 33–52). Moscow-Lennigrad: Uchpedgiz. (Original work published 1933).

Warden, D. A. (1976). The influence of context on children's use of identifying expressions and reference. *British Journal of Psychology, 67,* 101–112.

White, H. (1980). The value of narrativity in the representation of reality. In W.J.T. Mitchell (Ed.), *On narrative.* Chicago: University of Chicago Press.

Part II

ON CONNECTIVES

Part II consists of five chapters dealing with the integration function of connectives. The first three chapters are mostly devoted to the evaluation of the
functioning of connectives in comprehension; the last chapters are devoted to
production of connectives by children. The stress here is on the connectives'
semantic features, in view of the subjects' age and of the task characteristics.

In chapter 3 Caron defines the term *connective* and highlights the essential
characteristic of these words: They belong to a closed class. This suggests that
they are closely linked to fundamental cognitive processes. Caron draws up a
run-down on different interpretations of the role of connectives. From a logical
point of view, their linguistic meaning is equivalent to their logical meaning;
from a semantic point of view, the connectives express a limited number of
relations between states of the world. In a pragmatic approach, speakers and
listeners and their relationships to the propositional contents also have to be
taken into account. Caron reports a series of empirical results in support of a
procedural view: Connectives would be logistic tools acting on the representations through processing instructions (e.g., change in focus for *mais* "but",
focus attention on the state of things described in the clause following *si* "if").

In chapter 4, Noordman and Vonk postulate, like Gernsbacher, that the
building of the representation associated to a discourse is carried out by taking
into account the previous knowledge of the reader and the characteristics of
the text. Among the latter, the connectives activate procedures of segmentation, integration, and inference; each of which intervenes at one of the three
representational levels built by the reader: surface representation, propositional
representation, and mental representation, respectively. These different representations are elaborated online and are relatively dependent on each other.
The segmentation would take place on the surface representation, focusing
attention on the running clause and deactivating the elements of the previous
clause (cf. the example of "because"). The integration would be performed on
the propositional representation by bringing together concepts belonging to

49

different propositions. Finally, the interferences would draw on the readers/auditors' knowledge of the world in building a representation of the state of the world described in the text. The authors illustrate their ideas by bringing up a series of results concerning *because*, showing that such a connective would intervene in a complex manner at different levels and at different stages of sentence processing, by activating or deactivating the previously used items.

In chapter 5, Segal and Duchan, like Caron, outline the different functions of the interclausal connectives, but they focus on the conceptual function considered during production. They assume that the author of a narrative elaborates a story world that requires a "deictic shift," allowing the localization of the states and events in this world. Different linguistic means contribute to this deictic shift, in particular, the interclausal connectives. For example, *and* signals a continuity between the events, whereas *then* translates a discontinuity. In comprehension, the connectives would guide the reader (or auditor) in the building of the mental model. They would particularly indicate if and when the coming information is to be added or, on the contrary, must be distinguished from the previous information. More in general, they would specify the relationships between the elements of the mental model. The authors illustrate their conceptions by analyzing the occurrences of *but* in oral narratives produced by a five-year-old child and in two texts written by adults, one for the children and one for an adult audience. Data show that the use of *but* comes down to four types of conditions and that most of the examples can be interpreted in a three-part interpretive schema (e.g., the core meaning) that seems to be acquired early during the linguistic development.

In chapter 6, Braunwald, like McCabe and Peterson in chapter 7, is more particularly interested in the development of the expression of causality, particularly through the use of *because* and *so*. Braunwald reports an analysis of the diary data produced by her daughter Laura between the age of 15 and 42 months. This analysis aims at determining why, when, and how causal connectives (*because* and *so*) are acquired. The observed evolution goes from the juxtaposition of utterances that could be linked by causal connective (implicit causality) to the explicit use of *because* and then *so* which discards any ambiguity. According to Braunwald, the procedural knowledge necessary to express the interclause relations is acquired very early and children as young as 3 commit very few errors. This competence integrates linguistic, conceptual and social dimensions. It is rooted in the interest that 2- to 3-year-old children give to causes and consequences of their own behavior and that of others.

In chapter 7, longitudinal study conducted by McCabe and Peterson on seven children from the age of 27 months completes the case study reported by Braunwald. McCabe and Peterson recorded for several months the conversations between parent and children about past events. These longitudinal data allowed better understanding of how the use of connectives took place. Indeed, past research had shown that the use of *and, because,* and *then* was not modified between the ages of 4 and 9 years, and gave rise to very few mistakes. Consequently, children had to have acquired the ability to use these connectives at an earlier stage. Data of the longitudinal study confirmed the effects of the "parental scaffolding" on the use of connectives expressing causality. Indeed, the analysis of the exchanges between parents and children revealed that children answered parental prompting questions about causality several weeks before spontaneously using the causal statements. Moreover, the age of the first spontaneous use of the causal connectives was correlated to the number of causal connections uttered by the parents during conversations of the preceding months. McCabe and Peterson consider, therefore, that parental scaffolding enables causal connection and determines, at least partly, the more or less precocious age at which causal connectives are used.

Chapter 3

Toward a Procedural
Approach of the Meaning
of Connectives

Jean Caron
Université de Poitiers

The term *connective* is used "to characterize words or morphemes whose function is primarily to link linguistic units at any level" (Crystal, 1991, 74). Although their grammatical status can be variable (most of them are conjunctions, but some are usually classified as adverbs), their semantic function seems to be well defined; they denote some kind of relationship between the contents of the linguistic units they link. The most obvious units are clauses, but the link may hold between smaller units, such as phrases, or larger ones, such as whole paragraphs.

A common feature of those linguistic marks is that they belong to the *closed class*, that is, a class which, in every language, includes "a small number of fixed elements" so that "any change in membership of such a class happens only very slowly (over centuries) and in small increments" (Akmajian, Demers, Farmer, & Harnish, 1990, p. 20). This relative permanence across linguistic changes (as contrasted with the variability of content words along the time) leads one to think that their function is directly linked with some fundamental cognitive operations. Therefore, their study is particularly interesting for cognitive psychology, in that it can shed some light on the nature of elementary operations that take place in language production and comprehension and on the structure of cognitive representations.

This chapter, first, gives a brief overview of the psychological literature on connectives and of the problems they raise. In the second part, we discuss the main directions in which those problems have been approached and try to formulate an alternative theory. Experimental data will then be presented in support of this approach [1]. Reflections about the questions those views raise for cognitive science are offered.

FROM LOGIC TO PRAGMATICS

At first view, the function of connectives seems quite a simple one; they convey information about the kind of relationship existing between the states of things denoted by the linguistic units they link. However, such a definition is too simple. It raises problems as to the nature of those relationships, on one hand, and of the entities to which they are linked, on the other hand:

1. Some connectives seem to encode a purely logical, truth-functional relation, combining the truth values of propositions, without consideration of their content. They could be viewed as corresponding to the basic operators of propositional logic: conjunction - *and* -, disjunction - *or* -, and implication - *if*. (We shall not here consider the negation, *not*, which raises a lot of problems of its own).

2. Alternatively, connectives can be defined as expressing some physical relation, in the real world, between the states of things denoted by the clauses they link: temporal (*then*, *next*) or causal (*because*, *so*)—or a conceptual one, such as similarity or contrast, as is the case, for example, in adversative connectives (*but*, *although*, *however*), which express an opposition between the hearer's assumed expectations, and the actual state of things.

3. Finally, the relation may hold, not between the states of things denoted by the propositional contents of the clauses, but between speech acts. As Halliday and Hasan (1976) noticed, cohesive devices can be interpreted either in terms of the experiential function of language (i.e., representation of our experience of reality), or in terms of its interpersonal function (referring to the communication process); what they call their external versus internal function.

Combining Truth Values: The Logical Approach

Most of the early psychological studies of connectives have focused on the first class of connectives (*and*, *or*, *if*), assuming that they express something like a "mental logic", more or less similar to the propositional calculus of formal logic. Hence, the number of studies bearing on the truth tables, or on the inferential schemes, associated with those conjunctions. A variety of reasoning tasks have

---

[1]The experiments reported here have been carried out on French subjects. The correspondence of the connectives under study and their English counterparts is, at best, approximative; some uses of *mais*, *si*, *parce que*, and so forth, do not fully coincide with *but*, *if*, *because*, and so forth. Cross-linguistic studies are needed (e.g., Kail & Weissenborn, 1984). However, generalizations are not forbidden. As an example, the various uses of *si* in French can be found in other languages; the same sample of sentences with *si* could be translated with German *wenn*, and even in non-Indo-European languages, such as Finnish (*jos*) and Arab (*itha*) (Caron, Caron-Pargue, Micko, Tomeh, & Verdret, 1987; and see Footnote 2).

thus been designed to explore the logical development of children (see, e.g., Paris, 1975) or reasoning processes in adults (e.g. Falmagne, 1975). Not surprisingly, subjects generally fail to correctly achieve their logical task, and several types of hypotheses have been brought forward to explain this fact: incomplete truth tables (Wason & Johnson-Laird, 1976), specific inference schemas (Braine, Reiser & Rumain, 1984), and various biases in reasoning processes (Evans, 1982). More recently, Johnson-Laird's approach in terms of "mental models" (Johnson-Laird & Byrne, 1991) seems to fit with a wide range of data.

However, the problem we have to address is another one. Interesting as those studies may be, they rarely take into account the fact that experimental instructions are (necessarily) formulated in linguistic terms. A widely held (although rarely questioned) assumption is that there is no difference between the linguistic meaning of connectives and their logical counterparts.

In fact, linguistic connectives sometimes mean less than logical operators (in that they cannot give rise to the same inferences), sometimes more (i.e., implying a richer set of relationships, such as causal, temporal, etc.), and sometimes imply other kinds of relations, which do not seem truth-functional at all. *And* conveys other kinds of relations, along with the meaning that *p* and *q* are both true, depending on context: a temporal order, sometimes a causal relation, and even an contrastive one. *Or* can denote an inclusive disjunction, but sometimes an exclusive one. As for *If*, it takes on a wide variety of uses, from the seemingly logical ones (sometimes reducible to simple implication *if p, then q*; sometimes to equivalence *q if and only if p*), to adversative relations (although *p, q*), with puzzling cases where it does not seem at all to imply any logical relationship (as noticed by Austin, 1956).

A series of experiments by Fillenbaum (1977) have clearly shown how, in everyday language, those connectives depart from a truth-functional meaning. Their meaning depends heavily on the context. But what does "context" exactly mean? And what are the mechanisms by which this interaction is achieved? We shall return to that issue later.

Expressing Factual Relations: The Semantic Approach

A purely logical approach leaves aside a large number of connectives. Most of them are not (or, at least, not purely) truth-functional. They may express a number of relations between states of things or events in the world. These relations can be classified into four types (Halliday and Hasan, 1976): additive (*and, or*), temporal (*then, next*), causal (*because, so*), and adversative (*but, though*).

A number of experimental studies have focused on this semantic function, most of them in a developmental perspective (for a review, see, e.g., French and

Nelson, 1985). The order of acquisition of those different types of connectives seems to follow their relative order of complexity: additive < temporal < causal < adversative (Bloom, Lahey, Hood, Lifter, & Fiess, 1980). As for the time when children are able to fully grasp the underlying relations, data are more contro-versial. While most experimental studies conclude a rather late mastery of the "correct" use of connectives, French & Nelson (1985) have shown that, in familiar contexts, even 3-year-olds are able to display an almost perfect use of usual connectives. Rather than a progressive construction of semantic relations, cognitive development would imply a decontextualisation of those relations.

However, what is at issue in most researches—just like in studies on logical competence—is not really the functioning of linguistic connectives. These are generally assumed to simply denote factual relations, corresponding to some cognitive primitives, such as time or causality. Thus, the errors children make in understanding or producing connectives are interpreted—in the line of Piaget's (1924) first works—as evidence for their incomplete acquisition of those basic conceptual relations. (See Peterson & McCabe, this volume, for a discussion of this approach).

Since adult subjects can be assumed to have fully mastered those concepts, few studies are concerned with them. What has been chiefly explored is the role connectives play in the process of integrating information in texts. It can be shown, for example, that the presence of a connective at the beginning of a sentence makes this integration easier, as evidenced by shorter reading times (Haberlandt, 1982). A series of experiments by Townsend and Bever (Town-send, 1982; Townsend and Bever, 1978) explores this effect in more detail. A causal connective (*because, if, since*) gives rise immediately to thematic integra-tion, whereas adversative ones (*although, however*) delay this integration. The reader holds in memory the linguistic form of the sentence until complementary information has been given. More recently, similar results have been obtained by Ziti and Champagnol (1992) with French connectives expressing causal relations - *parce que* 'because', *puisque* 'since', or contrastive ones - *quoique* 'albeit' and *bien que* 'although'. However, some of their data cannot be explained by semantic properties only: *puisque* and *bien que* give rise to faster processing of the final clause than *parce que* and *quoique*. The authors ascribe this effect to the differences in illocutionary force of those pairs of connectives.

Pragmatic Aspects of Connectives

Thus, the semantic approach is incomplete. Connectives do not only express relations between propositional contents; they also implicate speakers and hearers and their own relationship to that content. That appears in at least three ways.

First, the same semantic relation can be expressed by several connectives, which differ only in the way the partners in the communicative act commit themselves to the content of the propositions. For example, conjunctions such as *because*, *although*, *if*, and *unless* imply different states of belief (Wing & Scholnick, 1981), and their comprehension by children progressively improves with age. It is also the case, as mentioned before, for causal or contrastive conjunctions in French. For example, *parce que* and *puisque* both denote a causal relation, but they differ in the speaker's and hearer's attitudes toward that relation and the clauses it links (Barbault et al., 1975). As we have just seen, this difference gives rise to changes in processing time (Ziti & Champagnol, 1992).

Second, the relation may hold, not between propositions, but between speech acts. For example, the use of *because* in Example 1, expresses a causal relation between the content of the second clause and the speech act (here, a question) expressed in the first one:

1. What is John's phone number, because I have to call him.

An intermediate case can be observed when, as in example (2), the second clause does not give the cause of the fact expressed in the first one, but rather the reason for asserting it:

2. John has left, because his car is not here.

Finally, connectives can play a role, not only in stating a specific relationship between clauses, but as conversational devices, marking the function of an utterance within discourse processes. Thus, studies of narrations in children show that *and* can be interpreted as "a generalized signal of cohesion between sentences and an indication that the narrator's conversational turn is not over" (Peterson & McCabe, 1988, p. 19), and that *but* "signals a change in level within a speaker's turn" (Peterson, 1986, p. 583). In such a view, connectives could be linked up with Roulet's *marqueurs de structuration de la conversation* (conversational structure markers) (Roulet, Auchlin, Moeschler, Rubattel, Schelling, 1987).

In summary, natural language connectives can fulfill a broad range of functions, and, accordingly, take on a number of different meanings. How can this polysemy, and plurifunctionality, be accounted for? A simple way of dealing with this problem would be to argue that we have "different connective meanings or functions which happen to be expressed by the same expressions" (Van Dijk, 1979, p. 449). But the generality of this phenomenon across languages rules out such an appeal to simple homonymy, even if "the pragmatic use of connectives may be accompanied by different phonological and syntactic constraints" (Van Dyk, 1979, p. 449.). Those differences are not always the case.

Obviously, those different functions and meanings of the same connective have something in common. The problem is to define this common element and to account for the way it interacts with context. It can be approached in several ways.

THEORETICAL APPROACHES TO POLYSEMY

Literal Meaning and Inferences

The most popular approach relies on a sharp distinction between semantics and pragmatics. It has its main source in Grice's theory of conversational maxims and implicatures (Grice, 1975). Given a conventional definition of the meaning of connectives, their semantically bizarre behavior can be accounted for by distinguishing between this literal meaning and the hearer's interpretation of the utterance, on the basis of general principles of communication and knowledge of the current situation. One would simply have to distinguish between meaning and use, that is between the allegedly simple semantic content of connectives and the inferences one has to draw to adjust the "literal meaning" they provide, with specific and general knowledge relevant to the situation.

Polysemy thus appears as a purely pragmatic phenomenon. At the semantic level, connectives have to be assigned one meaning; *if* simply means material implication, *and* logical conjunction, *because* causality, and so on. It is at the pragmatic level of interpretation that contextual information, and conversational rules, will lead to indirect interpretations. For example, the connective *and* merely implies logical conjunction (p and q are both true); but in some cases, the Grice's maxim of manner ("be orderly") leads to interpret the two events as ordered in time ("he went to Paris and stayed there for a month"), while Grice's maxim of relevance may even suggest a causal link ("he fell down and broke his leg"). A similar argument can be developed concerning other connectives.

Language understanding is thus conceived according to a two-stage model: a first stage of purely linguistic processing, followed by a stage of inferential procedures. Most students of language adopt this view, even if they disagree with some of Grice's assumptions (Sperber and Wilson, 1986). However attractive it seems, this conception raises several difficulties:

1. What is the output of the first stage of linguistic processing? Because it has to be the basis for inferences, it must be of a propositional nature. But connectives may link speech acts, and speech acts are not propositions. Moreover, some connectives (such as French *parce que* and *puisque*) differ only by their pragmatic features. Must these features be conceived as part of their logical form? The strict separation between semantics and pragmatics becomes problematic.

2. Inferential processes raise other problems. First, they imply (as noted previously) the existence of a literal sense, which is a purely theoretical construct. Moreover, the hypothesis lacks experimental evidence. Inferences take time, and they consume cognitive resources. As far as we know, no experimental data have shown, until now, the psychological reality of Gricean inferences. On the contrary, the hypothesis of a two-stage processing of meaning has been seriously challenged, concerning the understanding of metaphors (Ortony, Schallert, Reynolds & Antos, 1978) or of indirect speech acts (Gibbs, 1979). And there is some experimental evidence in favor of a direct "mapping from lexical representation onto mental models" (Marslen-Wilson & Tyler, 1987, p.59).

Metaphorical Use

A rather different approach is adopted by Sweetser (1990). Her main hypothesis (inspired from Lakoff) is that "not only our language, but our cognition and hence our language, operates metaphorically" (Sweetser, 1990, p.8). So, the same terms can be applied to different domains, while remaining conceptually the same. At least three domains can be distinguished; *content domain* (referring to physical or social events); *epistemic domain* (referring to our knowledge, and reasoning about it); and *speech acts domain* (where the relation holds between performances of speech acts). As an example (Sweetser, 1990, p.77), *since* can be interpreted in Example 3 as expressing real-world causality, in Example 4 as drawing a conclusion from a piece of knowledge, and in Example 5 as giving the cause of the speech act embodied in the main clause:

3. Since John wasn't there, we decided to leave a note for him.
4. Since John isn't here, he has evidently gone home.
5. Since you're so smart, when was George Washington born?

There is no reason, Sweetser argues, to consider the logical use as primitive. On the contrary, it seems more likely that the truth-functional meaning of

There is no reason, Sweetser argues, to consider the logical use as primitive. On the contrary, it seems more likely that the truth-functional meaning of connectives derives from their natural-language use which, in turn, has its basis in "the human perception and understanding of the world" (Sweetser, 1990, p.2). The primitive meaning applies to the content domain; and from there, it can be metaphorically extended to the other domains, giving rise to seemingly different meanings, but following the same pattern.

Although Sweetser often refers to Grice's maxims, her basic assumptions are of a different nature. She does not rely on inferential processes to derive the meaning of a given connective from a literal one, rather she argues for a direct mapping of the connective onto a particular domain. This recourse to metaphoric processes is interesting, but it raises two kinds of questions.

1. What are the mechanisms by which this mapping takes place ? The very notion of *metaphor* is, in itself, poorly understood. Most studies on metaphor (Ortony, 1993) focus on metaphorical uses of content words and approach them in terms of categorization (as does Lakoff, 1987). Can metaphorical use of abstract relations allow the same kind of treatment ?

2. The notion of metaphor still implies something like a literal meaning. For the author, this meaning should come from the content use, that is, the expression of relations between states of things in the real world (physical or social); or in Halliday and Hasan's terms, the external (or experiential) function of language should be more primitive than its internal (or interpersonal) function (Halliday & Hasan, 1976, p. 261). It does not seem to be necessarily the case. Data from children's language suggest that, at least for some connectives, pragmatic uses appear earlier and remain more frequent, than their content uses. For example, young French children use *parce que* ('because') mainly to give a justification for a speech act expressed in the first clause, as in:

6. Tire-toi de là, parce que c'est ma place.
   'Get out of there, because it's my place.'

Causal uses seem to appear at a later stage. Conversely, the first uses of *si* ('if') encode relations between real-world events; speech-acts conditionals (e.g., the contrastive use of *if*) occur much later. It is possible that the meaning of those terms has at first to be constructed in a particular context be it physical, social, or conversational. But the main issue is not in what occasion they are

Meaning Schemas and Meaning Effects

What obscures the problem is the notion of *literal meaning*, which in fact seems to be nothing but an *ens rationis*. This notion relies on a deeply rooted metaphor; words are conceived as containers, in which meanings are enclosed, and from which they are extracted when understanding an utterance. Hence the problem of explaining what we finally perceive is another meaning. Things may become clearer if we adopt another point of view, which could be called (since metaphors are inevitable) the *tool metaphor*.

Words can then be conceived, not as carrying meaning with them, but as tools for constructing meaning in a given context. In such a view, there is just one kind of meaning: the one that is consciously perceived. The output of linguistic processing is not a meaning, but a pattern of procedures which, applied to the current representation, will structure and modify it.

Let us explore the metaphor a little more. What is the function of a hammer? The first idea which comes in mind is pounding nails. But, in fact, a hammer can be used for a lot of other functions: cracking nuts (or other breakable things), beating something flat (a piece of leather or metal), making a hole in a wall and so forth. The primitive function is not one of those (as if a hammer was first designed to drive nails and then metaphorically used in other domains). It has to be defined in a more abstract way as in transferring a certain amount of kinetic energy on a given object. Such a transfer gives rise to a large variety of effects, according to the nature of the object that receives it; penetration into a resistant material yielding change in shape, internal structure, or physiological functioning. These are contextual effects, depending on some relevant properties of the object. What is common is not one of these effects, but an underlying general property, which can be abstractly represented as previously stated. People using hammers do not have to (and, in fact, do not) realize that abstract schema: they simply intend to achieve some particular effect.

One can define the function of words in a similar fashion, by distinguishing between the *meaning schema* associated with a given word (which can be conceived as a pattern of procedures) and the various *meaning effects* obtained when it applies to various contexts (Caron, 1988). Take, as an example, the conjunction *if*. Its primitive meaning is not material implication; no more than pounding nails is the hammer's primitive function. It has to be conceived in a way that may give rise to the logical interpretation, but also to other senses, according to context. We have already proposed (Caron, 1987) a tentative description (in part inspired by Ducrot, 1972), that could be formulated as follows:

If *p*, *q* instructs the hearer to:

a) restrict (temporarily) the domain of discourse to a *mental space* where *p* is the case

b) in this domain, consider *q* as relevant.

Contextual information will then be used to assign values to a number of specific parameters: (a) is *p* a fact or an assertion; (b) does the speaker commit him/herself to *p*; (c) what is the illocutionary force of *q*? Those parameters clearly followed from a multidimensional analysis of subjects' responses in a sorting task on a list of sentences (Caron, 1987.). Moreover, they fit rather well with the results of linguistic descriptions.[2]

The truth-functional value of *if* appears then as a particular case, where those different parameters take on default values: *p* and *q* are propositions, endowed with truth values, no speaker's commitment to *p* is taken into account, and relevance is reduced to truth. This meaning, far from being primitive, is, in fact, the highly elaborated product of a process of abstraction. Educated people are able to (and sometimes do) reason on such formal schemas; but it is a result of training, not a reflection of mind's structures.

Similar descriptions could be given for other connectives (see the following example for a tentative description of *but*). The general idea would be to consider them (among other terms) as giving procedural instructions for structuring the representation. The various meanings they give rise to are the effects of that structuration on the representational context on which they operate.

SOME EXPERIMENTAL DATA

The general hypothesis just presented is not directly testable. However, it offers a coherent framework for a number of experimental data, which show various effects of connectives on the processing of linguistic information and can hardly be interpreted on the basis of current models of psychological semantics.

Giving Instructions For Use of Information

Rather than simply providing information about the relation between the propositions they link, connectives appear to give "instructions for use"for the information supplied by these propositions. An illustration can be given by the French conjunction *mais* ('but'). (Caron, 1987, 1988). This connective is

---

[2]The same parameters, with slightly different weights, appeared in similar analyses of German *wenn* and Finnish *jos* (Caron et al, 1987).

generally considered as signaling an adversative (or contrastive) relation between the clauses it links. However, it is not always the case, as can be observed in spontaneous productions of children, and even of adults.

In a French replication of French and Nelson's (1985) experiment, we recorded the verbal productions of 3- to 6- year-old children, who were asked to describe what happened in familiar situations (Caron, Mendes-Maillochon, & Caron-Pargue, 1989). A number of uses of *mais* did not express a clearly contrastive relation, but simply a change in focus, introducing some interesting piece of information as in Example 7 or a specification of already given information as in Example 8:

7. Mon père il m'avait offert un petit bracelet tout rond, mais avec des petites étoiles.
  'My father, he gave me a little round bracelet, but with little stars on it.'
8. Et après je fais un gâteau, une galette . . . Mais cette fois c'est une galette à la fraise.
  'And after that I make a cake, a tart . . . But this time it is a strawberry tart.'

It must be mentioned that the same children, in other utterances, used *mais* in a contrastive sense. Should we conclude that they have not yet fully mastered the true meaning of *mais* and utilized it in a haphazard fashion? Or rather that, in its various occurrences, the connective is the trace of a common underlying mental schema?

Those observations can be completed by the results of a pilot experiment (Caron, 1983) in which we gave subjects (children and adults) a set of sentences, followed by *mais*, and asked them to complete those sentences with the first clause that came to their minds. A clearly adversative use of *mais* occurred only in about one third of the subjects' productions, such as in Example 9; but there were an equal proportion of productions that either expressed, as in Example 10, a limitation of the domain of validity of the first clause (e.g., limitations in time); or, as in Example 11, simply a useful piece of information, which must be taken into account together with the first clause:

9. Je nettoie les allées de mon jardin, mais les feuilles continuent à tomber.
  'I clean the paths in my garden, but the leaves keep on falling.'
10. Je supporte cet individu, mais ça ne durera pas longtemps.
  'I bear with this fellow, but it won't last very long.'
11. Les radiateurs maintiennent la chaleur de la pièce, mais il ne faut pas ouvrir les fenêtres.
  'The radiators keep the room warm, but you must not open the windows.'

Rather than searching for a far-fetched interpretation of Examples 10 and 11 in terms of some contrastive relation, it seems that a better way of capturing the meaning of *mais* is to conceive it as an instruction for use of the content of the first clause. Rather than conveying information about the kind of relation holding between the respective contents of propositions p and q, it would trigger a procedure for constructing the representation of the two clauses in memory; something like "mark p as requiring, for further use, the recall of q." Making use of p may consist in drawing inferences from it (the function of q is then to cancel some of these inferences. Such cases fit well in with the conventional adversative interpretation, as well as with the interpretation suggested by Ducrot, 1980), but it may also take on other forms, such as obeying an order, acting on an advice, and so forth.

An obvious prediction from that hypothesis is that, in a cued-recall task, subjects who recall p should tend to recall also q; the converse being not the case. This prediction was fully supported by the results of an experiment (Guyot, 1991) where subjects heard a series of short paragraphs, and then were asked to recall "the sentence where" a given word occurred.[3] The target sentences included two clauses, linked by *mais* for one group of subjects, by *et* for a second group, and simply juxtaposed for the third group, for example:

12. (The story is about a dolphin) Il se laissait manipuler par tout le monde, (mais/et/,) il avait une préférence marquée pour les enfants.
    'He allowed everybody to handle him, (but/and/,) he markedly preferred children.'

When the probe was taken from the first clause (*manipuler*), there was a significant difference between the three conditions. Among subjects who recalled (at least partially) the first clause, the amount of recall of the second clause was 66.5 % when the clauses were linked by *mais*; it was only 38.4 % with *et* and 35.2 % without connective. When the probe was in the second clause (*préférence*), the difference disappeared; 38.2 % with *mais* and 38.0 % without connective; whereas with *et*, recall was slightly poorer (21.6 %).

In each of the three conditions, there appeared a purely associative relation between the two clauses (averaging approximately 30 % of recall). But with *mais*, an interesting result is that the relationship of the two clauses in memory is asymmetric: p entails the recall of the other clause, but q does not. That observation rules out a purely associationist interpretation. It is not a matter of

---

[3]A first version of this experiment is mentioned in Caron (1987); the results given here are taken from a more recent, better controlled version.

simply linking clauses together (what, more or less, any connective can do), but of constructing a functional organization among them. Such an organization, which is a characteristic feature of *mais*, can hardly be explained in a propositional model of sentence processing.

Putting Information Into Perspective

Another aspect of this organization is the way information is "put into perspective" in memory; some pieces of information are foregrounded, other ones being backgrounded.

This effect appeared in an earlier experiment (Caron, 1985) on text recall. Two versions of the same text were prepared. The first (original) version included a number of connectives; in the second version, those connectives were deleted. Two groups of adult subjects were presented with those two texts and asked to recall them. The first result was that there was no significant difference in overall recall between the two versions; on the whole, the same number of propositions were correctly recalled in both conditions. Apparently, the absence of connectives did not prevent subjects from grasping the semantic relations between propositions and building a coherent representation of the text. But there were noticeable differences between the two texts in the detail of recall protocols. For some clauses, recall was poorer when the connective was deleted; in other cases, it was better. For example, *d'ailleurs* ('besides') entailed a better recall of the clause it introduced and often a re-ordering of clauses. Conversely, the presence of *même si* ('even if') to introduce the last clause of the text gave rise to a significant decrease in the recall of that clause.

In a more recent experiment (Caron & Bert-Erboul, 1993), we studied how various connectives can affect the accessibility in memory of the different constituents of the clauses they link. Subjects had to read short paragraphs, that included a sentence made up of two clauses linked by a connective.

13. La servante a allumé le feu, (*C*) la pièce est pleine de fumée.
'The maid has lighted the fire, (*C*) the room is full with smoke. '

(where (*C*) stands for a connective such as *parce que, puisque, si, car, mais* . . .). The next sentence contained a pronoun, which could have as its antecedent one of the four main components of the preceding sentence; subject or object of the first or of the second clause, (for example: [a] *she is now in the garden*, [b] *it has difficulty to burn*, [c] *it is badly ventilated*, or [d] *it stings our eyes*). Reading times were recorded for that sentence; connectives and target sentences were varied across groups of subjects.

Reading times for the target sentences were assumed to depend upon the greater or lesser availability in memory of the pronoun's antecedent, and, therefore, to reflect the effects of the different connectives on the foregrounding or backgrounding of information. In fact, reading times (for the same target sentence) showed significant differences among connectives. A detailed analysis of these results is out of place here, but it should be noted, for example, that *parce que* and *puisque*, although expressing the same causal relation, gave rise to different patterns in the processing time of pronouns; whereas *puisque* entailed foregrounding (i.e., shorter processing time) for the subjects of both clauses, *parce que* focused on the first clause only. Obviously, such effects do not reflect the whole procedural pattern connected with those markers, but they certainly are parts of it. Here again, such results are not predictable on the basis of a propositional model.

A comparable effect can be observed with the conjunction *si* ('if'). The procedural schema associated with this conjunction has just been described. It leads one to suggest that a clause introduced by *if* induces hearers to focus their attention on the state of things described by that clause. This can explain a number of logical errors classically observed in experiments on conditional reasoning (and, in particular, the tendency to consider as irrelevant those cases where the antecedent was false).

Another experiment (Caron, 1988) gives further evidence in support of this hypothesis. In this experiment, we used a variant of Wason's classical paradigm (Wason, 1966). Subjects were presented with four cards, bearing a letter on one side and a digit on the other. They had to choose what cards were to be turned over, to verify a rule of the form "If there is a B on one face, there is a 4 on the other face." The conditional rule was presented in four different forms:

a) Si p, alors q ('If p , then q');
b) p si q ('p if q');
c) p seulement si q ('p only if q');
d) p sauf si q ('p except if q').

The task was a difficult one, and the number of logically correct responses was almost zero. However, our aim was not to study the logical competence of our subjects, but to determine whether the conjunction *si* introduced biases in the subject's strategies. And, in fact, it did.

In each of the four conditions, an important proportion of subjects (from 46–55 %) chose only one card. Among them, the most frequent choice (48%–64%) was on the card introduced by *si*, irrespective of the logical structure of the rule (a random choice would have given 25%). When subjects chose two cards or more, the same pattern obtained concerning the first card they turned over. This kind of focusing effect, which cannot be explained by any of the various biases already mentioned by students of conditional reasoning (Evans, 1982), is clearly linguistic in nature and has nothing to do with the logical meaning of *si*. However, it fits well in our hypothesis.

Cognitive Operations in the Production of Connectives

If on one hand, connectives trigger in the hearer procedures for constructing a semantic representation, on the other hand, they can be conceived of as markers of the speakers operations on their own cognitive representations. Data from language production in problem-solving situations sheds some light on this kind of process.

A first example can be drawn from an experiment (Caron-Pargue, 1983) on children (ages 5 to 11), who had to explain to a peer how to tie a knot. It is not a trivial task because it is not possible to assign a stable referring expression to each of the two ends of the string as the left one and the right one change at each manipulation. However, most children manage to achieve the task by using different connectives; *et* ('and') and *et puis* ('and then') are consistently used to imply that the same system of reference is in use (i.e., that the left end of the string is still the same, even if it is now in the right hand). With *après* ('after that'), the partner is informed that a new system of reference has to be put in place. Those different additive connectives do not seem to be used in a haphazard fashion but are assigned different hierarchical levels in the co-ordination of representative units of a different nature. Rather than instructions consciously given to the partner, they appear as traces of the subjects' operations on their representations.

To characterize those operations, a suitable procedure is to study the contexts in which various markers are produced in verbal protocols during a well defined cognitive task. A systematic analysis of a number of linguistic markers (connectives, modals, interjections, verbs, etc.) is currently being carried on verbal protocols gathered in problem-solving situations (Caron-Pargue & Caron, 1989). Taking into account the linguistic context on one hand (the linguistic features of the marker's environment) and the situational context on the other hand (the characteristics of the problem situation in which they appear), the cognitive operations that give rise to the production of a given marker can thus be determined, along with the relevant contextual parameters on which they operate.

Connectives and modals are both associated with operations by which subjects organize and transform their representation of the problem, but their roles are somewhat different. While modals correspond to decision processes, whereby subjects withdraw from their representation to consider other possible representations, connectives mark processes whereby subjects are working within the current state of their representation to organize representational units.

In a first analysis of the most frequently used connectives in a set of adult protocols (Caron-Pargue & Baudet-Briquet, 1988), two broad classes of connectives were distinguished: Group 1, where *et* ('and'), *alors* ('then') correspond to the follow-up of the procedures and link elements into larger units, different connectives being assigned to different levels in the hierarchy of representational units, as suggested in the experiment previously discussed and Group 2, where *si* ('if'), *mais* ('but'), and *donc* ('therefore') appear during breaks in the problem-solving process and mark phases where subjects are working on their representation and trying to adjust it, by focusing on a problematic element.

In a later study (Caron-Pargue, 1992), more refined analyses were carried out to characterize in greater detail the contexts in which some of those markers occurred. Linguistic and situational features of the context were submitted to a correspondence analysis that yielded clear-cut oppositions between the four most frequent connectives, *si* ('if'), *parce que* ('because'), *comme* ('as'), and *une fois que* ('once').

The main opposition was between *si* and *parce que*. The former appeared in contexts where subjects withdrew from their current representation and introduced a new assumption to evaluate it. When using *parce que*, on the contrary, subjects focused on the current situation to analyze it and select a problematic element. The other two connectives were in an intermediate position on that first dimension (interpreted as *partial withdrawing*). They both marked the introduction of a new reference point; either a shift in temporal reference (*une fois que*) or an identification of the element at hand with another, already known, element (*comme*).

Such analyses permit a clearer view on the nature of cognitive procedures involved in the meaning schemas of those markers. Similar comparisons between the different contexts, in which a given connective occurs leads to a characterization of the main contextual parameters. They define the conditions of use of a given marker and of the various values they can take on, thus giving rise to a variety of meaning effects.

The Feasibility of Operations

We have spoken of the structuring function of connectives as if it were only a matter of organization among formal, contentless units. Obviously, this is not the case, and, at least as far as comprehension is concerned, the content imposes its own constraints; the kind of organization that the connective triggers must be feasible.

These contraints can be a matter of available knowledge; bridging inferences may be necessary for building an integrated representation suited to the structure required by the connective. This result appeared clearly in an experiment (Caron, Micko, & Thuring, 1988) in which subjects had to learn lists of sentences, each of which was made up of two, unrelated clauses linked by *parce que* (because), *mais* (but), *et* (and), or no connective at all. For example:

14. Le prêtre pouvait construire la nouvelle église (parce que/mais/et/Ø) l'ordinateur avait commis une grosse faute.
    'The priest could build the new church, (because/but/and/Ø) the computer had made a serious error.'

In a cued recall task, results were significantly better with *parce que*, while *mais* and *et* entailed poor recall. However, sentences with *mais* gave rise to a steady increase in recall when learning time was increased. Moreover, evidence for inferential processes could be gathered from the analysis of errors; the frequency of inferential errors was the same for *parce que* and for *mais* (and significantly lower for *et*). Clearly, differences in recall did not come from depth of processing, but from the difficulty subjects had in constructing a plausible representation.

A similar case can be made for young children, who seem perfectly capable of using and understanding usual connectives in familiar contexts (French & Nelson, 1985), although generally showing poor comprehension in experimental settings. However, more general factors may intervene, in relation to the representational abilities. As an example, in our study of verbal productions of young children 3- to 5-years-old (Caron et. al., 1989), we observed that the spontaneous use of *si* did not appear before 4 ½–5 years; in similar contexts, youngest subjects only used *quand* ('when'). We suggested that this use could be related to the new ability of children to handle several mental spaces in their representation, which can be paralleled by their developing theory of mind.

Interesting lines of research can be explored concerning linguistic development in children in relation to, not their logical competence, but their representational capabilities.

CONCLUSION

The procedural approach we have outlined in this paper aims to avoid the difficulties that arise from the two-stage model of meaning and to account for the polysemy of connectives without assuming a heavy apparatus of inferential processes. Rather than conveying information about states of things, connectives can be conceived as procedural instructions for constructing a semantic representation. In such a view, contextual information is not processed *after* the elaboration of meaning, but *before* it; the meaning schemas of linguistic markers determine the relevant features of context which have to be taken into account.

The mode of approach presented here raises some important issues for cognitive psychology. If the function of connectives (and, probably, of a large amount of other linguistic markers) is to trigger (or be the trace of) a pattern of procedures organizing the semantic representation, what are these procedures? Cognitive psychology, and, more generally, cognitive science, have until now assumed that primitive procedures must be conceived according to the model of those physical symbol systems as exemplified by digital computers. This amounts to considering that the functioning of human cognitive systems essentially consists in a formal computation on strings of symbols. A logical component (i.e., the formal rules that control those computational procedures) is thus assumed to lie at the heart of the system, and perceptual and motor processes follow from it. Perhaps it is more convenient to reason the other way around; to assume that human cognitive processes (and logical ones) have their root in sensorimotor coordinations. This was already assumed by Piaget and is argued by a number of current researchers (Clancey, 1993; Mandler, 1992). Although formal computation and logical reasoning are obviously possible, they are emergent properties of human mind, not basic ones.

Thus, elementary procedures that underlie language processing would come closer to perceptual and motor processes than to computational procedures (although amenable, as every process is, to computational simulations). The procedural schemas that have been proposed here for some connectives must be conceived in that way. Similar proposals can be found in current theories of cognitive linguistics (Talmy, 1988), and are akin to Culioli's theory of enunciative operations (Culioli, 1990).

This brings us to a second issue concerning the nature and structure of semantic representation. The most popular assumption is to conceive it in a propositional format that fits well with the computational approach discussed. However, a growing body of data support the idea of other kinds of representation, whose nature is analogical and continuous, rather than digital and discrete: from the studies on mental images, through the revival of Gestaltist ideas, to Johnson-Laird's mental models. A large number of semantic phenomena, including the functioning of connectives, can be explained by resorting to such kinds of representations.

Further research is needed to properly conceive this semantic representation and the processes by which it is organized and transformed. Such a task implies the consideration of a number of properties, which have not yet been sufficiently taken into account. For example, rather than the momentary activation of a body of knowledge, this representation has to be conceived as the product of the interaction with a world of biologically and culturally meaningful objects. It involves an interaction with other cognitive agents and involves the subjects' capacity for taking various points of view, focusing on such and such elements, and even withdrawing from their representation, to consider other possible worlds or mental spaces.

In conclusion, the study of connectives raises some fundamental issues that put into question some deeply rooted assumptions of current models of psychological functioning. Whether the cognitivist paradigm is able to take up this challenge, is still unclear. But cognitive psychology and, more generally, cognitive science, cannot do without seriously considering these problems.

REFERENCES

Akmajian, A., Demers, R. A., Farmer, A. K., & Harnish R. M. (1990). *Linguistics: An introduction to language and communication*. Cambridge, MA: MIT Press.

Austin, J. L. (1970). Ifs and cans. In J. L. Austin (Ed.), *Philosophical Papers* (Original work published 1956). (2nd ed., pp. 205–232). Oxford, England: Oxford University Press.

Barbault, M. C., Ducrot, O., Dufour, J., Espagnon, J., Israel, C., & Manesse, D. (1975). Car, parce que, puisque. *Revue Romane*, 2-X, 248–280.

Bloom, L., Lahey, M., Hood, L., Lifter, K., & Fiess, K. (1980). Complex sentences: Acquisition of syntactic connectives and the semantic relations they encode. *Journal of Child Language*, 7, 235–261.

Braine, M. D. S., Reiser, B. J., Rumain, B. (1984). Some empirical justification for a theory of natural propositional logic. In G. Bower (Ed.), *The psychology of learning and motivation*, Vol. 18, (313–371). New York: Academic Press.

Caron, J. (1983). Langage et argumentation: Etude d'enchaînements d'énoncés. In *La Pensée Naturelle* (pp. 229–240) (Actes du Colloque de Rouen, Sept.1981), Paris: P.U.F

Caron, J. (1985). Le rôle des marques argumentatives dans le rappel d'un texte. *Bulletin de Psychologie* [spécial Psycholinguistique textuelle], 38, 775–784.

Caron, J. (1987). Processing connectives and the pragmatics of discourse. In: J. Verschueren & M. Bertuccelli-Papi (Eds.), *The Pragmatic Perspective* (pp. 567–580) [Selected Papers from the 1985 International Pragmatics Conference] Amsterdam: J. Benjamins

Caron, J. (1988). Schémas de sens et effets de sens: La sémantique des termes fonctionnels. In: J. F. Richard (Ed.), *Actes du 3e Colleque International, "Cognition et connaissance: Où va la science cognitive?"* (pp. 283–297). Paris: Association pour la Recherche Cognitive.

Caron, J., Bert-Erboul, A. (1993). L'effet de connecteurs sur la disponibilité des informations en mémoire. In B. Claverie, E. Esperet & R. Jaffard (Eds.), *Actes du Colloque Sciences cognitives - Façade Atlantique*, pp. 131–136. Bordeaux, Université de Bordeaux II.

Caron, J., Caron-Pargue, J., Micko, H. C., Tomeh, B., Verdret, P. (1987). Analyse sémantique de connecteurs et de quantificateurs du langage naturel. Rapport final d'une recherche sous contrat CNRS (ATP 9.83.81)

Caron J., Mendes-Maillochon I., & Caron-Pargue J. (1989, July). A study of the production of connectives by preschool children. Poster presented at the 10th Biennial Meeting of the International Society for the Study of Behavioral Development, Jyväskÿla, Finland.

Caron, J., Micko, H. C. & Thuring, M. (1988). Conjunctions and the recall of composite sentences. Journal of Memory and Language, 27, 309–323.

Caron-Pargue, J. (1983). Langage et argumentation: Etude d'enchaînements d'énoncés. In: La Pensée Naturelle [Actes du Colloque de Rouen, Sept. 1981] Paris, P.U.F. (pp. 229–240).

Caron-Pargue, J. (1992). Connecteurs de subordination et opérations cognitives dans les verbalisations simultanées à une résolution de problème: si, parce que, comme, une fois que. Travaux Linguistiques du Cerlico, 5, 198–220.

Caron-Pargue, J., & Baudet-Briquet, N. (1988, October). Discourse organizers as cues for cognitive processes in a problem–solving task. 10th Advanced Course of the Fondation Archives Jean Piaget: Language and Cognition. Genève, Switzerland.

Caron-Pargue, J., & Caron, J. (1989). Processus psycholinguistiques et analyse des verbalisations dans une tâche cognitive. Archives de Psychologie, 57, 3–32.

Clancey, W. J. (1993). Situated action: A neuropsychological interpretation, response to Vera and Simon. Cognitive Science, 17, 87–116.

Crystal, D. (1991). A dictionary of linguistics and phonetics. (3rd ed.). Oxford: Basil Blackwell.

Culioli, A. (1990). Pour une linguistique de l'énonciation: Opérations et représentations. Paris: Ophrys.

Ducrot, O. (1972). Dire et ne pas dire. Paris: Hermann.

Ducrot, O. (1980). Les mots du discours. Paris: Ed. de Minuit.

Evans, J. St. B. T. (1982). The psychology of deductive reasoning. London: Routledge & Kegan Paul.

Falmagne, R. J. (1975). Reasoning: Representation and process in children and adults. New York, Wiley.

Fillenbaum, S. (1977). Mind your p's and q's: The use of content and context in some uses of and, or, and if. In G.Bower (Ed.), The psychology of learning and motivation, (Vol. 11, pp. 41–100) New York, Academic Press

French, L. A., & Nelson, K. (1985). Young children's knowledge of relational terms: Some ifs, ors, and buts. New York: Springer Verlag.

Gibbs, R. W. (1979). Contextual effects in understanding indirect requests. Discourse Processes, 2, 1–10.

Grice H. P. (1975) Logic and conversation. In P. Cole & J. L. Morgan (Eds.), Syntax and semantice, Vol. 3: Speech acts. New York: Academic Press.

Guyot, L. (1991). Le rôle du connecteur 'mais' dans le rappel indicé de phrases. Unpublished manuscript, Lab. de Psychologie, Univ. de Poitiers.

Haberlandt, K. (1982). Reader expectations in text comprehension. In J. F. Le Ny & W. Kintsch (Eds.), Language Comprehension (pp. 239–249). Amsterdam: North Holland

Halliday, M. A. K, & Hasan, R. (1976). Cohesion in English. London: Longman.

Johnson-Laird, P. N., & Byrne, R. M. J. (1991). Deduction. Hillsdale, NJ: Lawrence Erlbaum Associates.

Kail, M., &Weissenborn, J. (1984) L'acquisition des connecteurs: Critiques et perspectives. In: M. Moscato & G. Pieraut-Le Bonniec (Eds.) Le langage: construction et actualisation (pp.100–118). Paris: P.U.F.

Lakoff, G. (1987). Women, fire and dangerous things: What categories reveal about the mind. Chicago: University. of Chicago Press.

Mandler, J. M. (1992). How to build a baby: II. Conceptual primitives. Psychological Review, 99, 587–604.

Marslen-Wilson, W., & Tyler, L. K. (1987). Against modularity. In J.L.Garfield (Ed.), Modularity in knowledge representation and natural language understanding (pp. 37–62). Cambridge MA: MIT Press.

Ortony, A. (Ed.). (1993). *Metaphor and thought.* Cambridge: Cambridge University Press.

Ortony, A., Schallert D. L., Reynolds R. E., & Antos S. J. (1978). Interpreting metaphors and idioms: Some effects of context on comprehension. *Journal of Verbal Learning and Verbal Behavior, 17,* 465–477.

Paris, S. G. (1975). *Propositional logical thinking and comprehension of language connectives.* The Hague Netherlands: Mouton.

Peterson, C. (1986). Semantic and pragmatic uses of 'but'. *Journal of Child Language, 13,* 583–590.

Peterson, C., & McCabe, A. (1988). The connective 'and' as discourse glue. *First Language, 8,* 19–28.

Piaget, J. (1924). *Le jugement et le raisonnement chez l'enfant.* Neuchatel: Delachaux et Niestlé.

Roulet, E., Auchlin, A., Moeschler, J., Rubattel, C., & Schelling, M. (1987). *L'articulation du discours en français contemporain.* Bern: P.Lang.

Sperber, D., & Wilson D. (1986). *Relevance: Communication and cognition.* Oxford: Basil Blackwell.

Sweetser, E. E. (1990). *From etymology to pragmatics.* Cambridge: Cambridge University Press.

Talmy, L. (1988). Force dynamics in language and cognition. *Cognitive Science, 12,* 49–100.

Townsend, D. J. (1982). Thematic processing in sentences and texts. *Cognition, 13,* 223–261.

Townsend, D. J., & Bever, T. G. (1978). Interclause relations and clausal processing. *Journal of Verbal Learning and Verbal Behavior, 17,* 509–521.

Van Dijk, T. A. (1979). Pragmatic connectives. *Journal of Pragmatics, 3,* 447–456.

Wason, P. C. (1966). Reasoning. In B. M. Foss (Ed.), *New Horizons in Psychology.* Harmondsworth: Penguin.

Wason, P. C., & Johnson-Laird, P. N. (1972). *Psychology of reasoning: Structure and content.* London, Batsford.

Wing, C. S., & Scholnick, E. K. (1981). Children's comprehension of pragmatic concepts expressed in "because", "although", "if" and "unless". *Journal of Child Language, 8,* 347–365.

Ziti, A., & Champagnol, R. (1992) Effet des connecteurs sur le traitement en temps réel de propositions exprimant des relations de cause/effet. *L'Année Psychologique, 92,* 187–207.

❖ Chapter 4

The Different Functions of a Conjunction in Constructing a Representation of the Discourse

Leo G. M. Noordman
Tilburg University, The Netherlands

Wietske Vonk
Max Planck Institute for Psycholinguistics and Nijmegen University, The Netherlands

The notion of discourse representation has a prominent place in current linguistic theories on discourse and discourse processing. From a processing point of view, the discourse representation is the cognitive representation of the information in the text that readers construct when they process the text. One of the properties of the representation is that it is coherent. This coherence is achieved both by the text and by the reader's knowledge. On the one hand, sentences in the text are related with each other. The relations are expressed by all kinds of linguistic device such as conjunctions and anaphoric expressions. On the other hand, the reader's knowledge contributes to the coherence of the representation. Concepts in the text activate world knowledge on the basis of which relations between sentences are computed and integrated into the discourse representation. Conjunctions play an important role in a discourse representation. They have, in fact, several functions in the process of constructing the discourse representation. This chapter illustrates these functions for the conjunction *because*.

DIFFERENT FUNCTIONS OF A CONJUNCTION

A distinction is made between three functions of *because*: segmentation, integration and inference. First, the segmentation function. *Because* as a clause-in-

75

itial function word signals the segmentation between main and subordinate clause. It is supposed that this structural segmentation affects the parsing of the clauses and leads initially to differential processing and storage of the two clauses. This function is related to the syntactic word class of a conjunction. The second function of the conjunction *because* is its integrating function, which is related to the meaning of *because*. By indicating a causal relation between two clauses, the conjunction may facilitate the integration process for the two clauses. The third function relates to inferences. The conjunction *because* signals that a general causal relation between the events or states expressed in the two conjoint clauses has to be constructed. The understanding of Sentence 1 implies the proposition that, according to the writer of this sentence, in science, causal laws are more important than particular facts (c.f. Crothers, 1979).

1. History is not a science because in history particular facts are more important than causal laws.

This proposition is not explicitly expressed in the sentence; it is called an inference. An inferred proposition is activated or derived from the text on the basis of world knowledge in such a way that it is consistent with world knowledge. The inference process consists of deriving the proposition and checking it with respect to world knowledge. This inference process goes beyond the integration. Readers can understand Sentence 1 without making the inference that in science laws are more important than facts. If readers are satisfied with integration, they understand the propositions of the two clauses and the fact that there is a causal relation between them. But in this case, readers do not check this relation with respect to their knowledge. To illustrate this point, consider Sentence 2.

2. History is not a science, although in history particular facts are more important than causal laws.

If readers only integrate, they understand this sentence almost as Sentence 1. They understand the same two propositions and the fact that there is now a concessive relation between the two clauses. But only if readers derive the underlying proposition do they go beyond the integration process and make an inference. If they do, they detect that Sentence 2 is false: In science, particular facts are not more important than causal laws. This is evident for the reader who has the appropriate world knowledge. So making an inference is, in fact, deriving the relation underlying the sentence and checking it with respect to the knowledge base. Inference processes are deductions from the text on the basis of world knowledge.

The three functions correspond to different processes in the construction of the text representation. How do these functions affect the construction of the text representation? What can be expected on the basis of these functions for the processing of causally related sentences with a conjunction *because*? And how are these processes reflected in reading performance data?

Segmentation

The first function of *because* is its function as a segmentation device. *Because* as a clause-initial function word signals the start of a subordinate clause. Function words have, indeed, a segmenting function. They indicate the place where the reader has to start a new syntactic structure; they affect the parsing process (Clark & Clark, 1977). Fodor and Garrett (1967) demonstrated the segmentation function of a particular function word, namely, the relative pronoun. Omitting the relative pronoun in Sentence 3 increases the difficulty of processing the sentence, as was demonstrated in a paraphrase task.

3. The man (whom) the dog bit died.

According to Kimball (1973), grammatical function words, for example, conjunctions, signal the construction of a new clause. The reader starts the processing of a new clause. The clause that is closed is removed from working memory. The result is that the activation of the previous clause decreases. Consider again the sentence *History is not a science because in history particular facts are more important than causal laws.* The conjunction *because* should deactivate the concepts of the main clause.

Integration

The second function of a conjunction is its function as an integration device. It indicates how the current information has to be integrated with the previous information. The conjunction *because* indicates that the two sentences have to be related to each other in a causal way. Assuming that understanding a discourse is constructing a coherent representation, this function of the conjunction *because* should affect the reading process. What does the integration function imply for the processing of *because* sentences? Two questions can be addressed: How does the causal relation affect the integration process, and how does the presence of a causal conjunction affect the integration?

The first question is how the causality of the relation between the sentences affects the integration process. This question addresses the issue of how conceptual relations are integrated. One may compare the processing of causal relations with other, for example, additive relations. What are the predictions with respect to processing time? On the one hand, one may say that a causal relation is cognitively more complex than an additive relation. Indeed, a causal relation presupposes an additive relation: if "A because B" is true, then "A and B" is true as well. Accordingly, one may predict that causal sentences require extra integration, which should be reflected in extra processing time. On the other hand, one may hypothesize that causal relations are cognitively more fundamental than additive relations. This may be reflected in the way in which readers process text. Assuming that readers, in understanding a text, try to establish the coherence between the sentences, it is conceivable that they try to integrate the sentences by initially assuming more fundamental relations. In that case, causal sentences should require less reading time. Whatever the predictions based on the integration function are for the reading time, as far as recall is concerned, one may predict that the recall for causally related sentences is better than for less strongly related sentences. If causally related sentences require more integration and longer reading time than additively related sentences, one may predict that the longer processing results in a better storage. If, on the other hand, causal relations are cognitively more fundamental, one should predict that they will be better stored, independently of the predicted decrease in reading time.

Several studies in the literature suggest a processing advantage for causally related sentences over noncausally related sentences. Townsend and Bever (1978) investigated the processing of initial subordinate clauses that were introduced by different conjunctions. The conjunctions differed in the extent to which they explicitly signaled a causal event. In decreasing order of causality they were: *if, since, when, while,* and *though.* Having heard a fragment of such an initial subordinate clause, subjects had to perform either a task that measured the accessibility to the superficial form of the fragment or the accessibility to the meaning of the clause. As the connective more explicitly signaled a causal event, access to meaning was better and access to superficial form poorer. Thus, explicitly signaled causal subordinate clauses are processed more deeply. Townsend (1983) investigated the processing of complex sentences in which the final clause was introduced by one of the conjunctions *because, after, when, and, before,* and *although.* Subjects had to judge whether a 2–4 word verb–object phrase was similar in meaning to any part of the sentence that they had most recently read. The results indicated that the clausal meaning is more accessible for causal clauses than for noncausal clauses. That the causality of relations between sentences affects their processing has also been demonstrated by a number of other studies. Caron, Micko, and Thüring (1988) investigated the recall of unrelated sentences. The sentences were connected by conjunctions. They observed superior recall for sentences that were related by *because* than by *and*. Black and Bern (1981) found that causally related sentences in a narrative were better recalled than sentences that were not causally related. Causally related sentences are read faster (Haberlandt & Bingham, 1978) and were better recalled (Bradshaw & Anderson, 1982) than sentences that are not causally related. Keenan, Baillet, and Brown (1984) and Myers, Shinjo, and Duffy (1987) demonstraed that the effect of causal connectedness on memory for sentences is greatest for moderate levels of causality.

The second question with respect to the integration is how the presence of a conjunction affects the integration process. One may expect that the presence of the conjunction facilitates the integration process, because the conjunction indicates explicitly how the current sentence has to be integrated with the previous sentence. Readers do not have to compute the relation between the sentences purely on the basis of the propositions in the sentences; they are helped by the conjunction. As far as recall is concerned, one may assume that the presence of a conjunction facilitates the reproduction of the complex sentence. In the psycholinguistic literature, there is evidence for superior processing of sentences when the relation between them is explicitly expressed by a conjunction. Spyridakis and Standal (1987) found a recall advantage for the presence of logical connectives in a text that was neither too easy nor too difficult. Haberlandt (1982) found that the reading time for a sentence was shorter if it was introduced by a conjunction than when the conjunction was omitted, the greatest effect being observed for the first phrase of the sentence.

Inferencing

The third function of *because* is its function as a cue for inferences. How does *because* as a trigger for inferences affect the processing? The inference process consists in deriving a general causal relation between the events or states expressed in the main and subordinate clauses and checking that relation with respect to world knowledge. In the earlier Example 1, the conjunction *because* is a signal for the inference that in science laws are more important than particular facts. In terms of a syllogism, the inference is the derivation of the premise that closes the chain of reasoning. In terms of Toulmin (1958), it is the warrant. In general, in the sentence "A because B" the conjunction *because* is a signal to infer that B can be the reason for A. If this inference is made online, it should require additional reading time, since mental processes in general and inference processes in particular are assumed to require time. Accordingly, the general methodology to establish inferential processes is to compare the reading time for a sentence that requires an inference with the reading time for an appropriate control condition. For example, reading the sentence *The beer was warm* requires significantly more time in Example 4 than in Example 5.

4. Mary got the picnic supplies out of the car. The beer was warm.
5. Mary got the beer out of the car. The beer was warm.

This is evidence that Example 4 requires the inference that there was beer among the picnic supplies (Haviland & Clark, 1974). That the understanding of a conjunction requires an inference that takes additional processing time has been demonstrated for the conjunction *but* by Vonk and Noordman (1990). The conjunction *but* indicates that one has to construct a contrast of the following clause with the previous clause. This may be done by finding a dimension common to two entities on which the entities have opposing values. For example, Sentence 6, in a text about a girl who is looking for a room to rent, requires the inference that a large room is attractive and that not making music is unattractive for the girl.

6. The room was large, but she was not allowed to make music in the room.

The reading time for this sentence decreased if the preceding text already contained some of the information that had to be inferred.

Interplay Between the Functions

In the psycholinguistic literature, there is evidence for the effects of segmentation, integration, and inference. These effects have been investigated as isolated effects independent of each other and related to different linguistic expressions. For example, the segmentation effect has been investigated mainly for definite noun phrases and relative pronouns, but hardly for conjunctions. That the effects have been investigated for different linguistic expressions is no surprise because the functions are quite different indeed, as they deal with syntax, semantics, and pragmatics, respectively. But the three functions can presumably be triggered by the same linguistic device, such as a conjunction. The interesting question, then, is how these functions relate to each other and how they affect the processing of the discourse. There probably is a complex interplay between the functions with respect to the processes they initiate. For example, the effect of the conjunction as a segmentation device goes against the effect of the conjunction as an integration device: On the basis of integration, one would predict higher availability of the concepts from the previous clause; on the basis of segmentation, one would predict lower availability. Similarly, the role of the conjunction as trigger for an inference may go against the segmentation effect: The inference establishes the relation between the two clauses and should make the concepts in the previous clause more available. Furthermore, the integration process can take place without inferring the additional major premise. The reader may be satisfied by accepting that the writer intends to convey a causal relation without checking that relation to his/her knowledge, that is, without deducing the general premise. Finally, the conjunction *because* as an integration device may speed up the reading process, whereas as an inference trigger, it may slow down the reading process.

This chapter explores which processes and effects occur in understanding causally related sentences and gives an account of how these effects are related to each other. In this way, it gives a framework in which the different processes can be accommodated. To do so, it is necessary to start with a short overview of the process of understanding discourse.

DIFFERENT LEVELS OF DISCOURSE REPRESENTATION

From a psycholinguistic point of view, we can consider the understanding of discourse as a process of constructing a coherent discourse representation. But there is not only one single discourse representation. This is true for a number of reasons. One is the obvious reason that there are different ways in which readers understand a text, depending on the reader's knowledge and interest, depending on the use the reader wants to make of the information in the text, and so forth. But this is not the issue here. Even if a particular reader is reading a particular discourse with a particular purpose, different representations are being constructed. Several authors have proposed a tripartite distinction (Fletcher & Chrysler, 1990; Kintsch, Welsch, Schmalhofer, & Zimny, 1990; Klein, 1994; Van Dijk & Kintsch, 1983). Without claiming that the distinctions made by these authors are identical, there is considerable convergence among them. One may identify a surface representation, a propositional representation, and a mental representation. These representations differ in terms of what they contain as well as in terms of their time characteristics.

Surface Representation

The surface representation contains the surface structure: the words and sentences in the text. It is the representation that we retain in verbatim recall.

This representation is short lived, as has been demonstrated by, for example, Jarvella (1971). His subjects heard text fragments including sentences such as Examples 7 and 8:

7. With this possibility, Taylor left the capital. After he had returned to Manhattan, he explained the offer to his wife.
8. Taylor did not reach a decision until after he had returned to Manhattan. He explained the offer to his wife.

The phrase, *After he had returned to Manhattan,* is the target phrase and identical in both sentences, but in Example 7 it is part of the last sentence, and in Example 8 it is part of the first sentence. After having heard either the sentences of Example 7 or the sentences of Example 8, subjects had to report verbatim what they had heard. The correct recall for the target phrase was 54% when the phrase was part of the last sentence, and only 21% when it was part of the sentence before the last one. This means that only the information of the last sentence is fairly well available for verbatim recall. As soon as a sentence boundary is encountered, this information becomes less available in its verbatim form. It is replaced in working memory by the next sentence.

That the surface information is preserved only temporarily and is replaced by a representation that reflects the meaning rather than the surface structure of the sentences has been demonstrated by Sachs (1967). She used a memory task in which she presented subjects with sentences heard on headphones; an example is Sentence 9. After hearing this sentence, the subjects were presented with a test sentence that had to be judged as same or different with respect to the sentence that they had heard. This sentence was an identical sentence or a semantic change, as in Sentence 10, or different kinds of form change, such as an active–passive change as in Sentence 11 or a change of the order of the constituents as in Sentence 12.

9. He sent a letter about it to Galileo, the great Italian scientist.
10. Galileo, the great Italian scientist, sent him a letter about it.
11. A letter about it was sent to Galileo, the great Italian scientist.
12. He sent Galileo, the great Italian scientist, a letter about it.

These test sentences were presented at three different time intervals after the original sentence; either immediately after the original sentence, after 80 syllables of the continuing text, or after 160 syllables of the text. Immediately after the original sentence, the percentage correct was the same for the different conditions and was on the average about 90%. After 80 syllables and after 160 syllables, the percentage correct for the semantic changes was still about 90%, whereas the percentages of the identical and the form changes dropped to almost chance level. So, the surface information of the sentence becomes quickly lost in contrast to the meaning of the sentence.

Propositional Representation

The propositional representation contains the meaning of the sentences and is expressed in terms of propositions. That the meaning is represented was clear already from the experiment by Sachs. That the representation that is retained over time can be described in terms of propositions has been demonstrated by Ratcliff and McKoon (1978), for example. After studying a sentence such as Sentence 13 subjects were given a primed recognition test.

13. The bandit who stole the passport faked the signature.

The judgment that *signature* was in the sentence was faster when this target word was preceded by the word *bandit* than when it was preceded by the word *passport*. The words *bandit* and *signature* occur in the same proposition (faked, bandit, signature). Thus concepts that occur in the same proposition are better retrieval cues than concepts that do not occur in the same proposition, even if the latter are closer together in the surface of the sentence. Accordingly, sentences are stored in a propositional format. The propositional representation is still close to the linguistic information in the sentences.

Mental Representation

The mental representation contains not only information that is expressed by the propositions in the text, but also information that is inferred from the text on the basis of world knowledge. This information may be represented in the form of images, propositions, schemas, or otherwise; the crucial point is that it goes beyond the text-based propositions. The mental representation reflects the state of affairs in the world about which the text deals. This representation is referred to as a situation model (Van Dijk & Kintsch, 1983), or a mental model (Garnham, 1987; Glenberg, Meyer, & Lindem, 1987; Johnson-Laird, 1983). Because the word *situation model* biases toward an analogical representation, we will use the term *mental model*. Glenberg et al. (1987) found evidence for a mental model that reflects the situation in the real world. In a story about somebody who was preparing for a marathon and doing some exercises, either the associated Sentence 14 or the dissociated Sentence 15 was presented as a target sentence:

14. After doing a few warm-up exercises, he put on his sweatshirt and went jogging.

15. After doing a few warm-up exercises, he put off his sweatshirt and went jogging.

Subjects were tested in a probe recognition task for the word *sweatshirt*. The recognition task was administered either immediately after the target sentence, or after one or two additional sentences. The recognition times for the word *sweatshirt*, when presented immediately after the target sentence, did not differ between the associated and dissociated conditions. After one and two sentences, however, the recognition time was longer after the dissociated Sentence 15 than after the associated Sentence 14. This result is difficult to explain in terms of a propositional representation. Glenberg et al. argued that readers construct a situation model in which the protagonist has a salient role. As a consequence, concepts related to the protagonist are activated as well. Therefore, *sweatshirt* is activated in the associated condition, but not in the dissociated condition. The experiment demonstrates that the situation model is not constructed at once. The recognition time for *sweatshirt* immediately after the target sentence depends, on the surface of the sentences and not yet on a situation model.

The mental model does not have to be a picture-like representation analogous to the situation in the world. It may also consist of propositions derived from the situation in the world and particular concepts in the text. For example from the concept "pounding the nail" in Example 16 one may infer the instrument:

16. John was trying to fix the birdhouse. He was pounding the nail when his father came out to watch him and to help him do the work.

Readers of Example 16—falsely—recognized much more frequently that John was using a hammer than readers of the same sentence when *pounding* was replaced by *looking for* (Johnson, Bransford, & Solomon, 1973).

Time Characteristics of the Discourse Representations

The different representations are constructed in real time. Although it is too strong to claim that the surface representation is replaced by the propositional representation and that this representation is replaced by the mental representation, there is some temporal dependence among them. The propositional representation is based on the surface representation, and the mental representation is a further elaboration of the propositional representation. Under-standing a text can be considered a process in which these representations are constructed. These representations are partly parallel, partly sequential.

ROLE OF A CONJUNCTION IN CONSTRUCTING
THE DISCOURSE REPRESENTATION

The three functions that we identified for the conjunction *because*—segmen-tation, integration, and inference—can be considered to correspond to the three kinds of representation that we distinguished. *Segmentation* plays a role in the surface representation; it concerns the way in which the input is structured. *Integration* deals with the propositional representation; it concerns the way in which propositions are connected to each other. *Inferences* deal with the mental representation; they are deductions based on world knowledge. If the three functions correspond to the three kinds of representation and if these repre-sentations are more or less ordered in time, the three functions should manifest themselves at different moments in time. Segmentation effects should manifest themselves early in the processing, inferences relatively late, and integration effects in between.

Segmentation and Surface Representation

The conjunction *because* marks the beginning of a new clause. The reader terminates the processing of the previous structure and has to begin processing the new clause. The function of the conjunction in segmenting the input is to move the attention away from the previous clause to the current clause. Therefore, one may predict that the concepts in the previous clause are deactivated. Segmentation affects the input and is therefore supposed to occur as soon as the incoming clause is parsed; it should occur early in the subordinate clause. The crucial test to establish this kind of segmentation effect of the conjunction is to compare the activation of a word from the preceding clause right after the conjunction *because* with its activation after a control word that replaces *because* but that does not segment the sentence. The activation should be lower after *because* than after the control word. We do not know of any direct empirical support for this effect, but an experiment by Millis and Just (1994) may be relevant in this respect. They presented subjects with pairs of clauses, the first clause expressing the consequence of a particular action or event that was expressed in the second clause. The clauses were connected by the conjunc-tion *because* or unconnected and separated by a period as in Example 17.

17. The elderly parents toasted their only daughter at the party (because) Jill had finally passed the exams at the prestigious university.

At different moments during the presentation of this sentence, subjects had to say whether they had read a particular word. The target word of interest here was the verb of the first clause, in this example, *toasted*. When this target word was presented after the first word of the second clause (early presentation), the recognition time was longer in cases where *because* connected the two clauses than when no conjunction was used to connect the clauses. The opposite effect was observed when the target word was presented after the second clause (late presentation). It is difficult to explain why the conjunction in the early presentation condition led to longer recognition time than the period. But in any case the interaction effect suggests that the effect of the conjunction is different in the early condition than in the late condition. The effect in the late presentation condition is interpreted in the next paragraph as an integration effect; the effect in the early presentation condition might be interpreted as a segmentation effect. The conjunction *because* segments the incoming input and moves the processing forward from the previous clause to the next clause. Whatever the explanation is for the fact that this effect of *because* was stronger than the effect of a period, one should predict a segmentation effect of *because* if one compares the probe reaction time after *because* with the probe reaction time after a control word that does not segment clauses (e.g., varying Example 17, the sentence, *The elderly parents toasted their only daughter*, should be continued either by *because* or by *at the party*).

Integration and Propositional Representation

The second function of *because* is integration. Given that readers try to integrate the propositions of the current clause with those of the previous clauses, *because* should facilitate this integration process because it indicates the way in which the current clause is related to the previous clause.

If this integration with the previous clause occurs during the reading of the current clause, concepts in the previous clause should be activated during the processing of the current clause. The study by Millis and Just (1994) as well as experiments conducted in our laboratory (Cozijn, 1992) are relevant in this respect. As has been said already, when Millis and Just presented the target word after the second clause was read, the recognition times for the verb of the first clause were shorter when the two clauses were connected by the conjunction than when they were not connected. Millis and Just concluded that the conjunction integrates the second clause with the first clause, with the consequence that the concepts of the first clause are activated. This effect is not the effect of segmentation; it occurs later. Cozijn had similar results. He used texts in which two causally related clauses were connected by the conjunction *because* or were separated by a period, as in Example 18:

18. On his way to work that morning he was delayed (because) there was a traffic jam on the highway.

After reading the second clause, a target word was presented, in this case the word *morning*, and subjects had to say whether they had read that word. The recognition time was shorter when the pair of clauses was connected by the conjunction than when the clause did not contain the conjunction.

If the conjunction facilitates the integration, one would expect that the reading time for the second clause is shorter when it contains a conjunction. Indeed, Cozijn found a significant shorter reading time (corrected for the difference in clause length) for the second clause when it had a conjunction than when it did not. Millis and Just (1994) measured the reading time per word. The average reading time per word (excluding the last word of the clause) was shorter when the clause contained a conjunction than when it did not. The integrative effect of a conjunction has also been found for contrastive sentences that were connected by the conjunction *but* (Vonk & Noordman, 1987). In that study texts were presented in which two different opinions were presented, as in Example 19.

19. A public relations officer of the air force confirmed in a newspaper article that the safety devices of the basis were insufficient. [But] later in the article, the public relations officer said that there are no plans to improve the safety devices.

The presence of the conjunction was manipulated. The gaze duration for the phrase, *the public relations officer*, in the second sentence was shorter when this sentence started with the conjunction *but* than when the conjunction was left out.

If *because* facilitates the integration of the two clauses, one may assume that the performance on a question answering task is superior when the conjunction was present than when it was not. In the Millis and Just (1994) study, subjects had to answer questions that could be answered on the basis of the separate clauses. For example: "Did the parents have several children?" relates to the first clause of Example 17. The question answering accuracy was higher and the answer latencies were shorter when the clauses were connected by a conjunc-tion. This is interpreted as evidence for a better integrated representation.

The reading times, probe recognition latencies, and comprehension data indicate that the presence of *because* speeds up the integration process. The presence of the causal conjunction is a signal to the reader that the writer intended to express a causal relation. The reader accepts this relation and interprets the relation accordingly. In this way, the reader integrates the two clauses. The integration that is achieved is that the reader accepts the causal relation without checking it to his/her knowledge base.

Until now, we discussed how the presence of the conjunction *because* affects the integration. A final point to be discussed with respect to the integration of causally-related clauses is how the causality of the relation itself affects the integration. How are causal relations processed in comparison to other relations, for example, additive relations? Do causal relations require more integration time because they are more informative, or do they require less integration time because they are more fundamental relations in human cognition? Several studies conducted with Sanders (Sanders, 1992; Sanders & Noordman, 1996) give evidence for the latter conception. We presented a target sentence in two different texts. In one text, the sentences preceding the target sentence described a problem, and the target sentence described the solution. Consequently, the relation between the target sentence and the preceding context was a causal relation. In the other text, the target sentence described a situation that was comparable to situations described by the preceding context. The relation between the target sentence and the preceding context was an additive relation. The reading times for the target sentences were shorter when it formed a causal relation with the preceding context than when it formed an additive relation, suggesting that causal relations are more easily integrated with their context than additive relations.

Inference and Mental Representation

The understanding of a sentence with the conjunction *because* requires, in general, an inference, as was illustrated by Sentence 1. In a sentence, "A because B", the conjunction *because* is a signal to infer that B can be the reason for A. The effect of this inference is that the propositional representation is supplemented by derivations based on world knowledge, leading to a mental representation. Do readers make this inference online? According to most theories on inferences, this kind of inference is made online, because it is a backward, bridging inference that establishes local coherence. For example, McKoon and Ratcliff (1992) argued that inferences made online are those that establish local coherence and those that are based on immediately available knowledge. This is what they call the *minimalist theory of inferences*. However, bridging inferences are not always made online (Noordman, Vonk, & Kempff, 1992; Vonk & Noordman, 1990). We measured the reading time for the target *because* sentences. In one condition, the explicit condition, the *because* sentence was preceded by a sentence that expressed the inference, for example by Sentence 20:

20. In science causal laws are more important than particular facts.

In the other condition, this sentence was left out (implicit condition). The reading time for the *because* sentence was not different for the explicit condition and the implicit condition. On the other hand, the verification time for the inference sentence, presented after the text, required less time in the explicit condition than in the implicit condition. These results strongly support the conclusion that the inference was not made during reading. If it was, the explicit information had to have speeded up reading the target sentence. Similarly, if the inference was made during reading, the inferred information would have been stored as was the explicit information, and no effect should have been obtained in the verification times. On the basis of these data, we proposed a more parsimonious theory of inferences than McKoon and Ratcliff (Noordman & Vonk, 1993). The inferences we studied concerned propositions that were not familiar for the readers. These inferences were not made online, unless the reader's task required deep processing (Noordman, Vonk, & Kempff, 1992; Vonk & Noordman, 1990). On the other hand, when the inferences were familiar for the readers, the inferences appeared to be made online (Vonk & Noordman, 1990). The more parsimonious conception of inferences then claims that whether inferences are made or not does not so much depend on the characteristics of the inference, whether it is a backward inference or not, but that inferences are made if they correspond to the reader's knowledge.

To further test this theory, we conducted reading experiments with readers that differed in expertise with respect to the topic of the text (Noordman & Vonk, 1992). The inferences we studied were relations between concepts. A knowledge domain was selected in which the relations between concepts were familiar to experts and not to novices because the inferences should be familiar to the experts and not to the novices. Of course, the concepts themselves had to be familiar to both groups of readers. We selected the domain of economics. The experts were advanced students in economics; the novices were students who never had had any economics courses. In a number of elicitation experiments, we first investigated the knowledge in economics of experts and novices. On the basis of these experiments, we constructed knowledge graphs. The nodes in these graphs corresponded to the economic concepts; the links corresponded to the relations between the concepts. We constructed target *because* sentences using three concepts in such a way that the relations between the concepts were known for the experts but unknown for the novices, as in Sentence 21.

21. The American export has been suffering a decline in the last few months, because the rising inflation has produced a harmful effect on the competitive position of the U. S. A.

This sentence requires the inference that deterioration of the competitive position negatively affects the export. The target *because* sentences were presented in texts with an average length of nine sentences. In one condition, the explicit condition, the target sentence was preceded by a sentence that expressed part of the inference, for example Sentence 22.

22. Generally speaking the competitive position of a country has a strong influence on the volume of its exports.

In the implicit condition, this information was not given. The reading time for the target sentence was longer in the implicit condition than in the explicit condition for experts but not for novices. So, experts made the inferences and novices not. This experiment indicates that *because* is indeed a trigger for inferences. In addition, it demonstrates that whether the inferences are made online depends on the reader's knowledge. The conclusion is that the understanding of *because* sentences leads to inferences and to a more complete mental representation if the relations are familiar to the reader.

A final point should be mentioned. How does *because* as an integration device relate to *because* as an inference device? The experiment demonstrates that inferences are made if they correspond to the reader's knowledge. This does not mean that in those cases the inferences are made because they can be made automatically. On the contrary, the inferences require extra processing time. On the other hand, it has been argued that *because* speeds up the integration process. So the conjunction has antagonistic effects on the reading times. How do we reconcile the idea that *because* speeds up reading by facilitating the integration but slows down the reading by leading to an inference? The explanation may lie in the fact that the integration affects the propositional representation and the inference affects the mental representation. Because the inference is assumed to be a later process, it should manifest itself at a later moment during processing. And indeed, Millis and Just (1994) found that the reading time for the words in the target clause were read faster if it contained the conjunction *because* than when it did not. But this was true for all the words except the last word. The reading time for the last word was longer if the conjunction *because* connected the two clauses (although in one experiment, Millis and Just found that this effect depended on the causal relatedness of the sentences). These results may be interpreted that the inference takes place at the end of the sentence. The sentence wrap-up effect (Just & Carpenter, 1980) is, at least, partly due to inference processes.

SUMMARY AND CONCLUSION

Causal conjunctions, and other conjunctions as well, have a function in segmenting the input, integrating the propositions, and making inferences on the basis of world knowledge. The different functions correspond to different kinds of process in understanding text. The effects of these processes can be different. For example, segmentation can deactivate previous concepts, whereas integration can lead to an increase of the activation.

The different functions of a conjunction correspond to different kinds of representation that are constructed during the comprehension of sentences: the surface representation, the propositional representation, and the mental representation. Segmentation affects the surface representation, integration deals with the propositional representation, and inferences deal with the mental representation. Because these representations are constructed in real time during processing and because they have a certain temporal order, the different functions of *because* manifest themselves at different moments during processing. In that way, the different functions of the causal conjunction *because* are accounted for in the general framework of discourse understanding.

REFERENCES

Black, J. B., & Bern, H. (1981). Causal coherence and memory for events in narratives. *Journal of Verbal Learning and Verbal Behavior, 20,* 267–275.

Bradshaw, G. L., & Anderson, J. R. (1982). Elaborative encoding as an explanation of levels of processing. *Journal of Verbal Learning and Verbal Behavior, 21,* 165–174.

Caron, J., Micko, H. C., & Thüring, M. (1988). Conjunctions and the recall of composite sentences. *Journal of Memory and Language, 27,* 309–323.

Clark, H. H. & Clark, E. V. (1977). *Psychology and language.* New York: Harcourt, Brace, Jovanovich.

Cozijn, R. (1992, September). Inferential processes during the construction of a coherent text representation. Proceedings of the Center for Language Studies Conference. Tilburg, The Netherlands: Center for Language Studies.

Crothers, E. J. (1979). *Paragraph structure inference.* Norwood, NJ: Ablex.

Fletcher, C. R., & Chrysler, S. T. (1990). Surface forms, textbases, and situation models: Recognition memory for three types of textual information. *Discourse Processes*, *13*, 175–190.

Fodor, J. A., & Garrett, M. F. (1967). Some syntactic determinants of sentential complexity. *Perception and Psychophysics*, *2*, 289–296.

Garnham, A. (1987). *Mental models as representations of discourse and text*. Chichester: Horwood.

Glenberg, A. M., Meyer, M., & Lindem, K. (1987). Mental models contribute to foregrounding during text comprehension. *Journal of Memory and Language*, *26*, 69–83.

Haberlandt, K. F. (1982). Reader expectations in text comprehension. In J.F. Le Ny & W. Kintsch (Eds.), *Language and comprehension* (pp. 239–249). Amsterdam: North-Holland.

Haberlandt, K., & Bingham, G. (1978). Verbs contribute to the coherence of brief narratives: Reading related and unrelated sentence triples. *Journal of Verbal Learning and Verbal Behavior*, *17*, 419–425.

Haviland, S. E., & Clark, H. H. (1974). What's new? Acquiring new information as a process in comprehension. *Journal of Verbal Learning and Verbal Behavior*, *13*, 512–521.

Jarvella, R. J. (1971). Syntactic processing of connected speech. *Journal of Verbal Learning and Verbal Behavior*, *10*, 409–416.

Johnson, M. K., Bransford, J. D., & Solomon, S. K. (1973). Memory for tacit implications of sentences. *Journal of Experimental Psychology*, *98*, 203–205.

Johnson-Laird, P. N. (1983). *Mental models*. Cambridge: Cambridge University Press.

Just, M. A., & Carpenter, P. A. (1980). A theory of reading: From eye fixations to comprehension. *Psychological Review*, *87*, 329–354.

Keenan, M. F., Baillet, S. D., & Brown, P. (1984). The effects of causal cohesion on comprehension and memory. *Journal of Verbal Learning and Verbal Behavior*, *23*, 115–126.

Kintsch, W., Welsch, D., Schmalhofer, F., & Zimny, S. (1990). Sentence memory: A theoretical analysis. *Journal of Memory and Language*, *29*, 133–159.

Kimball, J. P. (1973). Seven principles of surface structure parsing in natural language. *Cognition*, *2*, 15–47.

Klein, W. (1994). *Time in language*. London: Routledge.

McKoon, G., & Ratcliff, R. (1992). Inference during reading. *Psychological Review*, *99*, 440–466.

Millis, K. K., & Just, M. A. (1994). The influence of connectives on sentence comprehension. *Journal of Memory and Language*, *33*, 128–147.

Myers, J. L., Shinjo, M., & Duffy, S. A. (1987). Degree of causal relatedness and memory. *Journal of Memory and Language*, *26*, 453–465.

Noordman, L. G. M., Vonk, W., & Kempff, H. J. (1992). Causal inferences during the reading of expository texts. *Journal of Memory and Language*, *31*, 573–590.

Noordman, L. G. M., & Vonk, W. (1992). Readers' knowledge and the control of inferences in reading. *Language and Cognitive Processes*, *7*, 373–391.

Noordman, L. G. M., & Vonk, W. (1993). A more parsimonious version of minimalism in inferences. *Psycoloquy* 4.8 1–4.

Ratcliff, R., & McKoon, G. (1978). Priming in item recognition: Evidence for the propositional structure of sentences. *Journal of Verbal Learning and Verbal Behavior*, *17*, 403–417.

Sachs, J.S. (1967). Recognition memory for syntactic and semantic aspects of connected discourse. *Perception and Psychophysics*, *2*, 437–442.

Sanders, T. J. M.(1992). Discourse structure and coherence: Aspects of a cognitive theory of discourse representation. Doctoral Dissertation, University of Tilburg, The Netherlands.

Sanders, T. J. M., & Noordman, L. G. M. (1996). The role of coherence relations and their linguistic markers in understanding expository text. Manuscript in preparation.

Spyridakis, J. H., & Standal, T. C. (1987). Signals in expository prose: Effects on reading comprehension. *Reading Research Quarterly*, *22*, 285–298.

Toulmin, S. E. (1958). *The uses of argument*. Cambridge: Cambridge University Press.

Townsend, D. J. (1983). Thematic processing in sentences and texts. *Cognition*, *13*, 223–261.

Townsend, D. J., & Bever, T. G. (1978). Interclause relations and clausal processing. *Journal of Verbal Learning and Verbal Behavior, 17*, 509–521.

Van Dijk, T. A., & Kintsch, W. (1983). *Strategies of discourse comprehension*. New York: Academic Press.

Vonk, W., & Noordman, L. G. M. (1987). On the effect of contrastive signaling in processing text. In G. Lüer & U. Lass (Eds.), *Proceedings 4. European conference on eye movements* (pp. 39–40). Toronto: Hogrefe.

Vonk, W., & Noordman, L. G. M. (1990). On the control of inferences in text understanding. In D.A. Balota, G.B. Flores d'Arcais, & K. Rayner (Eds.), *Comprehension processes in reading* (pp. 447–464). Hillsdale, NJ: Lawrence Erlbaum Associates.

Chapter 5

Interclausal Connectives as Indicators of Structuring in Narrative

Erwin M. Segal
and Judith F. Duchan
State University of New York at Buffalo

Discourse allows its users to share stories, build conceptual understandings, express attitudes and perspectives, and engage in vicarious experiences. Writers, speakers, readers, and listeners of discourse make use of a variety of linguistic devices to achieve these various purposes. The role that one such set of devices, *interclausal connectives*, can play in accomplishing the goals of discourse is reviewed in this chapter.

The discourse function of interclausal connectives has been a source of disagreement in recent times. Some researchers see connectives as peripheral to discourse and omit them from their study of the discourse structure and function (Kintsch, 1977; Stein & Glenn, 1979; Trabasso & Sperry, 1985).

Others researchers give connectives a minimal role—that of marking relations between adjacent clauses (Chomsky, 1957; Gleitman, 1965; Halliday & Hasan, 1976). It is this view that underlies the very name of these discourse elements: interclausal connectives. Chomsky (1957), in his classic work, *Syntactic Structures*, assigns a simple syntactic role to the coordinate conjunction subclass of connectives. These connectives serve to conjoin any two constituents of the same type from different sentences into a single sentence, provided the rest of the original sentences are identical. He notes that qualifications of this simple rule may be necessary. Gleitman (1965) takes up Chomsky's syntactic approach and defines those qualifications. The result is a highly complicated set of syntactic rules to account for the syntactic constraints for different connectives. Halliday and Hasan (1976) considered conjunctions that are intersentential, rather than intrasentential connectives. In their view, these

95

connectives are discourse cohesion devices that link adjacent sentences. Their view differs, in this respect, from Chomsky and Gleitman, but is similar in that the connectives link successive clauses, and their role is one of establishing structural ties between these clauses.

Another group of theorists have shown that connectives are sometimes used to mark larger, global units of discourse. They add to their interclausal role another function, one that involves discourse structuring (Schiffrin, 1987). In this view, connectives occurring between clauses have been called *discourse markers*.

We have argued that interclausal connectives can play an even more central role in discourse (Segal, Duchan, & Scott, 1991). For example, we found that connectives signaled the structural relations between elements in simple narratives and that they were thus crucial in building a coherent mental model for interpreting happenings in the story world. Without such connectives, the reader would not be able to build the intended model. We thus are more comfortable calling interclausal connectives *model-building connectives* so as to focus on their conceptual, rather than linguistic function.

This view of model-building connectives is associated with theorizing about the organization and function of narratives. We have proposed that tellers of narratives present and construct the narratives so that the audience (readers or listeners) can experience vicariously the events that make up the story. To do this, the teller derives the details of the story from a multidimensional mental model that represents aspects of a story world. It is proposed that the teller and the audience are each able to shift from a here-and-now perspective into a conceptual location within the world of the story. For example, in the story of *The Wizard of Oz* (Baum, 1900), both the writer and reader (viewer) walk down the yellow brick road with Dorothy and her friends. Those experiencing the story become engrossed in it, conceptually leaving their living rooms to join the events in the imaginary world of munchkins, witches, and wizards.

Our theory holds that this perspective shift to within the story world is necessary to interpret everyday deictic terms such as *I, we, this, today, recently, come,* and *here*. A major part of the meaning of these terms is determined by the situation in which they are used. *I* refers to the speaker; *this* refers to an object nearby; and *today* refers to the present day. In narrative, these deictic terms often are interpreted from a space–time–person origin within the story itself. *I* is a focal character in the story, *this* is a focal object or place; *today* is the time of the event being described. To meaningfully interpret these terms, the teller and reader must situate themselves within the world of the story.

In everyday discourse, interlocutors (speakers and listeners) interpret deictic terms from the here-and-now of their current situation. We claim that deictic terms in narrative discourse are interpreted from a perspective within the model. Interpreters thus experience the narrative world from a deictic center within it. This narrative discourse theory is called the *Deictic Shift Theory* (Duchan, Bruder, & Hewitt, 1995; Duchan, Meth, & Waltzman, 1992; Galbraith, 1995; Segal, 1990; 1995a; Segal, Bruder & Daniels, 1984; Segal, Duchan, & Scott, 1991).

This deictic shift is manifest in a variety of ways in discourse structuring—ways that affect interpretation of much more than deictic terms. One of the more obvious manifestations is through the use of definite noun phrases. The interpreter, upon hearing a definite noun phrase, is led to place the object identified into an accessible place in the story. Once the object is created and localized, pronouns can refer directly to them. Adverbial phrases are another way deixis is manifest in discourse. When such phrases are placed at the beginning of sentences, they often signal to the interpreter that there will be a deictic discontinuity in the story line. This could be a shift in space, time, or character.

In *The Pearl*, John Steinbeck (1954/1975) wrote "Kino squatted by the firepit and rolled a hot corncake and dipped it in sauce and ate it" (p. 5). Steinbeck has us witnessing Kino as he sits near a particular hot firepit, eating a corncake. While reading this phrase the deictic center in the story is with Kino at the firepit. Moreover, the firepit exists in the story, as a specific entity that lasts through the activity of eating corncakes and beyond. Once it is referred to by the author, it becomes a substantial entity within the story world. Its continuity is experienced as objects in the real world are, and it is expected to "behave" as a firepit throughout the story.

In this same example, there are two instances of *it*. By some interpretations, these pronouns refer to the word *corncake*. This construal casts them as anaphoric pronouns (Halliday & Hasan, 1976). That is, they stand for their antecedent—a word. The deictic shift view holds that the corncake exists in a mental model and the *it* refers to that mentally constructed entity, not the word that labels it.

Research on discourse deixis has shown how referring expressions tie to conceptual elements in the interpreters' models, rather than to lexical meanings associated with words in the text (Greenspan & Segal, 1984; Segal, 1995b; Wiebe, 1995). We have also identified how expressions can be interpreted from different perspectives within the same mental model. That is, interpreters can shift their perspective from an objective view of the events taking place in the story world to an observation of the world from the subjective perspective of a character within the story. Wiebe (1995) studied language devices that signal shifts from an objective orientation of a scene to a character's subjective interpretation of the same scene.

Consider this example: "She [Hannah] winced as she heard them crash to the platform. The lovely little mirror that she had brought for Ellen and the gifts for the baby!" (Franchere, 1964, p.3).

We, the readers, see Hannah wince and, with her we hear the objective crashing of something to the platform. We then enter the subjective world of Hannah's mind as she thinks about what it is that fell and what it means to her. Thus we shift our mental perspective from what is physically occurring to one that observes Hannah's subjective experience of it.

The role interclausal connectives play in discourse is clarified when they are viewed in the Deictic Shift Theory. In Segal, Duchan, & Scott (1991) we showed that narratives have a range of interpretations that vary depending upon the connectives they contain. The primary role for the connective *and* is to mark continuity between information in the upcoming clause and previously known events. When an *and* occurs, this signals to the interpreter that the events connected by the *and* are to be seen as a single conceptualized unit rather than simply as a concatenated string.

Then, in contrast with *and*, was found to signal discontinuity in the discourse line and not just to mark temporal relationships between adjacent clauses (Duchan, Meth, & Waltzman, 1992; Segal et al, 1991). Often the content following *then* requires a deictic shift. *Then* marks shifts in location or time, or it introduces a new character or redirects an interpreter to a previously identified one.

We also found (Segal et al, 1991) that causal connectives *so* and *because* often signaled a shift into a subjective perspective in addition to marking causal relations between events. A 5-year-old boy, Wally, used these connectives to explain the thinking process of his main character, a little lion (Paley, 1981):

> Once upon a time there was a little lion and he lived alone *because* his mother and father was dead. And one day he went hunting. And he saw two lions. And they were his mother and father. *So* he took his blanket to their den. *Because* it was bigger. (p. 9)

For each of the uses of the causal connectives, Wally accounts for the lion's behavior based on how the lion thinks about his experiences. He lived alone because he thought his mother and father were dead. *So* and the second *because* are part of a complex subjective argument by the lion for why he moved in with his parents (because their space was bigger than his) and what the move entailed (taking his blanket to their den).

From examples like this, one learns that what is connected by an interclausal connective is not always expressed directly in the text. Rather, it may be created from common knowledge applied to the mental model (Clark, 1992; Schiffrin, 1987; Stalnaker, 1978). The language of the story provides only a skeleton of the mental representations. Interpreters are free to, and indeed often are required to, fill in needed information to make sense of the text.

The role of connectives in narratives, then, is to guide the interpreter as to how to construct meaning for a text. They tell interpreters when to add information, and what they need to supply to make the text coherent. The connectives provide cues for how events and objects in the story relate to one another. In this way, connectives function to help interpreters build a mental model of the narrative.

To further develop the idea that the process of modelbuilding is guided by connectives, a detailed analysis is conducted how the connective *but* functions in several types of naturally occurring discourse. *But* offers us a nontrivial example of how a connective occurring in natural discourse adds significantly to the interpretation of the discourse. It also provides a concrete demonstration of different ways that analysts have represented the role of connectives in discourse.

Some previous accounts of *but* have cast its interpretation in terms of propositions surrounding the term. They often ignore the discourse contributions or functions of *but* and treat the connective as a logical operator signaling adversative, contrastive, or concessive relations that hold between propositions in the text (e.g., Bloom, Lahey, Hood, Lifter, & Fiess, 1980). Bloom, et al., assumed that children's acquisition of *but* involves their learning adversative relations between clauses and their using of *but* marks those relations.

Similarly, R. Lakoff (1971) identified one use of *but*, what she calls the "semantic opposition *but*," as marking a simple opposition between elements of a text. In this case, there are two opposing elements and *but* marks their contrast. In the sentence "John is tall, but Bill is short" (R. Lakoff, p. 133) the *but* marks the contrast in height between John and Bill.

R. Lakoff (1971) also pointed to instances in which elements of the text fail to directly illuminate the contrast existing between the clauses surrounding *but*. She attempted to solve this problem by claiming that preexisting presuppositions fill in the needed information. For example, she described one type of propositional relation between clauses surrounding *but* as requiring a presupposed expectation. The expectation allows the two clauses connected by *but* to be a valid grammatical structure. To interpret *John hates ice cream, but so do I,* one must presuppose that the usual case is that John and the speaker have different tastes in food and that this case is marked as unusual through the use of *but*. G. Lakoff (1971) incorporated the aforementioned analysis into a symbolic notation system that makes the presupposition explicit:

Assertion: S1 and S2
Presupposition: Expectation = (S1 implies not S2)

The S1 as applied to the aforementioned example about ice cream is *John hates ice cream.* S2 is *so do I* (hate ice cream). Because *but* is used rather than *and*, we are required to presuppose the expectation *If John hates ice cream, I will not.* But is thus used when S2 occurs in a context in which its opposite would be expected. This logical (semantic) analysis gives *but* the simple role of conjoining two clauses under the condition that Clause 1 and Clause 2 are contrastive.

Other, more recent accounts of *but* have given additional freedom to what *but* can mean (Schiffrin, 1987; Thompson & Mann, 1986). Thompson and Mann analyze *but* as a marker of *concession* in which a contrast in the mind of the reader is to be reinterpreted as a compatibility. They provide the following example in which they claim that the recipient of a letter is being invited to consider a new interpretation of a contrastive relation (Thompson & Mann, 1989, p. 440):

1. Your kind invitation to come and enjoy cooler climes is so tempting.
2. but I have been waiting to learn the outcome of medical diagnosis.
3. and the next three months will be spent having the main thumb joints replaced with plastic ones.

A typical reading of the aforementioned passage would have *but* signaling a contrast between going to *cooler climes* and being unable to go because of a *medical diagnosis* and need for surgery. Thompson and Mann, however, go one step further and suggest that the reader, after seeing the conflict between enjoying *cooler climes* and needing thumb surgery, comes to realize that the two goals are ultimately compatible (e.g., *The visit will have to be put off*). This interpretation is motivated by the presumed need of the letter's author to demonstrate sincerity in his refusal of the invitation—*but* helps show that thumb surgery is *not just an excuse for not visiting.*

Schiffrin (1987), like Thompson and Mann, allows for a rich interpretation of *but*. She analyzes an argument during a conversation into an abstract discourse structure and shows how *but* and the following clause fits that discourse structure. In some cases, *but* introduces a statement in support for an argument; in others cases, *but* introduces a new position. The role *but* plays for listeners is to signal that the point made following the *but* contrasts in some way with the information currently in focus. In Schiffrin's analysis, *but* marks the introduction of these contrasts. It does not, however, inform the interpreter as to what relations are being contrasted, nor does it provide a conceptual mechanism for creating such contrasts.

What we intend to demonstrate from the analyses that follow is how our constructivist deictic shift view expands on the semantic–syntactic function for the connective *but* provided in early renditions of formal logic frameworks, at the same time, limiting the possible interpretations provided within the more recent discourse inferential approaches. Further, analyses are aimed at arriving at a conceptual framework that gives *but* a stronger than usual role in the construction of plausible interpretations of narrative discourse.

The sources of *but* usage were the following texts: (a) *Wally's Stories* (Paley, 1981)—transcriptions of short oral narratives produced by a 5–year–old child; (b) *The Wizard of Oz* (Baum, 1900/1956), a well–known story written for children; and (c) *The Garden Party* (Mansfield, 1954), a short story written by an adult for an unfamiliar, adult audience.

The analyses were aimed at discovering what the producers of discourse were attempting to convey in the passages that contained the term *but* and how the term functioned to achieve their goal. We interpreted what was being conveyed by *but* in light of what was offered by the adjacent clauses surrounding it as well as what had been built up in the mental model from the text preceding it. From this information we derived a set of regularities that accounted for most of the situations in which *but* occurred.

A CHILD'S ORAL NARRATIVES

The first 10 occurrences of *but* were examined in a set of 20 oral stories told by a 5–year–old to his teacher over a period of a year (Paley, 1981). The stories ranged in length from 6–23 clauses. There were 13 instances of *but*, all occurring in clause-initial position. The analyses of the first 10 showed the following relational contexts in which *but* occurred.

A Failed Psychological Anticipation

In these cases, the character's goals, wishes, hopes, and expectations were not fulfilled. There were two instances that qualified under this relation. In the first example, a father's goal, mentioned in the third line, is to find his son on the moon. But his expectations are not fulfilled in line 6 (Paley, 1981, p. 65).

1.1 The father didn't see him
  2 and then he went out to find the boy.
  3 He thought maybe the boy flew up the moon
  4 because the boy was magic.
  5 So he went up there
  6 but still he didn't find him.

In example 2, the character with the blocked plan is the giant. He intended to lure children into the circle in lines 4–6, but failed in line 7 (Paley, 1981, p. 66):

2.1 There was a magic circle in the forest
2 and a giant lived inside.
3 There was a boy and his sister walking into the forest.
4 The giant tried to trick them
5 because if you stepped inside the circle
6 you turned into a spell.
7 But he couldn't trick them.

An Unexpected Outcome of a Situation

In information derived from the text of Wally's stories, as well as from the real world story logic gleaned from everyday life (called *verisimilitude* in Segal, 1995b), readers are led to to expect that a set of events would continue. The context in which *but* occurred was that in which these expectations were violated. There were three examples of these in Wally's stories.

In the first, knowledge from life would lead one to assume that if a person decides to remain with a caretaker, the caretaker should stay there. This would be especially true if that caretaker were a parent (this assumption is not made explicit in the text). But, in Wally's story this continued state was not fulfilled (line 4) (Paley, 1981, p. 12):

3.1 Once there was a man and a mother and two sisters and a brother.
2 First the oldest sister ran away.
3 Then the second sister decided to stay home with the father.
4 but he ran away too.

In the next example, about Snow White, *but* contributes to the story structure. Snow White was expected to have a sustained visit (implied). This is known only because *but* signals to us that there is an unexpected event. It is concluded that the visit was significantly shorter than expected (line 2) (Paley, 1981, p. 155):

4.1 and Snow White came to visit
2 but she didn't stay.

Finally, Wally leads his audience to believe that a man had one son (line 2, singular referent) and that this set of circumstances is likely to continue, but one finds in line 5 that he has two (Paley, 1981, p. 28):

5.1 Once upon a time a man went out to hunt
2 and his son went with him.
3 He found a lion
4 and the lion killed the boy
5 but the man had two sons
6 and one was still at home.

A Category That Contains an Element
With an Unexpected Property

A third use of *but* by Wally signaled the description of an unexpected attribute of an object or event already introduced in the story. There were three such cases in his stories. In one example, he relied on his audience knowing that under normal circumstances lions are visible, but this one was unusual in that it becomes invisible (line 3) (Paley, 1981. p. 46):

6.1 Then the father saw a lion.
2 He started to shoot
3 but the lion became invisible.

In the next example, Wally implies that orphaned children are not expected to have siblings at all, but this boy had many (line 2) (Paley, 1981, p. 155):

7.1 There was a little boy with no mother and no father.
2 But he had seven brothers and seven sisters.

In the next case, Wally implies that carrot seeds are usually not magic. But this one was exceptional (line 2) (Paley, 1981, p. 194):

8.1 A little boy planted a carrot seed
2 but he didn't know it was magic.

An Unexpected Consequence of a Changed State

This category is similar to the preceding one, but in this case the state of affairs is dynamic rather than static. Often a situation changes but the expected result is not obtained. Wally's stories contained three of these relations. In the first, a lion accepts a bargain (lines 2, 3, 4). The lion expects the boy to keep his word as expressed in the bargain, but he didn't (line 5) (Paley, 1981, p. 69):

9.1 Once a boy saw a lion in the forest.
  2 He said, "give me all your gold
  3 or I'll cut off your head."
  4 So the lion gave him all the gold
  5 but he still cut off his head.

In a second example, the *but* follows the coda of a story (Paley, 1981, p. 120):

10.1 "What words do you want to know?"
  2   "Lion, tiger, and wolf."
  3   "You already know them."
  4   "You just said them."
  5   "Then animal pretend talk must be English."
  6   So they lived happily ever after.
  7   But the man and lady know some words the boy didn't know.
  8   So they did have a lot to teach him.

The most salient interpretation of *but* in line 7 is at a level of metarepresentation. The coda, *they lived happily ever after* (line 6), is expected to create an end to the story, one state. This expectation is violated in line 7 with the story's continuation, and the violation is marked by a *but*, qualifying as an unexpected consequence of a changed state.

Uses of *but* found in the Wally stories extended over four relational contexts all having a three-part logical structure. An abstract representation of the components in the structure shows the first element as one that establishes the domain (D) within which the *but* operates. The second element sets up an expectation (E) which would normally follow from (D). This element is an expectation following from typical conditions and is necessary to interpret the third element as one that violates (V) expectations. The third element usually follows the expression of *but*. The four relational contexts are found in Table 5.1.

Although Wally was only 5–years–old, he worked in a sophisticated way with this abstract schema. In these stories, D, E, and V are sometimes explicit and often tacit. The relationship between D and V need not occur as an adjacency pair, as one might expect from a beginning user of this schema. Rather, Wally easily interspersed appropriate background material when needed. Wally was able to motivate for the reader the background needed to establish the logical structure of the *but* schema and its various subtypes.

The three elements (D, E, and V) comprise a logical structure, one we will be calling a *but* schema. Each of the elements within the schema is interpreted

TABLE 5.1
Four Relational Contexts of *but* Evidenced in the Stories of a 5–year–old

Domain	Expectation	Violation
hope, wish	should come true	is not fulfilled
situation	should produce certain results	unexpected outcomes
category	expected elements	unexpected elements
change	expected consequence	unexpected consequence

in relation to the other two. The *but* signals to the interpreter that a domain is being marked by the one producing the discourse and that the interpreter needs to determine what the domain is (D content). The interpreter must also determine what expectations are being associated with the domain (E content) and how they are being violated (V content).

One question that must be considered is whether the *but* schema found in the Wally stories were provided by Wally or are imputed to his text by the more sophisticated reader. First, it is found that Wally used *but* only sparingly and in contexts that allow for sensible interpretation. One abstract schema was found to be applicable in four and only four abstract, relational contexts. Furthermore, as is seen from the examples by adults presented here, these were the very same contexts that they used.

A STORY WRITTEN FOR CHILDREN

Next, the first 10 instances of *but* were analyzed in L. Frank Baum's *The Wizard of Oz* (Baum, 1900/1956). This story was written by an adult for children, so one would expect it to be more complicated than a story produced by a 5–year–old child and less complicated than one produced by an adult for an adult audience. The first 10 instances of *but* fell within chapters 1 and 2 of the story. All 10 fell within 2 of the 4 categories found in the Wally data—4 of the 10 were tied to situations that did not continue as would be expected; the remaining 6 described examples of a category that contained elements that had unexpected properties or that were contrastive with one another.

An Unexpected Outcome of a Situation

In the first example, the author describes how a house was at one time painted (Line 3), but has blistered, faded, and turned dull and gray (Line 4 and 5). Although a reader may assume that a fresh paint job will fade over time, the *but* leads one to conclude that whatever fading one might have expected cannot compare to the dreariness that actually occurred (Baum, 1900/1956, p. 10):

1.1 The sun had baked the plowed land into a gray mass, with little cracks running through it.

2 Even the grass was not green, for the sun had burned the tops of the long blades until they were the same gray color to be seen everywhere.

3 Once the house had been painted

4 but the sun blistered the paint and the rains washed it away

5 and now the house was as dull and gray as everything else.

The aforementioned text is interpretable within the 3-element *but* schema derived from our interpretation of Wally's stories, the domain (D), expectation (E), and violation (V) as:

D The house was beautifully painted
E One would expect it to remain in reasonable shape
V But it is blistered, dull and gray

In the next example, a description of a dynamic, dangerous situation, a storm, is provided. Storms upset those in them, but this one had an unexpected consequence (Baum, 1900/1956, p. 14):

2.1 It was very dark,

2 and the wind howled horribly around her

3 but Dorothy found she was riding quite easily.

The *but* schema offers the following interpretation of example 2:

D There was a storm in progress
E One would expect it to have violent consequences for someone in it
V But Dorothy was riding quite easily.

The example that follows, as with most of the others, conforms to the DEV schema. The girl thinks her dog is lost, but she is wrong (Baum, 1900/1956, p. 14):

3.1 Once Toto got too near the open trap door, and fell in

2 and at first the little girl thought she had lost him.

3 But soon she saw one of his ears sticking up through the hole . . .

And the DEV schema interpretation is :

D Toto was in danger when he fell through a trap door in a flying house

E The girl expected that he would be lost
V But he wasn't.

Dorothy, in the next example, expected the cyclone to continue its destructive activity (Baum, 1900/1956, p.14):

4.1 At first she had wondered if she would be dashed to pieces when the house fell again
2 but as the hours passed and nothing terrible happened,
3 she stopped worrying and resolved to wait calmly and see what the future would bring.

A DEV schema interpretation reveals:

D Dorothy was worried about her demise
E She expected to be dashed to pieces quickly
V But nothing happened

A Category Contains an Element With an Unexpected Property

Example 5 describes Dorothy's getting better as having a lonely quality (Baum, 1900/1956, p. 14):

5.1 Hour after hour passed away
2 and slowly Dorothy got over her fright;
3 but she felt quite lonely

A DEV schema interpretation is:

D Feelings tend to be unequivocal
E Dorothy felt better
V But she also felt lonely

In example 6, a typical situation accompanying a cyclone is first described. The *but* clause describes an exception to those circumstances (Baum, 1900/1956, p. 13):

6.1 In the middle of a cyclone the air is generally still
2 but the great pressure of the wind on every side of the house raised it up higher and higher . . .

DEV structure reveals the following possible interpretation:

D Cyclones have still centers
E One would expect a house in the center of a cyclone to remain stationary
V But, instead, this house, located in the cyclone's center was raised higher and higher

The following example takes the size of adults as its category focus (Baum, 1900/1956, p. 18):

7.1 . . . she noticed coming toward her a group of the queerest people she had ever seen.
2 They were not as big as the grown folk she had always been used to;
3 but neither were they very small.

Interpreted with the DEV schema:

D The people were not as big as grown folk
E So, one might expect them to be small
V But there were not very small either.

All of the previous examples fit comfortably into the DEV construction, with a domain established and an expectancy denied. In the next three examples, *but* signals to the interpreter to note a contrast. For these examples, one does not need to construct an expectancy to be denied.

In Example 8, Toto, the dog, is upset with the house's occasional tipping and spinning. Dorothy remains calm, in contrast to the reaction of Toto (Baum, 1900/1956, p. 14):

8.1 Toto did not like it.
2 He ran about the room, now here, now there, barking loudly;
3 but Dorothy sat quite still on the floor and waited to see what would happen.

The interpretation does not require a full DEV schema, but can be depicted as a contrast between two elements (A and B). *But* informs the reader to pay attention to the contrastive nature of the elements:

A. Toto ran around the room.

B. Dorothy sat quite still.
But—contrast Toto's behavior to Dorothy's.

In example 9, like example 8, the *but* marks a contrast provided to the interpreter and does not require a DEV schema for interpretation (Baum, 1900/1956, p. 20):

9.1 The men, Dorothy thought, were about as old as Uncle Henry, for two of them had beards.
 2 But the little woman was doubtless much older:
 3 Her face was covered with wrinkles,
 4 her hair was nearly white,
 5 and she walked rather stiffly.

And the contrast involves:

A. The adults look as old as Uncle Henry
B. The woman was much older.
But—contrast the age of the adults with the woman.

In a last example, there is again a contrast that is marked by *but*. A group of people approached Dorothy and stopped out of fear (Baum, 1900/1956, p. 20):

10.1 When these people drew near the house where Dorothy was standing in the doorway, they paused and whispered among themselves, as if afraid to come farther.
  2 But the little old woman walked up to Dorothy.

The contrast is as follows:

A. The people paused and seemed to be afraid
B. The woman was more adventurous
But—contrast the fear of the men with the adventurousness of the woman.

The use of *but* is quite informative in understanding this text. It seems that Baum uses *but* to point out to the children the implicit contrasts from which they can evaluate the occurrences of events in the story. These contrasts help establish feelings of suspense and involvement for them. It is known from the success over time of *The Wizard of Oz*, as well as from our analysis of the Wally stories, that children as young as 5–years–old appreciate the contrastive structure of *but*.

AN ADULT NARRATIVE

Katherine Mansfield's, *The Garden Party*, was selected as an example of an adult writing a narrative for an unfamiliar adult audience. The first 10 occurrences of *but* occurred in the first 5 pages of the 15-page story. The story contained 28 instances of *but* in total. The first 10 were classifiable into the same 4 categories as were the stories told by Wally: 2 were instances of *but* that failed psychological anticipation in which expressed goals, wishes, hopes, or expectations were not fulfilled; 4 were instances of unexpected continuation of situations; 3 examples were of a category that contained elements with unexpected properties; and there was one occasion that was an unexpected consequence of a changed state. None of the *buts* followed the abbreviated contrastive schema found in Baum's, *The Wizard of Oz*. Rather, they all conformed to the more elaborate DEV schema, involving a domain and its inherited expectations.

A Failed Psychological Anticipation

In these first examples, Laura, the main subjective character, was denied a goal and an expectation. (Mansfield, 1937/1954):

1.1 Laura wished now that she had not got the bread-and-butter
  2 but there was nowhere to put it, and she couldn't possibly throw it away. (p. 535)

The *but* schema for this passage reveals the following possibility:

D Laura has a concern about having bread and butter
E She wants to keep her bread and butter and she wants to put it down
V But there was nowhere to put it and she couldn't possibly throw it away (there are two clauses after the but, indicating that the scope of the E element spans two events.)

2.1 Good morning," she said, copying her mother's voice.
  2 But that sounded so fearfully affected that she was ashamed and stammered like a little girl . . . (p. 535)

Interpreted through the *but* Schema:

D Laura tries to sound authoritative by imitating her mother's voice.
E She would expect her mother's voice to sound authoritative.
V But, her imitation of it sounded affected.

An Unexpected Outcome of a Situation

In these examples, there is a break in the dialogic, subjective, or physical continuity. (Mansfield, 1937/1954)

3.1 "H'm, going to have a band, are you?" said another of the workmen...
2 "Only a very small band," said Laura gently.
3 Perhaps he wouldn't mind so much if the band was quite small.
4 But the tall fellow interrupted. (p. 535-536)

A *but* schema interpretation:

D Laura is in a discussion
E We expect to have the dialog continue.
V But the tall fellow interrupted.

4.1 And now there came a long, chuckling absurd sound.
2 It was the heavy piano being moved on its stiff castors.
3 But the air!
4 If you stopped to notice, was the air always like this? (p. 537)

A *but* schema interpretation:

D Laura is listening and reacting to human activities in the house
E One would expect her to continue to do this
V But she shifts her focus to more ephemeral matters outside.

5.1 "It's some mistake," she said faintly.
2 "Nobody ever ordered so many.
3 Sadie go and find mother."
4 But at that moment Mrs. Sheridan joined them. (p. 538)

A possible *but* schema interpretation:

D Sadie was asked to go and find her mother.
E One would expect her mother to be elsewhere.
V But she's right there.

6.1 "Yes, I ordered them. [canna lilies].
2 Aren't they lovely?"
3 She pressed Laura's arm.

4 "I was passing the shop yesterday,
5 and I saw them in the window.
6 And I suddenly thought for once in my life I shall have enough canna lilies.
7 The garden-party will be a good excuse."
8 "But I thought you said you didn't mean to interfere," said Laura. (p. 538)

An interpretation from the *but* schema:

D Mother said she wouldn't be involved in the planning.
E She is expected not to interfere.
V She interfered by ordering the canna lilies.

A Category Contains an Element With an Unexpected Property

There are no obvious constraints on what kind of element may have unexpected properties. Here we are informed that physical objects, knowledge bases, and proposed object locations have them. (Mansfield, 1937/1954):

7.1 His smile was so easy, so friendly that Laura recovered.
  2 What nice eyes he had, small but such a dark blue! (p. 535)

A *but* schema interpretation:
D He had nice, small eyes—ordinary properties.
E One would not expect his eyes to be unusual.
V But such a dark blue is notable.

8.1 . . . he turned to Laura in his easy way,
  2 "you want to put it somewhere where it'll give you a bang slap in the eye,
  3 if you follow me."
  4 Laura's upbringing made her wonder for a moment whether it was quite respectful of a workman to talk to her of bangs slap in the eye.
  5 But she did quite follow him. (p. 535)

A *but* schema interpretation:

D Someone of Laura's class is likely to have difficulty understanding lower class colloquialisms.

E One would not expect someone of Laura's class to understand it.
V But Laura did.

This example follows directly from the preceding one, (Ex 8)

9.1 "A corner of the tennis-court," she suggested.
2 "But the band's going to be in one corner." (p. 535)

Interpretation from the *but* schema:

D Laura's suggestion should be a good idea
E It would be expected to have a "bangs slap in the eye" effect.
V But there is a problem with it.

An Unexpected Consequence of a Changed State

In this last example, a daughter refuses to accept responsibilities granted her by her mother. (Mansfield, 1937/1954).

10.1 "Where do you want the marquee put, mother?"
2 "My dear child, it's no use asking me.
3 I'm determined to leave everything to you children this year.
4 Forget I am your mother.
5 Treat me as an honoured guest."
6 But Meg could not possibly go and supervise the men. (p. 534)

A *but* schema interpretation:

D The mother declines to make her usual decisions.
E She expects her daughter to take over.
V But daughter could not possibly do it.

One of the reasons that Mansfield's story was selected for investigation of *but* clauses is that it is known from previous study that much of the text was presented from a subjective perspective in the style of free indirect discourse (Banfield, 1982; Galbraith, 1995). This different style writing had the potential of presenting *but* in different contexts and logical frames than those in the other samples. It is found, however, that the logical and relational contexts were the same as those found in the other sets of examples, indicating that *but* plays a very similar role in three very different styles of narrative.

SUMMARY

There were only 4 types of conditions in which *but* was used across each of the different discourse contexts for the 30 examples (Table 5.2). *But* occurred in contexts in which there were expectations related to someone's thwarted plans, to situations, to unexpected or contrastive elements in a category or domain, and to changes in states. Within each of these relational contexts, *but* guides us to interpret the relevant text in relation to a particular aspect of a given situation—the domain of interpretation. The relational contexts are neither marked as such in the text, nor are they obviously identifiable units in the mental model under construction. Rather, they are conceptual entities that must be known or inferable by the interlocutors in order for the *but* to be interpreted. That *but* can be understood is, in itself, evidence for the need to go beyond the text in order to understand the text (Adams & Collins, 1979).

All but three of the *but* structures required a 3-part interpretive schema. When the word *but* is expressed in a text, the interpretation requires fore-grounding a domain, determining expectations of elements within that domain, and identifying violations of those expectations. This DEV schema was deriv-able for 27 examples studied.

Each element of the DEV schema needed to be abstracted from the text. The motivation to create the abstract structure is the need to understand the relationships triggered by the connective *but*. This structure, while abstract, is so important to text interpretation that even 5–year–olds seem to have learned its significance. Indeed, it is our judgment that 5–year–old Wally understood this abstraction and could not have placed *but* in interpretable contexts without an understanding of an underlying DEV schema and how to use it correctly.

Understanding the DEV structure requires the interpreter to set up a contrast between the unexpressed expectancy and its violation. The simpler structure that we uncovered in the remaining three *but* examples also requires the interpreter to identify and focus on a contrast, but, in this case, the contrast is based on elements explicitly expressed in the text. *But* allows a tension to be felt between the elements expressed, without the need for an expectancy to be denied.

The two structures, the full DEV structure and simpler contrast structure, both require considerable conceptual construction on the part of the inter-preter. A DEV interpretation requires providing a domain and its concomitant expectancies; the *contrast* structure requires identifying the contrastive ele-ments and the dimension upon which the contrast depends.

This empirical analysis of these 30 examples was classified into only 4 relational contexts. The small number of contexts and the considerable overlap

TABLE 5.2
The Four Relational Contexts and the Domains They Encompass

1. A Failed Psychological Anticipation

1. The father is looking for his son (CON, 1)*#

2. The Giant is luring children into the circle (CON, 2)

3. Laura has a concern about having bread and butter (AN, 1)

4. Laura tries to sound authoritative by imitating her mother's voice (AN, 2)

2. An Unexpected Outcome of a Situation

1. Caretakers stay with their charges (CON, 3)

2. Snow White was visiting (CON, 4)

3. A man had a single son (CON, 5)

4. The house was beautifully painted (ANC, 1)

5. There was a storm in progress (ANC, 2)

6. Toto was in danger when he fell through a trap door in a flying house (ANC, 3)

7. Dorothy was worried about her demise (ANC, 4)

8. Laura is in a discussion (AN, 3)

9. Laura is listening and reacting to human activity in the house (AN, 4)

10. Sadie was asked to go and find her mother (AN, 5)

11. Mother said she wouldn't interfere (AN,,6)

3. A Category That Contains an Element with an Unexpected Property

1. Lions are usually visible (CON, 6)

2. Orphaned children are not expected to have siblings (CON, 7)

3. Carrot seeds are usually not magic (CON, 8)

4. Feelings tend to be unequivocal (ANC, 5)

5. Cyclones have still centers (ANC, 6)

6. The people were not as big as grown folk (ANC, 7)

7. Toto was agitated (ANC, 8)

8. The adults look as old as Uncle Henry (ANC, 9)

9. The people paused and seemed to be afraid (ANC, 10)

10. He had nice, small eyes (AN, 7)

11. Someone of Laura's class is likely to have difficulty understanding lower class colloquialisms (AN, 8)

12. Laura's suggestion should be a good idea (AN, 9)

4. An Unexpected Consequence of a Changed State

1. A boy and a lion made a bargain (CON, 9)

2. Stories end with a coda (CON, 10)

3. The mother declines to make her usual decisions (AN, 10)

*CON = child's oral narrative
ANC = adult narratives to children
AN = adult narrative (to unfamiliar adults)
# numbers following code letters refer to example number in the above text.

of the findings from the different genres was surprising. It is not known if these findings are accidental to the set of examples chosen or whether they, in fact, are a complete taxonomy of relational contexts related to *but*. If this finding is universal, a theory is needed to explain its universality.

In conclusion, the following has been discovered from this analyses of the use of *but*:

1. The understanding of a particular use of *but* often requires consideration of information presented in clauses much earlier in the text than the clause just preceding the *but*.
2. Interpreting *but* often requires the incorporation of information about real world events—inferences depending upon the presumption of verisimilitude.
3. Interpreting the meaning of *but* in most cases requires that there be an exception to an expectation. This requires identifying the relevant domain within which both expectations and their violations can operate—a *but* schema.
4. There were only four relational contexts signaled by the *but* in these data. We have no principled reason to assume that these four represent a universal semantic or pragmatic taxonomy, but the possibility needs further exploration.
5. The *but* schema is functional for speakers and listeners of different abilities and across very different narrative styles.

CONCLUSIONS AND IMPLICATIONS FOR UNDERSTANDING HOW CONNECTIVES HELP STRUCTURE DISCOURSE

The aforementioned findings support a conceptual view of connectives, one in which terms traditionally thought of as connecting clauses, function instead to connect entities being constructed in a mental representation. The conceptual entities activated by the connectives may be found within the current model or may need to be brought to the model. The entities and their relations then become available to play a role in the evolution of the discourse content.

This analysis of connectives points out that the entities and relationships in the text are not simply propositions added to the interpreters' previously attained model. Instead, elements of the model must be reinterpreted. *But*, for example, always requires identifying a contrast between two different elements, either between the expectation and the occurrent exception or between explic-

itly expressed elements. Thus the interpreter must reorganize a previous interpretation to accommodate the meaning of the connective. This reorganization
is obvious in the DEV structure that requires a construction of the domain and
the expectancies therein. In the case of the simple contrast, the opposition
signaled by *but* requires that the first element be reinterpreted in light of the
opposition it marks.

Findings also, reveal that connectives often require interpreters to shift their
frame of reference from the "here-and-now" of the speaking/reading context to
the world of the discourse. The text is interpreted from a particular perspective
within the mental model. This goes beyond a traditional mental model approach
for representing discourse in that it requires a conceptual deictic shift into the
model, and, once there, it requires that interpretations be based on an internal
perspective on the events being presented in the discourse.

An example might clarify notions of how connectives work in structuring
discourse. One of the Wally stories begins as follows (Paley, 1981, p.4): "There
was a little boy with no mother and no father. But he had seven brothers and
seven sisters." Had there been an *and* in place of the *but*, one would interpret
the sibling sentence simply as an assertion of this family situation. The *but*
requires the reader to contrast the notion of being orphaned with that of having
many siblings and to see this juxtaposition as being focused upon and unexpected. In other words, one must reevaluate the status of the information in
the clauses in light of the information marked as unexpected by the *but*.

This example also poses for us the question about the source of the expectation. Who expected there to be no siblings? There are three possible sources
of this expectation: the interpreter, from general knowledge; Wally, as the
author of the story; or the little orphan boy. It cannot be the boy, because he is
the orphan with the siblings—he wouldn't be surprised. It is impossible to
discriminate between the other two. Nonetheless, the fact that one must ascribe
an expectation to someone makes the point that discourse, in particular
discourse containing *but*, requires taking a point of view.

This study of *but* has revealed that to understand discourse, one cannot treat
the sequences of information expressed by the text in a linear fashion. One of
the major functions of interclausal connectives is to help specify what the
nonlinear relations are among the elements of the mental model being created.
This role of connectives is consistent with our earlier work in which we studied
the relational nature of *and, then, because* and *so*, as well as *but* (Duchan, Meth,
& Waltzman, 1992; Segal, et al, 1991). Connectives in the studies were found
to signal different interpretive relations: continuity, discontinuity, causality, and
adversity. These required reinterpreting the current model in view of known
information and from a particular deictic perspective.

The analysis of *but* as well as *then* (Duchan, et al., 1992) reveals surprisingly few possibilities of relational contexts signaled by a particular connective. Much of the complexity arises from assuming the perspective within the model, rather than on multiple logical relations triggered by the connectives.

There is a general puzzle in natural language interpretation. One the one hand, linguistic elements must have a core meaning that is transituational, so that interpreters can understand the language when it occurs in novel situations. On the other hand, language must be sensitive to the specific nuances provided by different situational needs.

The tension between the two positions requires a diverse interpretation of the same structures. Findings presented here give a possible solution to this dilemma. A very circumscribed number of abstract relational contexts were found to be associated with a particular linguistic form (*but*) that can serve to structure an extremely large number of specific contextual domains (30 in this study). To the extent that connectives and probably other linguistic forms serve an abstract structuring role in a circumscribed way, they allow for a common basis of interpretation for diverse contexts. Since the structuring is abstract, the variations in context have the potential of giving particular linguistic forms the potential for shaping an infinite number of instantiations. This formulation supports the idea that there are but few syntactic possibilities underlying particular forms. This notion supplies a means of applying Chomsky's principle of sentences (Chomsky, 1965, p.8) "making infinite use of finite means" beyond syntax.

Chomsky's notion can be taken into the conceptual arena of interpreting connected discourse. Abstract conceptual structures are seen as being guided by closed class lexical items, such as connectives, and these abstract structures are seen as interacting with deictic perspectives to shape the specific interpretation of that text. Further work is needed on the notion that connectives provide a text with an abstract structure whose particulars are to be filled in, depending upon the specific perspective and context in which they occur.

REFERENCES

Adams, M., & Collins, A. (1979). A schema-theoretic view of reading. In R. O. Freedle (Ed.), *New Directions in Discourse Processing*, Vol. 2 (pp. 1–22). Norwood, NJ: Ablex.

Banfield, A. (1982). *Unspeakable Sentences: Narration and representation in the language of fiction.* Boston: Routledge & Kegan Paul.

Baum, L. Frank (1956) *The Wizard of Oz*, New York: Rand McNally & Co. (Original work published 1900).

Bloom, L., Lahey, M., Hood, L., Lifter, K., & Fiess, K. (1980). Complex sentences: Acquisition of syntactic connectives and the semantic relations they encode. *Journal of child language, 7,* 235–261.

Chomsky, N. (1957). *Syntactic structures*. The Hague: Mouton.

Chomsky, N. (1965). *Aspects of the Theory of Syntax*, Cambridge, MA: The M. I. T. Press.

Clark, H. (1992). *Arenas of Language Use*, Chicago, IL: The University of Chicago Press and the Center for the Study of Language and Information.

Duchan, J., Bruder, G., & Hewitt, L. (1995). *Deixis in narrative: A cognitive science perspective*, Hillsdale, NJ: Lawrence Erlbaum Associates.

Duchan, J., Meth, M., & Waltzman, D. (1992) THEN as an indicator of deictic discontinuity in adults' oral descriptions of a film, *Journal of Speech and Hearing Research*. 35, 1367–1375.

Galbraith, M. (1995). Deictic shift theory and the poetics of involvement in narrative. In J. F. Duchan, G. A. Bruder, & L. Hewitt (Eds.), *Deixis in narrative: A cognitive science perspective.* (pp.19–59). Hillsdale, NJ: Lawrence Erlbaum Associates.

Gleitman, L. (1965). Coordinating conjunctions in English. *Language, 41,* 260–293.

Greenspan, S. & Segal, E. (1984). Reference and comprehension: A topic-comment analysis of sentence-picture verification, *Cognitive Psychology*, 16, 556–606.

Halliday, M. A. K. and Hasan, R. (1976) *Cohesion in English*. New York: Longman.

Kintsch, W. (1977) On comprehending stories. In M. Just and P. Carpenter (Eds.) *Cognitive Processes in Comprehension*. Hillsdale, N.J.: Lawrence Erlbaum Associates.

Lakoff, R. (1971). If's and's and but's about conjunction. In C. Fillmore & D.T. Langendoen (Eds.), *Studies in linguistic semantics* (pp.114–149). New York: Holt.

Mansfield, K. (1954). The garden party. In *The Short Stories of Katherine Mansfield*, New York: Knopf. (Original work published 1937)

Paley, V. (1981) *Wally's Stories*. Cambridge, MA: Harvard University Press.

Schiffrin, D. (1987) *Discourse Markers*. New York: Cambridge University Press.

Segal, E. (1990). Fictional narrative comprehension: Structuring the deictic center. *The Twelfth Annual Conference of the Cognitive Science Society*, 526–533.

Segal, E. (1995a). Narrative comprehension and role of decitic shift theory. In J. Duchan, G. Bruder, L. Hewitt (Eds.) *Deixis in Narrative: A Cognitive Science Perspective* (pp. 3–17). Hillsdale, NJ: Lawrence Erlbaum Associates.

Segal, E. (1995b). A cognitive-phenomenological theory of fictional narrative. In J. Duchan, G. Bruder, & L. Hewitt (Eds.) *Deixis in Narrative: A Cognitive Science Perspective* (pp. 61–78). Hillsdale, NJ: Lawrence Erlbaum Associates.

Segal, E., Bruder, G., & Daniels J. (1984). Deictic Centers in Narrative Comprehension. Paper presented at Psychonomic Society Meeting, San Antonio, Texas.

Segal, E., Duchan, J., & Scott, P. (1991). The role of interclausal connectives in narrative structuring: Evidence from adults' interpretations of simple stories. *Discourse Processes, 14,* 27–54.

Stalnaker, R. (1978). Assertion. In P. Cole (Ed.). *Syntax and Semantics versus Pragmatics* (pp. 315–332). New York: Academic Press.

Stein, N., & Glenn, N. (1979) An analysis of story comprehension in elementary school children. In R. Freedle (Ed.) *New directions in Discourse Processing*. (Vol. 2, pp. 53–120). Norwood, NJ: Ablex.

Steinbeck, J. (1975). *The pearl*. New York: Bantam. (Original work published 1954)

Thompson, S. A., & Mann, W. C. (1986). A discourse view of concession in written English. In S. Delancey & R. Tomlin (Eds.), *Proceedings of the second annual meeting of the Pacific Linguistics Conference* (pp. 435–447).

Trabasso, T., & Sperry, L. L. (1985). Causal relatedness and importance of story events. *Journal of Memory and Language, 24,* 595–611.

Wiebe, J. (1995). References in narrative text. In J. Duchan, G. Bruder, & L. Hewitt (Eds.), *Deixis in Narrative: A Cognitive Science Perspective* (pp. 263–286), Hillsdale, NJ: Lawrence Erlbaum Associates.

Chapter 6

The Development of Because and So: Connecting Language, Thought, and Social Understanding

Susan R. Braunwald
University of California, Los Angeles

> *The child is father of the man.*
>
> —William Wordsworth

Many studies have found that preschool children use causal connectives correctly in their language production, albeit within a restricted range of linguistic and situational contexts (Bloom & Capatides, 1987; Byrnes, 1991; Eisenberg, 1980; French, 1986, 1988; French & Nelson, 1985; Hood & Bloom, 1979; Levy & Nelson, 1994; McCabe & Peterson, 1985). Diary data from my daughter Laura (henceforth L), from age 15–42 months, confirm this consistent finding and show how the ability to produce the causal connectives *because* and *so* emerged from discourse in the midst of her daily life. From the outset, L's use of interclause relations to express causality required the ability to integrate language, thought, and social understanding.

Both 3–year–old children and adults use the connectives *because* and *so* to mark a causal relation between two propositions. Yet, there is a vast developmental difference in their abilities to express causality. What can be learned from investigating the emergence of *because* and *so* in the language production of young children that is masked by the superior communicative competence of adults?

There are sound methodological and theoretical reasons for considering child language data as a source of insights that are not transparent in adult discourse (Byrnes & Gelman, 1991).

121

A developmental approach is inherently concerned with process, and so is especially suitable for detecting the relations among the ingredients of a complex system. . . . Studying development is thus a powerful methodological tool and potentially more revealing about the organization of a system than any attempt to infer it from the adult end product. (p. 4)

The data from L are the source of an explicit description of the development and marking of interclause relations with *because* and *so* that provide insight into the complexity and orderliness of a developmental process.

L acquired *because* and *so* during her third year as part of the organization of two complementary systems for expressing interclausal relations. One system involved the gradual emergence of connectives that differed in the meaning of the interclausal relations that they defined (Braunwald, 1985). The other involved the reciprocity in discourse between causal questions and answers (Blank, 1975; Hood & Bloom, 1979). Together, these two systems provided a developmental context for using language to acquire the meaning of *because* and *so* to express interclause relations. Thus, beginning in early childhood, L knew a procedural routine in discourse that reflected the immaturity of her causal reasoning but also allowed her to use language to learn from others about causality.

To understand why and how L's ability to use causal connectives emerged, it is necessary to envision her as a developing child. Therefore, I have divided this chapter into two main sections. First, I present a theoretical and developmental overview of L's acquisition of *because* and *so*. I discuss two current concepts from developmental psychology, intersubjectivity and decontextualization, that provide a theoretical perspective for the ideas in this chapter. Next, I describe and illustrate the emergence of *because* and *so* in L's language production. In the second section, I propose three general insights about the emergence of causal interclause relations that were derived from the developmental overview. I use additional examples from L's diary to illustrate the theoretical basis for these insights about <u>why</u>, <u>when</u>, and <u>how</u> causal connectives are acquired.

Method

Subject. L is the second–born daughter of college–educated parents. She is 2 years, 9 months younger than her older sister, Joanna. Her mother was her primary caregiver; L and her family spoke English.

Examples. The examples come from a hand-recorded daily diary of L's language acquisition, which her mother kept during the early 1970s. The diary is a cross-contextual record of L's spontaneously produced emergent language, and the data reflect the upper limit of her communicative competence. Examples, which occur in children's average language use at a later age, are found as rare events at an earlier age for L.

There are approximately 8,300 speech events in the diary for the 27–month period for L between the ages of 15 and 42 months. The length and complexity of a speech event varies from single word utterances to conversations involving multiple turns. Additional information about this diary case study is available elsewhere (Braunwald & Brislin, 1979).

DEVELOPMENTAL OVERVIEW

Between 15 and 42 months, L was an avid explorer of a social, emotional, and physical world that was novel and challenging to her. As she lived through the developmental transition from toddler to preschool child, she discovered the connectives *because* and *so* in the practical context of learning and talking about cause and effect in the course of her everyday personal experiences. During her third year, L developed the ability to produce *because* and *so* as intentional causal markers with contrastive meanings in discourse and in complex sentences.

Theoretical Orientation

Intersubjectivity. Intersubjectivity refers to a basic human experience of successful interpersonal engagement. During infancy, intersubjectivity involves finely tuned exchanges of affect (Stern, 1985) and the establishment of a joint focus of attention. Bloom (1993) proposed that toddlers acquire language in order to maintain intersubjectivity: "Children learn language... because they strive to maintain intersubjectivity with other persons—to *share* what they and other persons are feeling and thinking" (p. 245, italics in original). According to Bloom, toddlers develop language to express and interpret messages that cannot be conveyed without words.

As a toddler, L's language functioned to maintain intersubjectivity because her messages were simple and context dependent. L and her mother could even exchange causal information if her mother could discern the topic from the situation or prior shared experience.

Context-dependent causality. (L, 1;10.8, is afraid of the neighbor's dog. The dog is barking.)[1]

> L: Doggie barking. Worried. (L expresses internal state—The doggie is barking so I'm worried.)

---

[1]In the examples, the child's age is stated in years, months, and days. L, J, M and F refer respectively to Laura, Joanna, their mother and their father.

M: Worried? (M knows that L is afraid of the dog.)
L: Worried. (L confirms her internal state.)
M: It's okay. He can't get through the fence. (M provides a causal reason why L is safe.)

Between 24–36 months, L's context-dependent language began to be inadequate as a means to maintain intersubjectivity. She started to explore a realm of experience that required language as an explicit means of communicating about thoughts and feelings that could only be shared through language. Causal connectives emerged in this developmental context as a function of a process of decontextualization.

Decontextualization. The term, *decontextualization*, can be used with a general and a specific meaning. In a general sense, decontextualization describes a developmental process that has been observed in cognitive development and in language acquisition. New abilities emerge in a specific and limited context of use. Development involves the gradual generalization of these context-specific abilities to novel contexts of use. In this general sense, decontextualization refers to a basic explanatory principle that accounts for development as a function of incremental changes in competence over time (see Braunwald, 1985; French, 1986, 1988; French & Nelson, 1985; Levy & Nelson, 1994, for theories that apply this principle to the acquisition of causal connectives).

Decontextualization can also be used in a more specific, but related, sense to refer to an important step in language acquisition. The meaning of children's early language is embedded in the immediate context of the "here and now." With development, language becomes freed from the "here and now" or decontextualized. That is to say, language bears the burden of conveying shared meaning in a relevant exchange of thoughts and feelings. The data from L highlight the importance of intersubjectivity and decontextualization as the basis for the emergence of connectives, including *because* and *so*. As L's language developed into a more creative and powerful means for maintaining intersubjectivity, connectives became necessary to define the nature of the relationship between her thoughts. Connectives emerged in L's language production beginning with *and* at 1;11.12 and throughout her third year as a function of the decontextualization of language in both senses of the term (see Braunwald, 1985, for the order of emergence).

Causal Connectives. The connectives *because* and *so* in natural language consist of two components of meaning, a causal component and an order component (French, 1986, 1988; French & Nelson, 1985). Both *because* and *so* mark the relation between two propositions as causal. The difference in their meaning relates to the order component (French, 1986, 1988; Hood & Bloom, 1979). *Because* expresses the relation effect-cause (Hood & Bloom, 1979) or consequence-antecedent (French & Nelson, 1985). Conceptually, *because* always (Byrnes, 1991) "explains *why* a cause brings about an effect" (p. 356 italics in original). *So* expresses the relation cause–effect or antecedent–consequence with a meaning of "in order that," "so that," or "therefore." Pragmatically, *because* and *so* are used when the speaker is certain of the truth of both the antecedent and the consequence (Byrnes, 1991).

L's Development of *Because* and *So*

Like the children Dunn (1988) observed, L's initial interest in causality emerged in the midst of her family life and reflected her concern about practical, psychological matters. The emergence of causal connectives in L's language production offered a unique glimpse at how a young child talked about causality in the naturalistic contexts of her daily life.

Antecedents in the Second Year. The foundation of the communicative competence and psychological need for the development of causal connectives was in place by L's second birthday. Her vocabulary contained 899 words, including 215 verbs (Braunwald, 1995). Her mean length of utterance (MLU; based on consecutive utterances in the diary data) was 3.68 (Braunwald, 1993). Her thoughts were elaborated as sequences of utterances on a topic or as turns in discourse. Her interest in the cause and consequences of behavior was emerging as a theme in her language production (Dunn, 1988).

Three unusual speech events, with *why*, *how come*, and *because* respectively, suggest that by 21–22 months, L was already attending to causal words in the language she heard.

Why: (L, 1;8.24, and J, 4;5.24, both have recipe cards from the newspaper. J wants L's.)
> J: Laura, where'd you put your card?
> L: Card *why?*
> J: Where's your card?
> L: *Why?*

How come: (L, 1;9.7, is pushing her stool toward the hot stove.)
> M: It isn't a good idea to put that (the stool) there. It's hot.

L: *How come,* Mama? *How come?*
M: *Because* it's hot.

Because: (L, 1;10.2, and J, 4;7.2. M gave L a piece of candle wax to feel.)
    L: No take me Laura's. No take Laura's away, Dee-Dee (L's name for
    J).
    J: I won't.
    L: Mine *because.* Dee-Dee *because.*
    J: *Because why?*
    L: *Because* (at least 10 times).

L's use of these causal words did not signal the advent of connectives. However, it foreshadowed the psychological necessity of developing the ability to talk about causality.

Beginning at about 19 months, L produced successive utterances on a topic that could have been joined together with a causal connective to form a complex sentence. The need for explicit marking with because or so was implied from the order of the clauses in relation to the context of use (e.g., because at 1;8.25, as L played with a doll, "Quiet!" "Laura baby sleep" [Be quiet because Laura's baby is asleep] and so at 1;10.15, as L is filling a toy pan with water, "This is hot coffee," "Have to careful" [This is hot coffee so I have to be careful]). L's production of these causally related thoughts suggests that she developed a rudimentary social as well as sensorimotor understanding of causality prior to the emergence of an explicit linguistic procedure for its expression.

L continued to use implicit causal relations until 28 months (e.g., at 2;4.1, as J and her friend are laughing at L, "Don't laugh I bite my tongue" [Don't laugh *because* I bit my tongue]). Descriptions of implicit causal relations overlapping developmentally with their explicit expression have been reported in other studies of the initial acquisition of causal connectives (Bloom & Capatides, 1987; Braunwald, 1985; Hood & Bloom, 1979).

Emergence of Because and So in the Third Year. L acquired *because* and *so* during her third year as part of a reciprocal process in discourse of asking causal questions and providing explanatory information. Her participation in discourse served the dual purpose of eliciting and providing information about causality.

Eliciting causal information: (L, 2;4.14, notices that the salt and pepper shakers are above the stove. They are usually kept on a table.)

L: *How come* you put salt and pepper up there? *How come? Why?*
M: *Because* I didn't want them on the table.

Providing causal information: (L, 2;4.16, and F are discussing L's day at school. Fred cries everyday.)
    F: *Why* did Fred cry?
    L: *Because* he want her mommy.

In her shifting roles as questioner and respondent, L was mastering simultaneously the structures in discourse for asking and answering causal questions.

Beginning at 2;0.18, L began to form an association between the words *why* and *because*, with *why* eliciting *because*. She often asked someone to say "why" and answered with "because."

Form of because: (L, 2;0.18, is sitting across the table from M. There is no eliciting event. L has used *because* once before at 1;10.2; see previous example.)
    L: *Why? Because. Because* Nanny Edith coming. *Because* Nanny
        Mickey come here. *Because* (at least 20 times). *Because* Nanny
        Mickey coming. (pause) *Because* Nanny Edith coming.
    M: *Because* what, Laura?
    L: You say *why.*
    M: *Why?*
    L: *Because* Nanny Mickey coming.

One day later, L answered J's *why* question with a version of the sequential form "*because*...coming" which she had practiced.

First meaningful use of because: (L, 2;0.19, and J, 4;9.19, have been fighting. Both girls were screaming and are now being comforted by M.)
    J: *Why* did you pull my hair?
    L: *Because* daddy, mommy coming.

Two weeks later, L used the word *because* flexibly in discourse with M, although her language and reasoning were simple.

First flexible use of because: (L, 2;1.3, is dribbling water down a picture window and watching it make a design.)
    L: That beautiful? (Is that beautiful?)
    M: *Why* do you think that's beautiful?

L: *Because* that go window. (Because the water makes a design on the window.)

M: Oh, you think it's beautiful.

Between 2;1.3 and 2;2.19, L occasionally used because in both an implicit and explicit form. Two months after her first practice of the form, L produced a complex sentence with *because*.

First complex sentence with because: (L, 2;2.19, is trying to roll up her car window.)

L: Roll up my window *cause* wind blowing.

M: Okay, *cause* wind blowing.

Later complex sentence with because: (L, 3;1.12, is looking at the wind blowing the trees.)

L: We shouldn't go out, but I need to *because* I hafta go to school.

As the second example indicates, L could use because in a linguistically complicated sentence as long as the topic did not tax her conceptual understanding.

For more than a year (2;2.19–3;3.25), L always used *because* in complex sentences with the clause order B because A. L's extreme preference for B because A clause order in complex sentences (102 of 104 speech events) suggests that she attended to the temporal order of discourse in which the question *why* was followed by an answer marked with *because*.

The acquisition of *so* as a causal connective was more complex than *because*. Connectives with homonymous forms are learned later and first appear in a nonconnective context (Bloom, Lahey, Hood, Lifter, & Fiess, 1980). L produced *so* as an intensifier during the same month that *because* emerged (e.g., at 2;0.5, after seeing a newborn, "Baby *so* tiny"). From 2;1.27-3;6, L sometimes used *so* intensifier as if it were associated with the expression of causality (e.g., at 3;3.15, as L is examining a new kind of flower "Look it that flower," "It's *so* nice," "I wanna see that beautiful flower *cause* it's *so* nice").

The two meanings of *so* as a connective emerged simultaneously, but L used *for* to express the meaning "in order that" from 2;2.18–2;5.27 and reserved *so* for the meaning "therefore."

For meaning "in order that": (L, 2;2.18, was with the babysitter all day because M is sick. She made a picture for M which she is showing to her.)

L: That *for* you feel better. I made that for you feel better.

M: Oh thank you. It's beautiful.

So meaning "therefore": (L, 2;2.20, is showing M a throw-away newspaper. The day before she saw a man throw it out of a truck and ran to get it.)

> L: Somebody dropped that paper.
> M: Yes, somebody dropped that paper.
> L: *So* I got it. *So* I got it.
> M: Yes, you did.

Beginning at 2;2.3, L sometimes used *so* with a meaning that was indeterminate between "in order that" and "therefore" (cf. French & Nelson, 1985).

L first used *so* meaning "therefore" in an incorrect complex sentence, which she immediately repaired with the correct causal connective, *because.*

Repair of meaning: (L, 2;3.22, has been running on a neighbor's lawn. She is speaking to her mother. There is a bird in the tree overhead.)

> L: Can't go up there *so* bird up there. Can't go up there *cause* bird up there. *So* can't go up there.

This informative repair suggests that L recognized that the clause orders B because A and A so B differed in their meaning. At 2;4.8, L produced her first complex sentence with the causal connective *so* (on a personal topic).

By 2 years, 6 months, L seemed to be consolidating her understanding of the meaning of *so* as a causal connective. She used the meaning contrastively with *because.*

Contrast in Meaning of because and so: (L, 2;5.25, is sitting on a beach and playing with F. She is wearing a paper hat.)

> L: I have a hat *so* I won't get sun in my eyes. (L gives the hat to F but promptly discovers that the sun is too bright.)
> L: You look perfect. There Jack, you look pretty. Sun coming in my eyes.
> F: Okay, you wear it.
> L: Okay, *because* sun coming in my eyes.

L also discontinued the substitution of for to express the meaning "in order that" and incorporated this meaning into her use of the causal connective *so.*

So meaning "in order that": (L, 2;6.3, asks M's friend to hold a picture up while she gets tape.)

> L: Could you hold this (her picture) up *so* it won't fall.

In sum, at least for L, the causal connective *so* was more difficult to master than *because.* However, by her third birthday, she knew how to use these connectives correctly. L learned how to mark interclause relations with *because* and *so* through discourse (cf. Levy & Nelson, 1994) and practiced using these connectives in her solitary and social play.

DEVELOPMENTAL INSIGHTS

The emergence of *because* and *so* in L's language production demonstrates three basic insights about causal connectives that are highlighted in the *in vivo* developmental process. These data show <u>why</u>, <u>when</u>, and <u>how</u> causal connectives become necessary to define the relationship between thoughts in successive clauses.

<u>Why</u>: Causal Connectives are Necessary to Delineate the <u>Explicit</u> <u>Meaning</u> of the Interrelations Between the Thoughts in Two Clauses.

The concepts of *intersubjectivity* and of *decontextualization*, in both senses of the term, are relevant to an understanding of <u>why</u> causal connectives become necessary as explicit markers of interclause relations. The presence of a connective is critical to the establishment of intersubjectivity when the topic is decontextualized from the "here and now" and the speaker's intended stance is not apparent from the discourse, the order of the clauses, or the existence of shared knowledge in common.

TABLE 6.1
The Marking of Interclause Relations

Ambiguous—Unmarked Interclause Relations

  1. (L, 2;1.5, is going to ride a pony later in the day and is apprehensive.)

      L: I big girl ride pony. I big girl ride pony.

      M: Yes, you're a big girl.

      L: I very big girl.

      M: Okay, have fun.

      L: Not going yet.

  2. (L, 2;1.17. J is nagging to go to the pony park.)

      L: I rode pony. I big girl ride pony.

Explicit—Marked with <u>Because</u> in Discourse

  3. (L, 2;5.1, The family is discussing a possible trip to the pony park.)

      L: I'm big girl ride ponies, right, mom. Cause I'm big girl.

      M: Right.

Explicit—Marked with <u>Because</u> in Complex Sentence

  4. (L, 2;7.18. M is suggesting what L could wear.)

      M: You could wear your osh-koshes (overalls). They're not dirty.

      L: I haven't made caca in um (them) cause I'm a big girl. I'm a big girl.

Table 6.1 shows that explicit marking with a connective avoids ambiguity and facilitates the successful exchange of meaningful thoughts. In Examples 1 and 2, the meaning of the decontextualized sentence "I'm big girl ride pony" is ambiguous because the interclause relation is not specified. A number of connectives including *and, because, so, since, when,* and *if* would make sense at the juncture between the clauses "I big girl" and "ride pony." Even though the two clauses are integrated into a single unit, the interclausal relation between them cannot be determined without a connective.

In Example 3, the choice and placement of the connective *cause* makes L's stance toward riding a pony clear. Together, the two sentences express the relation between the clauses and, hence, L's intended meaning: "Being a big girl" is the reason why L can ride a pony. In Example 3, *Cause* is a "discourse connective" in a "discourse fragment" that expresses the intersentential relation, "causation" and is comparable to examples from adults' speech (see Warner, 1985).

In Example 4, *cause* is a subordinate conjunction that defines an intrasentential relation between two clauses in a complex sentence. The subordinate clause introduced with *because* describes the antecedent event and explains why (Byrnes, 1991). In Example 4, "being a big girl" is the reason why L no longer soils her pants. (The immediate repetition of "I'm a big girl" as an independent clause reinforces L's perception of herself as competent.)

When: The Procedural Knowledge to Produce Because and So to Mark an Interclause Relation in Discourse and in Complex Sentences is Developed During Early Childhood.

During her third year, L learned a procedural routine for marking causal interclause relations with *because* and *so*. She rarely made a mistake in the choice between *because* and *so* to express the correct order of the causal relations. There are 254 speech events with *because* (191) and *so* (63) as connectives. Only 6 of them (2%) involved substitution errors of *because* and *so*. Table 6.2 presents these substitution errors. In Examples 5 and 6, L's substitution errors with *so* are ambiguous. They could be interpreted as examples of child-logic in which L meant "therefore" and "in order that" respectively.

The correctly executed procedural routine created a framework that contained increasingly complex language and thought as a function of L's development. Table 6.3 illustrates the zenith of L's communicative competence with *because* and *so*. As can be seen from these examples, the presence of causal connectives in L's speech was an integral part of her ability to engage in socially

TABLE 6.2
Substitution Errors with *Because* and *So*

<u>Because</u> *Instead of* <u>So</u>

1. (L, 2;2.15, put her toy helicopter in a kitchen drawer in order to hide it from J.)

   M: Oh no, Laura, we'll never find your helicopter there.

   L: *Cause Dee-Dee got it. Cause Dee-Dee got it.* (So Joanna won't get it.)

2. (L, 2;4.10, is walking up the garden stairs with M. L had been playing with a bug and identified it, "This is a bug," L was not stung by a bee.)

   L: One those bees sting me. One those bees sting me. *Cause I'm angry one those bees sting me.* (So I'm angry that one of those bees stung me.)

3. (L, 2;4.25, and M are looking at a picture of a swimming pool in a magazine.)

   M: Do you like swimming pools?

   L: Yep, I don't wanna go in deep water. *Cause stay stepies.* (I don't wanna go in the deep water so I stay on the steps.)

4. (L, 2; 5.5, is taking off a pair of new shorts.)

   L: Those are so dirty *cause* need to get washed, right? (Those are so dirty so they need to be washed, right?)

<u>So</u> *Instead of* <u>Because</u>

1. (L, 2;6.0 is in bed; earlier in the day M warned her to stop eating grapes or she would have a tummy ache.)

   L: My tummy hurts so I ate too much grapes. *That's why.* (My tummy hurts *because* I ate too many grapes.)

2. (L, 2;8.5, is walking by M with an arm full of blocks.)

   M: Laura, keep the blocks in the playroom.

   L: I'm making a crutches so you can walk on crutches. (I'm making crutches *because* you can walk on them.)

   M: You're walking on a what?

   L: Some crutches.

appropriate commerce with people. L was talking about familiar, culturally transmitted experiences such as borrowing, requesting a favor, and not getting lost.

In sum, the data from L support the finding that the procedure for selecting between *because* and *so* seems to be error-free in young children's causal language production (Bloom & Capatides, 1987; Byrnes, 1991; Eisenberg, 1980; French, 1986; French & Nelson, 1985; Hood & Bloom, 1979;). However, L's command of this procedural knowledge revealed other sources of error.

How: Competent Use of Causal Connectives
Involves a Complex Integration of Language,
Thought, and Social Understanding.

L's essentially error-free command of the procedure for using *because* and *so* as
causal connectives provided a window into her mind. In L's case, errors
occurred in the content and language that she produced within the general
framework of well constructed interclause relations. These errors involved the
complexity of the developmental interface among language, thought, and social
understanding.

Table 6.4 contains examples of conceptual and pragmatic errors, which are
qualitatively childlike. It demonstrates that L's childlike causal reasoning
occurred in her explanations of her personal worldview. "What's interesting
about Laura's language is no longer the acquisition of syntax, but the way in
which she uses language as a social and intellectual tool. Her 'choice of words'
reflects an entire worldview. This worldview... is qualitatively different from an
adult's" (from the diary note for L at 3;3.29). In effect, L's causal questions and
explanations revealed the naivete of her theories about the physical and social
world in which she lived (Byrnes, 1991).

TABLE 6.3
Correct Procedural Knowledge of *Because* and *So*

Explanation of Internal State

   1. (L, 3.5.28. Part of a conversation about L sleeping through the night.)

      L: I did a good sleeping job, right?

      F: Right.

      L: But daddy, I was sad.

      F: Why?

      L: *Cause I wanted someone to sleep with me.*

Psychological Justification in Social Negotiation

   2. (L, 3;4.13, noticed her mother's stapler on the dinning room table.)

      L: Can I use your stapler *cause I don't have one.*

      M: Yes, you can borrow it if you put it back on my desk.

      L: I'll put it right in the zipper (pencil box with a zipper) *so nobody'll steal.*

   3. (L, 3.5.13, is trying to change a bandaid.)

      L: Someone would you take my other bandaid off *cause I wanna switch bandaids.*

Thoughts about Contingencies

   4. (L, 3;0.7, is no longer in the shopping cart.)

      L: I should go with you *because I might get lost.*

TABLE 6.4
Errors in the Relation Between Language and Thought

Childlike Causal Reasoning

1. (L, 2;7.7 has just opened a box of new clothes.)

    L: I won't bump my eye anymore *because* I got new clothes.

    M: You won't bump your eye anymore *because* you got new clothes? (M is perplexed by L's logic.)

    L: Yep.

2. (L, 2;8.25. M was leaving L alone in the playroom and had not closed the door. L is genuinely afraid of monsters.)

    L: A monster is coming. A purple monster will come in so you don't leave the door open.

3. (L, 3;4.29, is telling M all about a stuffed-toy that "really talks like people." [The toy is not present].)

    L: My rabbit will never grow up.

    M: I see.

    L: *Because* he's a toy rabbit. But he's not really a toy rabbit.

    M: He isn't. *How come?*

    L: *Because* he doesn't like anyone except me.

4. (L, 3.5.11, is squinting at the sun which is rising.)

    L: My colors make the sun.

    M: Your colors make the sun?

    L: Yeah, cause I go like that, see. (L demonstrates how she squints.)

Pragmatic Errors

5. (L, 3;4.6, is telling M about an incident with F. L fails to specify the referent of *it* for M.)

    L: Daddy made me upset.

    M: *Why* did he make you upset.

    L: *Because* he said I did *it* on purpose and I did *it* by accident.

6. (L, 3;5.1, screamed yesterday after she had been put to bed and kissed goodnight. L uses the "I screamed" redundantly.)

    L: You *know why* I screamed?

    M: No

    L: *Because* I was cranky when I went to bed *that why* I screamed. Daddy you *know why* I screamed? *Cause* I was cranky that why I screamed. (*Because* I was cranky when I went to bed, I screamed.)

L's pragmatic errors (Examples 5 and 6, Table 4) reflected her inaccurate assessment of her listener's perspective—that is to say, her failure to gauge appropriately how much her listener knew about the topic. In Example 5, L failed to specify a referent for the pronoun *it*. She used *it* to refer to a past event as if she and her listener shared some prior, common knowledge. However, her mother did not know what happened between L and her father. Despite L's clear contrast of *on purpose* and *by accident* in her explanation, her pragmatic error prevented her from establishing intersubjectivity with her mother ("I don't know what *it* refers to, but apparently L annoyed F," from diary context note).

In Example 6, L was redundant and repeated old or given information which her listener already knew from the prior discourse ("that why I screamed"). This pragmatic error may have occurred as an erroneous strategy to clarify her meaning in the clause order Because A, B. When L substituted *since* for *because* in the clause order Since A, B, she did not make this mistake (e.g. at 3;5.25, as L is turning to let F pat her sunburn "Since you're a doctor, put your cold hands on it").

During her third year, L gradually learned how to ask causal questions and to offer explanations. Her emergent interest in communicating about cause and effect was motivated by and contributed to her quest to understand aspects of human behavior that are experienced internally and personally. L began to use *because* and *so* to explain her own internal states and motivation and *how come* and *why* to request this same information from others.

By 3;6 there was an observable disparity between L's procedural competence with causal interclause relations and the childlike quality of the thoughts and feelings which she expressed. But the intricate organization among language, thought, and social understanding was clearly underway. The same two developmental principles, the need to maintain intersubjectivity and decontextualization, would continue to operate as a source of L's future progress.

FINAL THOUGHTS

Analyzing child language diary data is analogous to being an archeologist of the mind. Incremental changes and informative errors were pieced together to define a coherent developmental process based upon the changing pattern of L's interweaving of language, thought, and social understanding:

• **implicit causality**—the use of separate, sequential utterances to express a causal relation between the thoughts in two propositions

• < **form**—the discovery and practice of the form of causal words as a function of attention to input language

• < **meaning**—the association of a form with its causal meaning as a function of participation in discourse and practice in play

• < **function**—the intentional use of causal words in discourse to mark specific interclause relations

• < **procedure**—the correct use of causal connectives to create a linguistic framework for the conceptual expression of causality

- < complex content—the increased developmental complexity of the language and thought packaged into the procedural framework.

The data from L reveal the emergence of the requisite skills that provided a foundation for using *because* and *so* correctly in discourse and in complex sentences. Although a description from a case study is not generalizable, these data provide valuable insight into a complex developmental process. They explain the repeated finding that young children control the procedure for using *because* and *so* correctly in their language production even though their causal reasoning is childlike.

In adults, the ability to use causal connectives is a *fait accompli*. Thus, the data from L are a source of developmental insight that is not apparent from adults' competent language production. These data clarify <u>why</u>, <u>when</u>, and <u>how</u> causal connectives become necessary as explicit markers of the meaning of interclause relations. Adults' competence with causal interclause relations begins with 2 to 3–year–old children's intense interest in the cause and consequences of their own and other people's behavior and the reason why events in their environment occur.

REFERENCES

Blank, M. (1975). Mastering the intangible through language. In D. Aaronson & R. W. Rieber (Eds.), *Developmental psycholinguistics and communication disorders* (pp. 44–58). New York: The New York Academy of Science.

Bloom, L. (1993). *The transition from infancy to language: Acquiring the power of expression*. New York: Cambridge University Press.

Bloom, L., & Capatides, J. (1987). Sources of meaning in the acquisition of complex syntax: The sample case of causality. *Journal of Experimental Child Psychology, 43*, 112–128.

Bloom, L., Lahey, M., Hood, L., Lifter, K., & Fiess K. (1980). Complex sentences: Acquisition of syntactic connectives and the semantic relations they encode. *Journal of Child Language, 7*, 235–261.

Braunwald, S. R. (1985). The development of connectives. *Journal of Pragmatics, 9*, 513–525.

Braunwald, S. R. (1993, March). *Differences in two sisters' acquisition of first verbs*. Poster presented at the Biennial Meetings of the Society for Research in Child Development, New Orleans, LA.

Braunwald, S. R. (1995). Differences in the acquisition of early verbs: Evidence from diary data from sisters. In M. Tomasselo, & W. E. Merriman (Eds.), *Beyond names for things: Young children's acquisition of verbs* (pp. 81–111). Hillsdale, NJ: Lawrence Erlbaum Associates.

Braunwald, S. R., & Brislin, R. W. (1979). The Diary Method Updated. In E. Ochs & B. B. Schieffelin (Eds.), *Developmental pragmatics* (pp. 21–42). New York: Academic Press.

Byrnes, J. P. (1991). Acquisition and development of *if* and *because*: Conceptual and linguistic aspects. In S. A. Gelman & J. P. Byrnes (Eds.), *Perspectives on language and thought: Interrelations in development* (pp. 354–93). New York: Cambridge University Press.

Byrnes, J. P., & Gelman, S. A. (1991). Perspectives on thought and language: Traditional and contempory views. In S. A. Gelman & J. P. Byrnes (Eds.), *Perspectives on language and thought: Interrelations in development* (pp. 3–27). New York: Cambridge University Press.

Dunn, J. (1988). *The beginnings of social understanding*. Cambridge, MA: Harvard University Press.

Eisenberg, A. R. (1980). A syntactic, semantic and pragmatic analysis of conjunction. *Papers and Reports on Child Language Development, 19*, 70–78.

French, L. A. (1986). Acquiring and using words to express logical relations. In S. A. Kuczaj & M. D. Barrett (Eds.), *The development of word meaning: Progress in cognitive development* (pp. 303–338). New York: Springer-Verlag.

French, L. A. (1988). The development of children's understanding of "because" and "so." *Journal of Experimental Child Psychology, 45*, 262–279.

French, L. A., & Nelson, K. (1985). *Young children's knowledge of relational terms: Some ifs, ors, and buts.* New York: Springer- Verlag.

Hood, L., & Bloom, L. (1979). What, when, and how about why: A longitudinal study of early expressions of causality. *Monographs of the Society for Research in Child Development, 44* (6, Serial No. 181).

Levy, E., & Nelson, K. (1994). Words in discourse: A dialectical approach to the acquisition of meaning and use. *Journal of Child Language, 21*, 367–389.

McCabe, A., & Peterson, C. (1985). A naturalistic study of the production of causal connectives by children. *Journal of Child Language, 12*, 145–159.

Stern, D. N. (1985). *The interpersonal world of the infant: A view from psychoanalysis and developmental psychology.* New York: Basic Books.

Warner, R. G. (1985). *Discourse connectives in English.* New York: Garland Publishing.

Chapter 7

Meaningful "Mistakes": The Systematicity of Children's Connectives in Narrative Discourse and the Social Origins of this Usage About the Past

Allyssa McCabe
University of Massachusetts Lowell

Carole Peterson
Memorial University, St. John's, Newfoundland

Interviewer: Have you ever spilled anything?
Ben (9 years): That's what happened last year. I looked right at it *and* I got it.
Interviewer: Oh, really? Tell me about it.
Ben: See, I was painting *and* the glue wouldn't come off *so* I got mad at it *and* I threw the bottle *and* I went to pick it up *and* I looked into it *and* I tried to squirt it *and* I got it right in the face. My teacher asked me what happened *and* I told her that the glue had got me in the face *and* she laughed at me *and* I said "That ain't funny. What if you got it in your face?" *And* she said, "I'd cry." *But* I said, "I'm not a bawlbaby." I got mad too. (Example from corpus of Peterson & McCabe, 1983)

DEVELOPMENT OF SEMANTIC AND PRAGMATIC USAGE OF CONNECTIVES: AN OVERVIEW

In personal narratives of real past experiences, like Ben's narrative, as well as in many other kinds of discourse, children knit sentences together using various connectives such as *and*, *then*, *because*, *so*, and *but*. In a series of studies, Carole

Peterson and I have examined, in great detail, various aspects of the way in which children use these connectives to serve both semantic and pragmatic functions. We began by examining development descriptively, using cross-sectional data. Recently, we have begun to examine development longitudinally, which allows us to ask whether children or their parents initiate usage of particular connectives. In this chapter, descriptive work and some preliminary findings from more recent directions of research are presented.

In the relatively short narrative just presented, there are no fewer than eleven uses of *and*. One might expect that children would use *and* less as they grew older and more adept at understanding and expressing connections using more specific terms (e.g., *because* to express causal relationships). However, that is not the case (Peterson & McCabe, 1987). In fact, between the ages of 4 and 9 years, children actually increase the percentage of sentences they connect with *and*. While 16% of all narrative sentences produced by 4–year–olds are connected by *and*, a full 33% of those produced by 9–year–olds are so connected (Peterson & McCabe, 1987).

What is more, there is no change in the kinds of more specific relationships they denote using this all-purpose connective (Peterson & McCabe, 1987). Specifically, they connect two temporally sequenced events with *and* about a third of the time (e.g., "I threw the bottle *and* I went to pick it up"). Twenty percent of the time they use *and* to connect two causally related events (e.g., "Grandpa told me to put it someplace else *and* I did"), another 20% to connect events where one event enables another to happen (e.g., "Somebody went straight by them on the road *and* they crashed"), and a third 20% where there is no relationship more specific than that of simple coordination (e.g., "Pam and Barbara was fighting *and* Daddy was at work"). About 10% of the time, sentences were related by antithesis that would have been more aptly denoted by use of *but* (e.g., "He stole all my slips and gave it to Mom and my mom gave them back to me").

Puzzled by these counterintuitive findings, Carole Peterson and I compared all independent narrative clauses connected by *and* with those that were not connected in any way—simply juxtaposed. This was done for 1,081 sentences produced in personal narratives of 4-year-olds and 3,025 sentences produced by 9-year-olds. Using standardized scores, no main effect of age or meaning was found. Children aged 4–9 years either used *and* or no connective at all the same proportion of times. Sentences with and without *and* are equally likely to refer to clauses that are coordinate, temporally sequenced, causally related, antithetically related, related through enabling, or restatement. There was only one significant effect of any kind, a significant interaction between connective and meaning. A higher proportion of *and*-connected sentences involved some type of temporal succession whereas a higher proportion of juxtaposed sentences involved coordination relationships.

In that same study (Peterson & McCabe, 1988), sentences within narratives of past personal experiences were compared with those that fell outside of narrative in conversations about present or future (nonnarrative) matters. Sentences within narrative boundaries were far more likely to be connected by *and* than were sentences falling between narratives, in conversation largely about the here-and-now. This systematicity suggested that *and* served some kind of pragmatic narrative function.

Peterson and McCabe (1991b) pursued this line of research by focusing just on sentences within narratives. They broke down narrative clauses into those that encoded events (e.g., "My teacher asked me what happened *and* I told her that the glue had got me in the face") and those that encoded nonevent information, such as orientation ("It was 4 o'clock in the morning") or evaluation ("I got mad too"). Children were more likely to simply juxtapose sentences when they linked timeline events with off-the-line information or evaluation clauses. In contrast, when they returned to timeline events, children were likely to use the connective *and*. In fact, *and* prefaced a timeline event 87% of the time it was used; *and then* prefaced timeline events 88% of the time; and *and so* did so 95% of the time those connectives were used in narratives. *Then* always introduces timeline events. Less than 14% of the time did any of these four connectives introduce off-the-timeline clauses. There is, in other words, great systematicity in the way children use these seemingly ubiquitous connectives to signal an upcoming event.

To further complicate matters, although children increasingly use *and* when, they should more appropriately use *but* (Peterson & McCabe, 1987); as we have said, when children do use *but*, it is often semantically inappropriate (Peterson, 1986; Peterson & McCabe, 1991a). For example (Peterson, & McCabe, 1991, p. 452):

Interviewer: I bet you see the sun come in the morning from your room.
   Child: But I saw the zoo. . . (A narrative about a zoo followed)

What this child was doing was using the connective *but* for the pragmatic purpose of opening a new narrative about a topic other than the one proposed by the interviewer. There are other pragmatic uses to which children put connectives:

Change of focus functions to move away from a chronological recapitulation of events (e.g., "And then I fell down *but* you know what?").

Chronology violation (e.g., We went to Florida *but* first we went to Texas").
Endings signal a termination of narration (e.g., after a narrative about a car accident and how many people died, "So they dead right now too.").

To complete the description of the ways in which children use connectives in personal narratives, the extent to which children employed connectives for semantic versus pragmatic functions was assessed. Peterson and McCabe (1991a) found that children aged 4 to 9 years match connective form to meaning in a general way. There are virtually no significant age effects in usage. Over 90% of the time children use *because, then,* and *and then* for some kind of semantic purpose. Of these semantic uses, *because* is employed over 70% of the time to denote causal relationship between two clauses. The rest of the time it denotes enabling, coordinate, or antithetical relationships. *Then* and *and then* are used about half of the time to express temporal relationship between two clauses, half the time to refer to the other kinds of relationships. Seventy-three percent of the time it is used, *but* denotes some kind of semantic relationship, usually antithesis (71%). *So* is used 67% of the time semantically, usually to refer to causal relationship (61%).

Much of the remaining use of connectives is for one of the aforementioned pragmatic reasons. Specifically, we found extensive pragmatic usage of *so* (31%), *but* (22%), because (9%), *and then* (5%), and *then* (3%). The most common pragmatic usage is of *but* and *so* to begin a new narrative topic.

Once one separates systematic pragmatic usage of connectives from true mistakes, one finds that children make very few real mistakes in this way. Only 5% or less of all connective usage that we have examined falls into the category of genuine mistakes serving neither semantic nor pragmatic function (e.g., "And all of the people comed to the party and so Barbara didn't come to the party.").

Because age changes are minimal between 4 and 9 years, children must develop connectives prior to that time, as in fact they have been observed to do (Bloom, Lahey, Hood, Lifter, & Fiess, 1980). Thus we have now turned our attention to providing an account of how children develop the ability to use connectives in the context of conversing with their parents. Our first step in this direction is an account of the development of causal connective usage, a matter of considerable cognitive, as well as linguistic, interest.

PARENTAL SCAFFOLDING EFFECTS:
THE CASE OF *BECAUSE* AND *SO*

Semantic Function of Causal Connectives

Piaget (1930/1972) emphasized the many kinds of mistakes children make in understanding all kinds of causal thinking, especially in sentence completion tasks (Piaget, 1928/1972). This confusion of children younger than 7 or 8 years about how to use *because* correctly received much support (Bebout, Segalowitz, & White, 1980; Corrigan, 1975; Emerson, 1978; Homzie & Gravitt, 1976; Johnson & Chapman, 1980; Katz & Brent, 1968; Kuhn & Phelps, 1976), although some investigators found almost errorless comprehension by first graders (Scholnick & Wing, 1982; Wing & Scholnick, 1981). There is some evidence that even preschoolers' performance on such tasks can be improved by using detailed and explicit task instructions and modelling procedures (Peterson & McCabe, 1985).

To a degree, children's ability to use causal language correctly depends on the kind of causal relations encoded. Many researchers have noted children's ability to express and understand psychological before physical causality (Corrigan, 1975; Donaldson, 1986; Fein, 1973; Hood & Bloom, 1979; Johnson & Chapman, 1980; McCabe & Peterson, 1985; Piaget, 1928/1972) and physical before logical causality (Corrigan, 1975; Piaget, 1928/1972).

Shifting from assessment of comprehension to analysis of spontaneous production of causal connectives presents an even more optimistic picture of young children's causal expertise. Few errors have been found in the spontaneous productions of *because* and *so* by children aged 2;6 to 3;6 (Hood & Bloom, 1979) or 3;6 to 9;6 years (McCabe & Peterson, 1985). Regardless of Piaget's (1928/1972) claims to the contrary, preschool children are no more apt to spontaneously produce reversals of cause and effect or otherwise err when they use *because* or *so* than are adults (McCabe & Peterson, 1988). Even on elicited production tasks, preschool children have been found to produce very few inversions of cause and effect (Donaldson, 1986). Moreover, many children's errors using causal language are in fact better understood as servicing the kind of pragmatic, discourse-level functions such as marking the beginning or ending of a narrative or departures from, returns to, or violations of a chronological sequence of events that we discussed above (Peterson & McCabe, 1991a, 1991b).

In producing causal language about past personal experiences, children encode a number of semantic relationships. Almost 75% of correct semantic use of *because* and over 90% of correct semantic use of *so* encodes some sort of *psychological causality*, meaning the relation of motive for an action with a consequence (McCabe & Peterson, 1985). Sometimes this consisted of reference to explicit intentions (e.g., "She wanted to hurt him *so* she hit him."). Even more often, children implicitly referred to intentions (e.g., "I scratched her *so* she scratched me."). Children also referenced the relation of an emotional state to some outcome (e.g., "She was mad *so* she hit him."). They encoded directives (e.g., "Daddy said, 'Get that girl out of here and get her to the hospital!' *So* we went to the hospital.") and also reasoning (e.g., "She adopted us and everything *so* she was really our real mother.").

Despite the fact that in talking about real past experiences, there was ample opportunity to encode physical causality involved in car wrecks and injuries, children aged 4–9 years seldom did so (McCabe & Peterson, 1985). Of 454 semantically correct uses of *because* and *so*, children only encoded physical causality (e.g., "The cut was all dirty because there was pencil lead down there.") 24 times, or just about 5% of the time. Other, less frequently discussed kinds of causality were almost as frequent as this kind. Children gave explanations (e.g., "My dad didn't get to go because he had to work."), made logical connections (e.g., "Tame rabbits don't run away. This rabbit doesn't run away, so it must be tame."), connected abilities to actions (e.g., "I couldn't swim, so I just walked in the water."), and drew moral conclusions (e.g., "You shouldn't throw rocks because that will break windows."). About half of the time, children encoded highly predictable causal relationships in their talk about the past—the kind of causality parents are always announcing to their children—but almost as frequently, children denoted uncommon relationships.

In short, competence in producing spontaneous causal language seems to develop as early as 2;6, although errors persist in laboratory tasks assessing decontextualized comprehension throughout early elementary school years. The question remains: How do children come to acquire an understanding of causal language at such a young age? One possibility is that parental conversation with children is a source of development of their so-called spontaneous concepts of causality. This question is investigated by considering parent–child conversations about causality that occurred in the past. This approach obviates nonverbal demonstration of causal relationships that might accompany talk about present causality and that could assist children's understanding. We focus here exclusively on parental talk as a source for child competence.

General Parental Scaffolding Effects in Past Research

Because of considerable evidence that parents scaffold many aspects of narrative performance in young children (Eisenberg, 1985; Sachs, 1982; Snow & Goldfield, 1982), it was hypothesized that parents would precede their children's spontaneous causal usage with causal conversation about past events. Parents differ in the manner in which they discuss past events with their children (Engel, 1986; Fivush & Fromhoff, 1988; McCabe & Peterson, 1991, Peterson & McCabe, 1992, 1994; Reese & Fivush, 1996). In general, the extent to which parents talk extensively with 2;3–2;7-year-old children about past experiences predicts the ability of those children to talk extensively and coherently about past experiences themselves later on at 3;6 (McCabe & Peterson, 1991) and 6;0 years of age (McCabe & Peterson, 1990). More specifically, the extent to which parents question children regarding *where* and *when* predicts children's subsequent skill in providing such information "spontaneously" to adults who are interested in their stories but who do not actively scaffold these stories (Peterson & McCabe, 1994). The number of causal/conditional terms (*because, so, when, if, while, until*) used by mothers when children are 30–35 months old tends to be related to the number of such terms used by the children themselves at 41–46 months. There are similar relationships for maternal and child usage of orienting terms and evaluative intensifiers (Fivush, 1991). Scaffolding effects are quite specific to the type of information stressed by individual parents. If parents habitually question their children about contextual more than action information, children later on disproportionately "spontaneously" produce such information to nondirective adults. If parents stress action sequences, children later on "spontaneously" produce more advanced plots in their narratives compared to the aforementioned children of parents who emphasize context (Peterson & McCabe, 1992, 1994).

The central question of this chapter is whether parents discuss causality with their 2-year old children, and, if so, whether they discuss causality with their children *before* those children produce it, or *afterward*, in response to an understanding that must have developed in a purely cognitive manner (e.g., through perception and manipulation of objects).

Ten Caucasian, middle-class children and their parents served as subjects originally. The children were recruited close to their second birthday (i.e., between the ages of 25 and 27 months). All were from 2-parent families. Three children had to be dropped from this original sample because in two cases the children produced causal usage from their earliest transcripts and in one case the mother never prompted her child for causal language during the duration of the study. In those three cases, the scaffolding hypothesis could not be tested. This left 7 parent–child pairs.

Parents were given a tape recorder approximately every other month beginning when their children were 27 months old, on average. Parents were all asked to elicit narratives about real past personal experiences from their children but differed in the extent to which they complied with such requests. Bimonthly recording ended when children were 3;6 years old. After that time, parents were asked to record their conversations about past events with their children every 6 months. Instances of causal language in the parent–child conversation were identified and scored reliably. One person scored all parent–child conversations, and a second person also scored 15% of those conversations inde-pendently. Estimation of reliability for scoring categories of parent–child inter-action was based on 18 agreements among 21 decisions (85.6%).

All parent tapes were scored for form of causal language (statement, *yes/no* question, or *why* question) and content, or type of causality discussed (motive of other people, child's motive, emotions, pragmatic explanation, physiological causality, physical causality, reasoning, logical causality, ability, evidential cau-sality). Children's causal exchanges were also scored (i.e., no response, inap-propriate response, appropriate immediate or eventual response, appropriate statement of causality without parental prompting). Coders noted the age of the child at the time of parent's first production of, as well as the child's first appropriate response to, a *yes/no* question ("Is that why you wouldn't talk to me—because you were tired?") or *why* question ("Why did you grab Amy's overalls?"). Coders also noted the age at which parents first made causal statements to children, as well as the age at which children first produced a causal statement to their parents without having been prompted.[1]

Parental Scaffolding of Causal Talk

As is shown in Table 7.1, there is a wide range of ages for children's first spontaneous expression of causality to their parents: from 30 to 66 months. As is also shown in Table 7.1, in all seven cases, children responded to parental prompting questions about causality at least 1 month prior to spontaneous causal statements, with the mean delay between prompted and unprompted causal expression equaling 10 months. This variable was considerably skewed, however, and the median delay was 5 months. There seemed to be no consistent pattern for parents to produce *yes/no* questions before *why* questions, nor for children to respond appropriately to one form before the other. Maternal statements of causality generally appeared at about the same time as did other forms of causal talk.

But while there was remarkable inconsistency in the age at which children first "spontaneously" talked about causal links with their parents, there was equally remarkable consistency in the fact that parents increased their discus-sion of past causality with their child 5 or 6 months before their children's spontaneous production of causal language. As is shown in Table 7.2, parents made remarkably infrequent mention of causal connections 7 to 12 months before their children would produce causal language on their own. Such causal

---

[1]Children in our sample almost never asked *why* questions themselves. This rarity, coupled with focus of the chapter on parental question, led us to exclude the few examples we found from further analysis.

TABLE 7.1
Ages at Which Causal Language is Produced

Child	Range of Months Scored	First Mom Statement	First y/m?	First why?	Child First Responds to: y/n	Child First Responds to: why	First Statement to Mom
Ned	26–38	26	27	26	27	33	38
Cara	28–31	29	29	28	29	29	30
Terry	27–66	30	–	48	–	48	66
Kelly	28–34	–	28	28	28	28	34
Harriet	27–33	28	27	27	27	31	32
Leah	26–48	26	26	27	26	31	48
Carl	26–34	29	–	27	–	27	34

language was even more infrequent before this time frame. For example, there were only .08 parental mentions of causality 7 months before each child began to talk about it independently. Six months prior to independent production, parents mentioned causality .21 times per narrative (i.e., in one out of five narratives). But 5 months prior to independent production (regardless of age), parents mentioned causality .52 times per narrative, a level that was maintained thereafter (.56, .64, .52, .44 at 4, 3, 2, and 1 month prior to independent production, respectively). Thus, 5 months prior to children's spontaneous production, parents began to question or inform their children about causal links in at least half of their narrative conversations. As is also shown in Table 7.2, often such questions had to be repeated, recast in simpler forms, answered by the parents themselves, or even abandoned, but some were, in fact, successfully answered by children. The most frequent exchange was for parents to ask *why* something happened, to get no appropriate response, and to abandon the issue (33 instances). The second most frequent exchange was for parents to ask *why* something happened and for children to respond appropriately (28 instances). The third common phenomenon was for parents to simply make some causal statement themselves (22 instances). Ten instances of parents asking a *why* question and successfully rephrasing it as a yes/no question and 4 instances of *why* rephrased as a *what* question were also noted. Despite their frequent frustrations, however, parents persisted in asking such questions.

To account for individual variation, children were ranked in terms of the age at which they first spontaneously produced a causal statement to their mother (i.e., "x" in Table 7.2). Parents were then ranked for their relative stress on causal connections. First, the frequency with which they produced causal questions or statements prior to this age was determined. Then, because parents differed considerably in terms of the number of tapes they contributed to the

Table 7.2
Parents' Causal Language to Children

Age	No. of kids	No. of narr.	Why statement	y/n question	Why → resp.	Eventual resp.	What & resp.	y/n & resp.	Self answer	abandon	Why → trans.
x	7	51	5	2	9	1	0	1	2	3	2
x-1	4	27	2	0	5	0	1	1	0	2	1
x-2	5	27	1	1	3	0	0	1	2	6	0
x-3	2	14	3	0	0	0	1	0	1	4	0
x-4	4	25	1	1	2	0	0	3	0	6	0
x-5	4	25	1	0	2	0	0	2	0	6	2
x-6	4	19	0	0	2	0	0	1	0	1	0
x-7	2	13	0	0	1	0	0	0	0	0	0
x-8	2	6	0	0	0	0	0	0	0	0	0
x-9	1	5	0	0	0	0	1	0	0	0	0
x-10	1	6	1	0	0	0	0	0	0	0	0
x-11	1	6	0	0	0	0	0	1	0	0	0
x-12	2	19	4	0	3	0	0	0	0	3	0
x-13 through 39	1[a]	100	4	1	1	2	0	0	2	2	1

[a] in each age, except for x-18, where $n = 2$

Note. x = age at which child spontaneously produces causal connectives to parents
Y/N Question: The parent asks a yes/no question.
why → resp: Parent asks a why (or "how come") question and child gives an appropriate causal answer.
why → eventual resp: Parent asks why question, child doesn't respond at first but does eventually.
why → what & resp: Parent asks why, child doesn't respond appropriately, parent at some point converts to a what question, asking for the same information, and child does respond to this what question.
why → y/n/ resp: Parent asks why question, child doesn't respond appropriately, parent at some point converts to a y/n question and child responds.
why → self answer: Parent asks why question, child doesn't respond, parent ends up answering the question herself.
why → abandon: Parent asks why question, gets no appropriate response, and whatever happens next (she may throw in y/n questions, what questions, or reformulations of why), the child doesn't give her an appropriate answer and she gives up, i.e., abandons.
why → trans: Parent asks why question and it is impossible to assess the appropriateness of the child's response since we can't understand the transcript.

study, we divided this frequency of parental causal connections by the total number of tapes used to assess parental causal talk (specifically, all tapes that parents contributed with some causal language included). It was this relative production of causal links per conversation that was ranked for parents. We converted to ranks in each case because of the fact that one child was quite delayed in the production of causal talk, which created a pronounced skew in our data, and so interval measures were counterindicated. The age of first spontaneous causal connection was positively correlated with the relative number of causal connections parents made per conversation in months prior to that spontaneous production (Spearman's rho [5 = .85, p < .01]).

Psychological causality has been defined as the relation of motive for action with a consequence (McCabe & Peterson, 1985; Piaget, 1928/1972, p. 7) and includes references to the motives of others, or of the children themselves, to the relation of an emotional state to some outcome or vice versa, or to reasoning (drawing a conclusion from some piece of information). *Physical causality* is defined as the relation of cause and effect where the cause is rooted in the objective physical world and people are involved only to the extent that they are considered physical or physiological objects. *Logical causality* connects a result clause derived from a definitional prior clause. Some kinds of causality fall into none of these major types (i.e., pragmatic explanations, evidential uses of causal language to explain the speaker's motive for making some comment, and references to physical ability as the cause of some kind of outcome event). The following types of causality were found to be (the examples are real ones) discussed in the parent–child conversations about past events:

(a) *Motives of Others*
    M: Why did he push you?
    C: 'cause he hit me.
    M: Why did he hit you? Why?
(b) *Motives of Child*
    C: I didn't want to go to the fire engine.
    M: Why not?
    C: Because the clowns were scary.
(c) *Emotional*
    C: He was crying next day.
    M: Crying?
    C: Yeah
    M: Why was he crying?
    C: He wanted his mother.

(d) *Pragmatic Explanation*
   M: Were you at the library?
   C: Yeah
   M: Yeah. Outside of the library?
   C: No.
   M: Why not?
   C: Because (garbled)
   M: Yes, that was outside the library when he climbed on the motorcycle.

(e) *Physiological*
   M: You have a cold because you got wet.

   M: Why were you eating a popsicle yesterday?
   D: Because my tummy was getting a little bit upset.

(f) *Physical*
   M: We had a failure didn't we? We were whipping some?
   C: Cream.
   M: And it didn't?
   C: Work
   M: Why? Do you remember why?
   C: Because the machine was broken.

(g) *Reasoning*
   M: What do you play with at Grandma's house? Do you remember?
   C: I don't know.
   M: Because you were doing really well considering you haven't been
       to grandma's house since last August.

(h) *Evidential*
   M: How do you know it wasn't dead?
   C: 'Cause it was flying.

(i) *Logical*
   M: You can look at the movie but you can't touch it. If you stand up
       and touch it the other children won't be able to see it, will they?
       Because you'll be in their way, right?

A total of 118 instances of causal language from parents were coded. Parents stressed an understanding of others' motives most of all, followed by discussion of children's own motives for various actions. Specifically, parents discussed various types of causality in the following descending order of frequency: Motives of others (42 instances), motives of child (22), emotional consequences (22), pragmatic explanations (12), physiological (9), physical consequences (6), reasoning (3), evidential (1), logical (1). Thus, 72.8% of the instances of parent causal language concerned psychological causality (motives of child or others or emotional consequences), whereas only 12.7% concerned physical or physiological causality. The remaining 14.5% concerned logical or other causality that fell into neither physical nor psychological categories.

Parents predate their children's so-called spontaneous expression of causal links by approximately 5 months. While this effect falls under the category of scaffolding effects generally associated with Vygotskian theorizing, it necessitates a revision of what Vygotsky (1962) himself argued concerning the specific issue of causal language. He contrasted what he called spontaneous causal expressions with ones in which elementary school-aged children were instructed by teachers. Parents scaffold their children's emergent causal language by asking questions, repeating or revising such questions, occasionally answering those questions themselves, or abandoning them. Children respond to parental causal questions before they make statements of causal connection without such prompts, Vygotsky's so-called spontaneous causal expressions.

While there was consistency in the fact that parents preceded children's productions by 5 or 6 months with talk that invited causal thinking and talking, there was remarkable variation in the age at which children spontaneously produced causal language. This, in itself, supports the notion that parental scaffolding enables causal connection. However, there is further evidence to support this conclusion in that the more parents stressed causal links in their conversations with their children, the younger the age at which children produced causal links without prompting.

Regardless of the degree to which causality was emphasized in conversations about the past, the type of causality stressed by all parents was psychological causality in various forms. Discussion of the motives of other people in past events dominated such conversations, followed closely by discussion of children's own motives for past behavior and emotions and their antecedents or consequences. Such a focus accords well with the subsequent emphasis of older children (in different samples), for whom psychological causality dominates in narratives of past personal experiences (McCabe & Peterson, 1985).

There are important theoretical and practical consequences of these findings. To begin with, the origin of children's causal expressions seems at least, in part, to be parental discussion of causal links, which begins some time during the pre-school years. That there is such wide variation in when parents begin to focus on causal links with their children means that some children will produce causal links at 2.5 years and that other children will not do so until 3 years later. This kind of individual variation means that children exposed to early and frequent parental conversation about past causality are likely to have an advantage in answering the kinds of inferential questions about the motivation of storybook characters often tested for in schools (Barr, Kamil, Mosenthal,

& Pearson, 1991). Even more importantly, children whose parents emphasize past psychological causality are not likely to suffer the kinds of deficits in social cognition that have been implicated in such disorders as conduct disorder with aggression (Spivack, Platt, & Shure, 1976).

CONCLUSION

Far from emerging "without apparent external cause; self-generated," which is the American Heritage Dictionary's (1969, p. 1248) definition of "spontaneous," children's so-called spontaneous causal talk about past motivations, emotions, and physiological antecedents and consequences appears after considerable parental discussion and prodding for such connections. This first step in accounting for the origins of children's connective usage has been fruitful. It remains to be seen, however, how very young children develop the ability to use causal connectives pragmatically in the context of conversing with their parents. For example, researchers have begun to examine the extent to which parents use connectives pragmatically in conversation with their children. For example, one mother began a conversation with her child by asking, "So, tell Mommy did you go to the doctor this morning?" This use of *so* as a conversation opener takes the work full circle from the extensive examination of pragmatic usage within children's own conversational turns to the interpersonal pragmatic usage of connectives noted long ago by other researchers (Eisenberg, 1980; van Dijk, 1979).

In sum, by the tender age of 4 years, children are extraordinarily systematic in their use of connectives in their own monologic narratives, despite the fact that extensive pragmatic usage has given rise to the impression that their connective usage is error-ridden. As demonstrated, most of their so-called "errors" are very meaningful "mistakes."

REFERENCES

American Heritage Dictionary of the English Language. (1969). Boston: Houghton Mifflin.

Barr, R., Kamil, M. L., Mosenthal, P.B., & Pearson, P.D. (1991). *Handbook of Reading Research, Vol. II*. Whiteplains, NY: Longman.

Bebout, L. J., Segalowitz, S. J., & White, G. J. (1980). Children's comprehension of causal constructions with 'because' and 'so'. *Child Development, 51*, 565–568.

Bloom, L., Lahey, M., Hood, L., Lifter, K., & Fiess, K. (1980). Complex sentences: acquisition of syntactic connectives and the semantic relations they encode. *Journal of Child Language, 7*, 235–261.

Corrigan, R. (1975). A scalogram analysis of the development of the use and comprehension of "because" in children. *Child Development, 46*, 195–201.

Donaldson, M. L. (1986). *Children's explanations, A psycholinguistic study*. Cambridge, UK: Cambridge University Press.

Eisenberg, A. R. (1980). A syntactic, semantic, and pragmatic analysis of conjunction. *Papers and Research in Child Language Development, 19,* 70–78.

Eisenberg, A. R. (1985). Learning to describe past experiences in conversation. *Discourse Processes, 8,* 177–204.

Emerson, H. (1978). Children's comprehension of "because" in reversible and non-reversible sentences. *Journal of Child Language, 6,* 279–300.

Engel, S. (1986, March). The role of mother-child interaction in autobiographical recall. In J.A. Hudson (Chair), *Learning to talk about the past.* Symposium conducted at the Southeastern Conference on Human Development, Nashville.

Fein, D. A. (1973). Judgments of causality to physical and social picture sequences. *Developmental Psychology, 8,* 147.

Fivush, R. (1991). The social construction of personal narratives. *Merrill-Palmer Quarterly, 37* (1), 59–81.

Fivush, R., & Fromhoff, F. A. (1988). Style and structure in mother-child conversations about the past. *Discourse Processes, 11,* 337–355.

Homzie, M., & Gravitt, C. (1976). Children's reproductions: Effects of event order and implied vs. directly stated causation. *Journal of Child Language, 4,* 237–46.

Hood, L., & Bloom, L. (1979). What, when, and how about why: A longitudinal study of early expressions of causality. *Monographs of the Society of Research on Child Development, 44,* No. 6.

Johnson, H., & Chapman, R. (1980). Children's judgment and recall of causal connectives: A developmental study of "because", "so", and "and". *Journal Psycholinguistic Research, 9,* 243–60.

Katz, E. W., & Brent, S. B. (1968). Understanding connectives. *Journal of Verbal Learning and Verbal Behavior, 7,* 501–509.

Kuhn, D., & Phelps, H. (1976). The development of children's comprehension of causal direction. *Child Development, 47,* 248–251.

McCabe, A., & Peterson, C. (1985). A naturalistic study of the production of causal connectives by children. *Journal of Child Language, 12,* 145–159.

McCabe, A,. & Peterson, C. (1988). A comparison of adults' versus children's spontaneous use of because and so. *Journal of Genetic Psychology, 149,* (2), 257–268.

McCabe, A., & Peterson, C. (1990). *Keep them talking: Parental styles of interviewing and subsequent child narrative skill.* Paper presented at the Fifth International Congress for the Study of Child Language, Budapest, Hungary.

McCabe, A., & Peterson, C. (1991). Getting the story: A longitudinal study of parental styles in eliciting oral personal narratives and developing narrative skill. In A. McCabe & C. Peterson (Eds.), *Developing narrative structure* (pp. 217–253). Hillsdale, NJ: Lawrence Erlbaum Associates.

Peterson, C. (1986). Semantic and pragmatic uses of 'but'. Journal of Child Language, 13, 583–590.

Peterson, C., & McCabe, A. (1985). Understanding "because": How important is the task? *Journal of Psycholinguistic Research, 14,* 199–218.

Peterson, C., & McCabe, A. (1987). The connective 'and': do older children use it less as they learn other connectives? *Journal of Child Language, 14,* 375–381.

Peterson, C., & McCabe, A. (1988). The connective and as discourse glue. *First Language, 8,* 19–28.

Peterson, C., & McCabe, A. (1991a). On the threshold of the storyrealm: Semantic versus pragmatic use of connectives in narratives. *Merrill-Palmer Quarterly, 37* (3), 445–464.

Peterson, C., & McCabe, A. (1991b). Linking children's connectives use and narrative macrostructure. In A. McCabe & C. Peterson (Eds.), *Developing narrative structure,* (pp.29–54). Hillsdale, NJ: Lawrence Erlbaum Associates.

Peterson, C., & McCabe, A. (1992). Parental styles of narrative elicitation: Effects on children's narrative structure and content. *First Language, 12,* 299–321.

Peterson, C., & McCabe, A. (1994). A social interactionist account of developing decontextualized narrative skill. *Developmental Psychology, 30* (6), 937–948.

Piaget, J. (1928/1972). *Judgment and reasoning in the child*. New Jersey: Littlefield, Adams.

Piaget, J. (1930/1972). *The child's conception of physical causality*. New Jersey: Littlefield, Adams.

Reese, E., & Fivush, R. (1996). Parental styles of talking about the past. Manuscript submitted for publication.

Sachs, J. (1982). Talking about the there and then: The emergence of displaced reference in parent-child discourse. In K. E. Nelson (Ed.), *Children's language* (pp. 1–28). Hillsdale, NJ: Lawrence Erlbaum Associates.

Scholnick, E. K., & Wing, C. S. (1982). The pragmatics of subordinating conjunctions: A second look. *Journal of Child Language*, 9, 461–79.

Snow, C. E., & Goldfield, B. A. (1981). Building stories: The emergence of information structures from conversation. In D. Tannen (Ed.), *Analyzing discourse: Text and talk* (pp. 127–141). Washington, DC: Georgetown University Press.

Spivack, G., Platt, J. J., & Shure, M. B. (1976). *The problem-solving approach to adjustment*. San Francisco: Jossey-Bass.

van Dijk, T. (1979). Pragmatic connectives. *Journal of Pragmatics*, 3, 447–456.

Vygotsky, L. (1962). *Thought and language*. Cambridge, MA: M. I. T. Press.

Wing, C. S., & Scholnick, E. K. (1981). Children's comprehension of pragmatic concepts expressed in *because, although, if,* and *unless*. *Journal of Child Language*, 8, 347–65.

Part III

FROM SEGMENTING TO RELATING

The three contributions in this part deal mainly with written production and stress the segmentation problems, even thought the study of segmentation has to be conducted simultaneously with the study of integration. It is interesting to note that centering on the written production allows the authors to analyze the use of punctuation marks, a set of linguistic devices whose impact on the comprehension processes only gave rise to a limited number of studies.

In chapter 8, Fayol defends the idea that, in written production, punctuation marks and connectives belong to the same functional paradigm. Both are used, first of all, to indicate the level of the link between the states or events expressed by two adjacent clauses and also, possibly, to indicate the nature of this link. To support this view, Fayol uses data issued from research both with children and with adults. A corpus analysis and the experiments carried out on children's productions clearly show that they use punctuation marks and connectives in a systematic way. The experiments confirmed that the frequency of punctuation markers used is inversely proportional to the degree of continuity between the events referred to. Similar relationships have also been brought forward as to the use of connectives. The experiments conducted with adults confirmed that, even with the increasing number of markers (punctuation or connectives), the frequency and the nature of markers strongly remained determined by the strength of the links between states and/or events evoked by adjacent clauses. In conclusion, Fayol proposes a model of the use of punctuation marks that accounts for both the observation about their acquisition and their diversity in adult language.

In chapter 9, Heurley discusses the division of a text into paragraphs and questions the problem of the relationship between the paragraphs in a text and the blocks or chunks in the mental representation. He reports a series of data showing that the effect of paragraphing on the readers' processing does not systematically confirm that paragraphs are signaled to help the reader in building a mental model of the described situation. In fact, the occurrence of

155

paragraphing also depends on factors concerned with the composition process. Heurley proposes an integrated approach, taking into account both the writer's and reader's capacities and demands. To support this viewpoint, he reports on four experiments based on production and comprehension of procedural texts. These experiments show that suprasentential textual organization depends on the referent's structure, the author's familiarity with the field, and the production strategies. The resulting blocks of information are units of the planification process. Their adjustment to the reader's needs appears occasional rather than systematic. Consequently, Heurley proposes to consider the information block as an encoding unit of the structural/semantic organization, different from the paragraph marking in the surface structure.

The viewpoint developed by Bestgen and Costermans in chapter 10 is very close to Fayol's, but it concerns the temporal markers in narratives. Indeed, instead of considering these markers exclusively in a semantic/conceptual perspective, they first treat them as cues for discourse segmentation. Temporal markers would signal discourse structure, like punctuation markers, by introducing degrees of continuity–discontinuity. Moreover, speakers/writers would use the various temporal expressions to mark the discourse structure in narratives in the same way they use spatial expressions in descriptions. To test these predictions, Bestgen and Costermans carried out a corpus analysis and experimental research with adults and children. Results show that, from the age of 8 , people use temporal expressions in correlation with the hierarchical structure of the narratives and, in particular, according to the discontinuity strength between the linked elements. They conclude by proposing, within the frame of Gernsbacher's model, some ideas concerning the impact that different temporal expressions should have on the online processing during text comprehension.

❀ Chapter 8

On Acquiring and Using Punctuation: A Study of Written French

Michel Fayol
Université de Bourgogne

All discourse refers to an underlying referent (that which is described, related, or argued about) that is represented mentally in a coherent fashion by the individual producing the message. This mental representation (mental model, according to Johnson-Laird, 1983; model of situation, according to Van Dijk & Kintsch, 1983) is always multidimensional, i.e., has many relationships linking its elements. However, language production, whether oral or written, is strictly linear and time-dependent. This means that, at a given time, only one piece of information can be related (Grimes, 1975; Levelt, 1981, 1982, 1989). It follows that one of the main problems confronting a speaker or writer is how to present information in a linear format (i.e., to linearize information) when such information is rarely stored in a linear structure in the mental model (except for simple narratives, whose linearization is more or less determined by the chronological order of events; even then, there are episodes that group related elements together; Fayol, 1985).

PUNCTUATION MARKS AND CONNECTIVES: A SINGLE PARADIGM

The linearization process involves at least three different kinds of operations: defining a starting point, selecting a path, and marking the surface structure. First, the speaker/writer must select a starting point or origin that corresponds to a particular point of view (i.e., the beginning of a narrative or the starting point of a description; Bronckart, 1985); the rest of the information in the text

157

must be situated with respect to that origin (Costermans & Bestgen, 1991). Second, he or she has to determine a path that can be retained in working memory with the least amount of effort (Levelt, 1982; Linde & Labov, 1975). This path may or may not be easy to determine; although it is easy to define in simple narratives, it is much more difficult to elaborate in argumentative discourse or text. Third, he or she must establish and mark the relationships between the statements in the text. Indeed, according to the "nextness" principle (Ochs, 1979; Segal, Duchan, & Scott, 1991), unless otherwise indicated, two linguistic items that are close "on the text/discourse surface," go together (i.e., are strongly related to each other). However, two consecutive statements in an oral or written discourse may (a) pertain to successive states or events that are strongly related to each other in the mental model of the situation being described or (b) pertain to states or events that are weakly related to each other in that mental model. Hence the need for a system of marks to indicate the strength and/or nature of the link between adjacent statements. Only a set of very specific marks is capable of governing (or controlling) the application of the nextness principle. This set of marks is the punctuation/connectives paradigm.

A Functional Model of Inter-Propositional Marks

An elementary correspondence between a system of marks and a conceptual opposition regarding the relatedness of facts is assumed to be the initial framework upon which the development and use of punctuation and connectives is based. In this framework, a mapping is assumed to exist between a related/unrelated opposition between events and/or states in the mental model and an opposition between two signifiers (e.g., either mark 1 vs. mark 2 or simply no mark vs. mark 1, whatever it is). These cohesion–segmentation marks are held to be the traces of the coherence relations in the underlying mental model. This framework is a working hypothesis that constitutes a plausible model to account for young children's behavior, its developmental patterns, and even the diversity of the punctuation/connective marks and their usage by adults.

This basic framework can be extended and modified in several ways:

1. by making it more complex through the gradual appearance of different degrees of relatedness between events — the simple "related–unrelated" opposition is extended across a coarsely or finely graduated scale (e.g. highly related, moderately related, weakly related, or unrelated) that depends on the subject's cognitive discrimination capabilities for the topic at hand;

2. by gradual differentiation of the various concepts expressed by the para-digm of connectives: causality, succession, simultaneity, and so on;
3. by extension of the paradigms of punctuation marks and connective marks; and
4. by a consistent and conventional mapping between different degrees and kinds of relatedness on the one hand, and different punctuation and connective marks on the other.

In the functional perspective presented in this chapter, a punctuation mark can be defined as any mark that provides indications about the structural links between adjacent elements of a text (Nunberg, 1990). Punctuation is a linguistic micro-system composed of a limited number of marks forming a partial hierarchy, which for "pausal marks" is very clear-cut. Indeed, the precedence order "*indentation* (beginning of a new paragraph) > *period + capital letter > semi-colon > comma > space* (between words)" is easy to define for these marks (Catach, 1994; Damourette, 1939; Drillon, 1991), but is more complicated for other marks such as a dash or suspension points.

The situation is not so clear-cut for connectives. The term connectives refers to a variety of linguistic forms (Corblin, 1987; Schneuwly, 1988), including adverbial phrases, coordinating and subordinating conjunctions, and relative pronouns, whose function is to indicate, with a varying degree of precision, the existence of a relationship between two discursive segments, whose span is also variable.

The Function(s) of Punctuation Marks and Connectives

Understanding the function of connectives in discourse production is not a straightforward matter. First, many inter-propositional links are not marked explicitly. Second, the fact that a connective is used does not mean that the semantic information that is actually being conveyed corresponds to what is generally considered as its assumed meaning. For example, in *Paul sortit de la maison de son ami. Après il regagna son domicile* ('Paul left his friend's house. Afterwards, he went home'), the connective *après* ['afterwards'] is not essential to marking the sequence of events. We can legitimately wonder what is (are) its function(s) (Costermans & Bestgen, 1991; Fayol, 1986). Third, there are problematic cases of connectives in both written and spoken French. For example, it is possible to find *puis après* [literally 'then afterwards'], in which case we can wonder what the individual roles of the two connectives are. Determining the meaning of connectives is even more difficult knowing that *puis ensuite* ['then then'] and even *puis avant* ['then before'] are currently observed, but not *après ensuite* ['afterwards then'], which casts doubts about the possible role(s) of *puis* ['then'].

Considering the above observations, the first and foremost function of punctuation marks appears to be to indicate the strength of the link between two adjacent statements or utterances. The same appears to be true for connectives. However, in addition to this primary function of marking inter-statement and inter-utterance links, connectives appear to play another role: within certain limits, they may also mark the nature of the link (e.g. *if* may mark a logical link; *then*, a chronological one). Investigators often focus solely on this second function.

Therefore, punctuation will be considered here as merely one particular way of marking inter-statement and inter-utterance links, with connectives being another, complementary way. Punctuation marks and connectives are segmentation and cohesion markers, both being surface representations of the underlying coherency relations between adjacent states and/or events. Since there are some important differences between the two, both as to the elements belonging to the paradigm and the functions they fulfill, this chapter mainly deals with punctuation, even though connectives are included in most studies, with focus, in particular, on the acquisition of punctuation in children and its usage in adults.

ACQUISITION AND USAGE OF PUNCTUATION MARKS

Very little information is available on the use of punctuation by adults who are not professional writers. Most of the data concerns authors of novels or different types of texts, or the history of the punctuation mark paradigm (Catach, 1994; Bruthiaux, 1993). On the other hand, there are some published studies dealing with the acquisition of punctuation by children (Fayol, 1981; Kress, 1982; Lurçat, 1972; Schneuwly, 1988; Shaughnessy, 1977; Simon, 1973). The majority of these studies concern the period between the second and the fifth years of elementary school and are either corpus analyses or experimental studies (see, however, Schneuwly, 1988).

Corpus Studies

Corpus analyses have provided coherent results regarding both the frequency and the form of punctuation marks. The consensus is not as clear, however, in regard to their functions.

Punctuation marks are rarely observed in the first year of elementary school (Fayol, 1981; Lurçat, 1972; Simon, 1973). From the second year on, their frequency and diversity begin to increase rapidly: The period appears in second grade, whereas the comma emerges in fourth grade. Children also use many nonconventional marks, including the period alone (without capital letters), capitalization alone (without periods), and indentation alone. Fayol (1981) analyzed 205 texts written by children in the second through fifth grades and noted the proportion of each type of mark. The results (Table 8.1) showed that a decrease in the use of a period alone, capitalization alone, and indentation was accompanied by an increase in the number of periods with capitalization and a greater number of commas. Even though nearly all punctuation marks were found very early, most of the 7- or 8-year-olds used only one mark. The older children commonly used two or even three different marks. Thus, the developmental pattern seems to be standardization and diversification.

The study of the functions of punctuation marks is a more difficult one. Indeed, a given mark can only be defined with respect to the other marks in the paradigm. The value of the period or the connective *and*, for instance, changes with the degree of complexity of the set to which it belongs. This principle, based on De Saussure's (1916) work, can account for certain observations concerning children's written productions.. Second graders, for example, have been found to use different marks to express the same opposition between conceptually linked or unlinked states or events.

The writing samples of the second and third graders presented in Table 8.2 show that different marks perform the same function for young children. At the location where the author of sample 2 used a period and capitalization, the authors of samples 3 and 4 started a new paragraph. In all cases, a punctuation mark was used to mark the boundary between two new, unrelated announcements (Fayol, 1987, 1991). Writing samples 1 and 2 provide another example of how inter-propositional marks are employed by young children. Both

Table 8.1
Percentages of Different Punctuation Marks as a function of Grade in School

Punctuation Marks	School Grades			
	2nd	3rd	4th	5th
Indentation (new paragraph)	24	8	5	7
Period or capital letter	35	28	5	1
Period and capital letter	30	50	61	69
Comma	11	14	29	22

Note. From Fayol (1981). Reprinted with permission.

Table 8.2
Examples of Personal Experience Narratives Written by 6- to 10-year-old children

---

1. *Je suis allé chez ma mémé/mon cousin et moi on a joué au château/et on la fait tombé/le soir on a mangé la soupe/* (6 y-0);
   'I went to my grandma's/my cousin and I played castle/and we knocked it down/in the evening we had supper/'

2. *Je suis allé à la piscine./Dimanche je suis allé au rugby./Samedi je suis (allé?) chez ma maman./Le mercredi j'ai été au cathéchisme./ Dimanche à huit heures je suis parti en colonie/et j'ai été faire du ski* (7 y-0);
   'I went to the pool./Sunday I went to rugby./Saturday I (went?) to my Mom's./Wednesday I went to church./Sunday at eight o'clock I left for camp/and I went skiing'

3. *Un dimanche j'ai été chez ma tata manger./Un jour ma mémé est venue repasser chez moi./*

   Je joue tout le temps au ballon./

   Un jour j'ai joué à la corde./

   Un jour j'ai été au zoo/ (7 y-0);

   'One Sunday I went to eat at my aunt's./ One day my grandma came to iron at my house./

   I always play ball./

   One day I played jump rope./

   One day I went to the zoo/'

4. *J'étais dans ma baignoire/j'ai fait tomber la chopine (= petite bouteille)/elle est un peu cassée./*

   J'étais dans mes escaliers/et j'ai tombé sur le nez/et j'ai comme un bouton/ (8 y-0);

   'I was in my bathtub/I dropped the bottle/it's a little broken./

   I was on my stairs/and I falled on my nose/and I have like a bump/'

5. *Mon papa et moi nous sommes allés à la pêche./Nous sommes arrivés à la rivière./Nous avons monté les gaules./Nous avons lancé les gaules dans l'eau./Tout-à-coup le bouchon s'enfonce/mon papa tire/le poisson s'en va/* (8 y-0);
   'My dad and I went fishing./We arrived at the river./We set up the fishing rods./We threw the fishing rods in the water./All of a sudden the float sinks/ my dad pulls/ the fish gets away/'

6. *Un jour chez ma mémé j'allai(s) en vacances chez elle./Le soir je suis allé me coucher/j'ai rèvé./Le lendemain matin je me suis levé tôt./J'ai pris mon vélo/et j'ai été en faire du vélo/C'était dans une descente/j'avais pas vu/qu'il y avait un hérisson/j'ai marché sur ses piquants/alors une roue de mon vélo a été crevée./* (8 y-0);
   'One day at my grandma's I was on vacation at her house./At night I went to bed/I had a dream./The following morning I got up early./I took my bike/and I went for a ride/It was downhill/I didn't see/that there was a hedgehog/I rode over his spines/so I got a flat tire.'

Note. "/" indicates clause boundaries. From M. Fayol (1981). Reprinted with permission.

of these authors used the opposition between *et* ['and'] and another mark (in Sample 1, a space between propositions, and in Sample 2, a period and capitalization). In both cases, *et* expresses the existence of a link between events (Bloom, 1970; Bloom, Lahey, Lifter & Fiess, 1980; Braunwald, 1985; Jeruchimovicz, 1978; Peterson & McCabe, 1987), while the absence (or the weakness) of a link is marked either by an inter-propositional space or by a period and capitalization. These data show that, even in young children, we are able to find examples of connectives and punctuation performing complementary functions.

Writing Samples 5 and 6 show that coexisting in the same production, one can find some portions of text that are systematically punctuated with periods and capitalization and others that are under-punctuated. The former seem to correspond to scripts (Fayol & Monteil, 1988; Schank & Abelson, 1977) or highly conventional and predictable sequences of states or events, essentially linked by juxtapositions of chronologically consecutive relationships. In contrast, the latter describe sequences of facts linked by causal or means-end relationships. Native French-speaking adults would probably have used commas to separate the events in these causal sequences. Because the correct use of the comma has not been acquired by children at this age, they rely on the inter-propositional space. However, in all cases, punctuation becomes sparser or weaker (e.g., the comma marks an interevent break that is not as strong as the period) when the adjacent propositions relate events or states that are more closely linked.

Analysis of the co-occurrences of punctuation marks and connectives has shown that certain connectives (e.g. *et* ('and') appear more often without punctuation, while others (e.g., *après* ('afterwards') and *enfin* ('finally') are usually used along with strong punctuation marks (indentation for *enfin*; period and capitalization for *après*), while the use of punctuation is more variable with others (i.e., *alors* ('so'); Fayol, 1981, 1986).

The results of these corpus analyses confirm that, even in the writing of younger children, punctuation marks, whether conventional or not, are employed to indicate the strength of the link between the states or events described in adjacent propositions. They play a complementary role, with connectives, in performing this function. The developmental pattern can be characterized by standardization and diversification in the form of punctuation marks, although the functions of the punctuation remain unchanged. However, corpus studies provide incomplete, and thus controversial data that can only be viewed as hypotheses. To gain a more complete understanding of this issue, several experimental studies were conducted.

Experimental Studies

Two series of experiments were conducted to test the hypothesis that the frequency and strength of punctuation marks decrease as the strength of the link increases between the states or events described in two consecutive propositions.

In Experiment 1, Fayol and Lété (1987) asked subjects aged 7, 9, 11 and 13 years (second, fourth, sixth, and eighth graders, respectively) to copy over and correctly punctuate short, unpunctuated written narratives. Each narrative related a single episode with seven constituents derived from the Mandler and Johnson (1977) schema: Setting, Initial Event, Reaction, Goal, Attempt, Result, and Ending (Table 8.3).

The hypothesis was that, because the events form a causal chain (a goal induces an attempt that leads to a result), punctuation would be less common and weaker in the middle than at the beginning or end of an episode. The results were consistent with this prediction: for children at the ages of 9, 11, and 13, but not 7, punctuation marks were significantly more frequent and stronger between the Setting and the Initial Event, between the Initial Event and the Reaction, and between the Result and the Ending, than between any of the other propositions.

In Phase 2 of this study (Fayol & Lété, 1987), the same narratives were presented with either the same connective *et* ('and') inserted at different interpropositional locations, or with different connectives *et* ('and'), *alors* ('so'), *après* ('afterwards') inserted at the same interpropositional location (Table 8.3). The hypothesis was that the presence of certain connectives (namely, *et* and *alors*) would lead to the use of fewer and weaker punctuation marks. The results were consistent with this prediction: *et* nearly systematically triggered the disappearance of all punctuation marks; *alors* led to the more frequent use of a comma at the expense of a period and capitalization, especially in the older subjects; and *après* did not significantly modify the distribution of punctuation marks.

Table 8.3

Narrative Writing Samples Used to Study the Distribution of Punctuation Marks as a Function of the Presence or Absence of Connecties

Annie. (1) *Annie ne savait pas quoi faire ce jour là* (2) *un joli petit chat entra dans sa chambre* (3) *Annie était surprise et très contente* (4) *elle voulut s'amuser avec le chaton* (5) *elle lui mit la tunique de sa poupée (elle reçut un coup de griffe sur la main* (7) *elle bouda jusqu'à la tombée de la nuit.*

(1) 'Annie did not know what to do that day' (2) 'a pretty little cat came into her room' (3) 'Annie was surprised and very happy' (4) 'she wanted to play with the cat' (5) 'she put her doll's dress on it' (6) 'she got scratched on her hand' (7) 'she sulked until nighttime'

(a) Type 1 versions have no punctuation or connectives.

(b) Type 2 versions have the connective *et* between propostions (3) and (4).

(c) Type 3 versions have either *et, alors,* or *après* between constituents (5) and (6).

Note. From M. Fayol and Lété (1987). Reprinted with permission.

This first series of experiments thus confirmed that (a) the frequency of punctuation marks is inversely proportional to the strength of the link between states or events (the data were not as consistent concerning the strength associated with each of the marks used, due to the rare and late use of the comma and other marks such as the semi-colon and the dash) and (b) very early in the development, connectives and punctuation fulfill complementary functions that vary from one connective to the next. However, contrary to the results of corpus analyses, no significant modification was observed before the fourth grade in the relative proportion of each punctuation mark, either as a function of where it was located in the narrative or what connective was used. This absence of the hypothesized variations is probably due to the fact that the task proposed (copy and punctuate a text, and, thus, understand it) was not suited to second graders.

Chanquoy (1989) used another method with second graders. She gave them a chart showing their school schedule for a week and then asked them to write a composed version of it to send to some pupils in another school. The chart separated the days (Monday through Tuesday and Thursday through Saturday), the half days (mornings and afternoons),[1] and the disciplines within the same half day (for example, math and French). The only punctuation mark analyzed in the compositions was the period (which was or was not followed by capitalization) because it was the only one that was both frequent and used by all children. As predicted, periods situated at high–order boundaries significantly outnumbered all others (by frequency of occurrence: periods separating days > periods separating half-day > periods separating disciplines).

Thus, both corpus analyses and experimentation have shown that, right from the onset of written composition (second grade), children use punctuation and certain connectives in accordance with our hypotheses. Punctuation marks increase in frequency as the strength of the link between consecutive states and/or events decreases in the mental model of the referent. As far as the connectives studied are concerned (*et, alors, après*), some (*et*) are very rarely associated with punctuation marks, while others (*après*) are very frequently so. The developmental pattern is an increasing standardization of punctuation marks reaching an advanced level as early as the third grade and the appearance of new marks for expressing finer degrees of linkage.

ADULT USAGE OF PUNCTUATION

Through the acquisition and use of new punctuation marks and new connectives, adults have at their disposal a much broader paradigm of marks than do

---

[1] French children have a full school day on Monday, Tuesday, Thursday, and Friday and a half day on Saturday morning.

young children. One question that might be raised concerning this broader paradigm is whether adults accord approximately the same values to punctuation marks as do children and whether the hierarchy of marks they employ corresponds to the one linguists propose. An initial series of experiments was devoted to answering this question by first considering punctuation marks alone and then examining punctuation marks in conjunction with a limited number of connectives.

Another question raised concerns the use of punctuation marks during written composition. Once again, the hypothesis tested was that the frequency and strength of punctuation is inversely proportional to the strength of the link between the states and/or events described in adjacent propositions. To verify this hypothesis, adults were given scripts with a predefined hierarchical organization and asked to compose the corresponding texts. To analyze these texts, an index of the punctuation strength at each inter-propositional location was computed by multiplying the frequency of each mark at that location by the strength of that mark (as defined in a preceding experiment).

Value and Hierarchy of Punctuation Marks

The first two experiments verified that punctuation marks (and, to a lesser extent, connectives) are organized along a continuum representing the strength of the link (or break) between the pairs of events and/or states to which they apply. To test this hypothesis, two studies were conducted using a metalinguistic evaluation method.

In the first study (Fayol & Abdi, 1988), a list of twelve punctuation marks written on a sheet of paper were given to 36 students. They were asked to use a subjective scale (ranging from 0 for a "very strong link" to 7 for a "very weak link") to evaluate the strength of the link or separation associated with each mark. The results are shown in Figure 8.1 along with the data reported by Van De Water and O'Connel (1986), who studied the duration of pauses associated with the punctuation marks used by English and German authors of sermons that were broadcast on the radio.

They found a clear hierarchy in the pause and punctuation mark association. Certain marks were systematically associated with long pauses; others were associated with short pauses. The results of these studies suggest that punctuation marks are organized along a continuum representing inter-event and/or inter-state relatedness and that they are associated with pause durations, which also vary along the relatedness, dimension (see also Foulin, Chanquoy, & Fayol, 1989 for similar findings regarding the relationship between punctuation marks and pause duration in writing).

In another study designed to examine the relationship between punctuation marks and connectives (Fayol & Abdi, 1990), pairs of propositions such as *La nuit tombait/l'enfant courait* ('Night was falling/the child was running') were presented with verbs in the imperfect tense (the French *imparfait*). The two propositions were connected with one of the following marks: space (no mark at all), comma, period and capital letter, *et, alors, après*. Students were asked to evaluate the strength of the link between the two propositions in each pair, using a 6-point scale. As expected, the connectives and punctuation marks formed a continuum of inter-event link strength, something like: *et* > comma > *alors* > period > *après* (that is, *et* marks a stronger link than comma, and so on). *Après* appears to mark a very weak, purely chronological link.

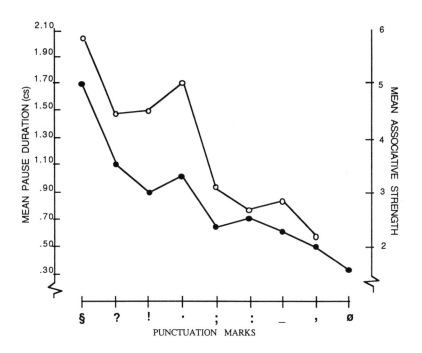

FIG. 8.1. Mean pause duration (•—) and mean associative strength (▭—) as a function of punctuation marks.

In summary, these two empirical studies showed that punctuation marks and, at least, certain connectives are organized along a continuum representing the strength of the link between the states and/or events described in adjacent propositions. The next study was designed to investigate how punctuation marks were used by adults composing script-based texts.

Use of Punctuation Marks in Texts

The general hypothesis here was that the frequency and types of punctuation marks used in compositions would be highly correlated with the strength of the link between the events and/or states related in two successive propositions. From this hypothesis, it was predicted that (a) the more semantically or discursively related the two states and/or events, the sparser and weaker the punctuation marks and (b) inversely, the less related the two states and/or events, the more frequent and the stronger the punctuation marks.

Two studies were conducted, dealing with "script-based" texts (Fayol & Abdi, 1988). A script is a representation in long-term memory of familiar events that take place in a conventional, highly regular order. The advantage of scripts is that the individuals in a given culture know them well enough to agree on their constituents and on the order in which they occur.

The first experiment took place in two stages, both of which used script frames as the material. In the first stage, students received two lists of scripted events (Going to the restaurant; Going to the dentist) in a counterbalanced order and presented as shown in Table 8.4. Subjects were asked to classify the states or events in a frame by "putting together the ones that go together." The following groupings were used to establish a hierarchical structure containing clusters of propositions at different levels (for similar approaches, see Mandler, 1987; Pollart-Gott, McCloskey, & Todres, 1979; Rotondo, 1984). This hierarchical structure is shown in Figure 8.2 as an inverted tree with propositions 1, 2, 3, ..., 27 as its leaves. The branches join together at various heights in the tree in such a way that the higher they meet the weaker the link, and the lower they meet, the stronger the link. The theory predicts that this hierarchical structure will be the main determinant of the frequency and types of punctuation used.

In the second stage, a different group of university students was given the same lists of events, presented as lists of propositions (as in Table 8.4), and then asked to compose a text in "proper French" by using punctuation marks and connectives and changing verb tenses, but without modifying the order of the reported events. The types of marks occurring at each inter-propositional location in the written productions were analyzed. Connectives were disregarded due to difficulties in statistical processing.

Table 8.4
List of the propositions Given for the Sorting Task and for the Text Production Task

Annie Visits the Dentist
1. Annie has a toothache.
2. Annie thinks about it.
3. Annie calls the dentist.
4. Annie is happy.
5. Annie can go to the dentist now.
6. Annie arrives at the dentist's.
7. Annie goes into the waiting room.
8. Annie sits down.
9. Annie takes a magazine.
10. Annie tries to read.
11. Annie is in too much pain to read.
12. Annie looks at the other patients.
13. Annie goes into the dentist's room.
14. Annie sits on the dentist's chair.
15. Annie closes her eyes.
16. Annie opens her mouth.
17. Annie feels the vibrations.
18. Annie hears the noise of the instruments.
19. Annie is not in pain anymore.
20. Annie gets up.
21. Annie listens to the advice of the dentist.
22. Annie pays.
23. Annie goes out relieved.
24. Annie goes back home.
25. Annie feels better.
26. Annie will be able to go to work.

Note. From M. Fayol and H. Abdi (1988). Reprinted with permission.

The analysis dealt with both the frequency of the punctuation marks and the weighted value of each one. This value was computed from the data collected in the previous experiment (Figure 8.2) by applying a correspondence analysis to transform the ordinal scale of subjects' evaluations into the interval scale required for statistical analysis (for a detailed explanation, see Bestgen, 1992; Bestgen & Costermans, 1994; Fayol & Abdi, 1988). For each interpropositional location, a total punctuation weight was computed by multiplying

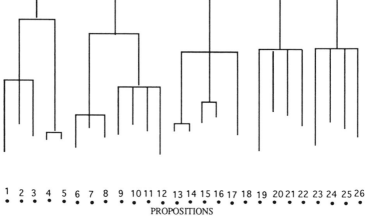

PROPOSITIONS

FIG. 8.2. Annie script: Inverted tree showing the degrees of relatedness between adjacent propositions.

the frequency of each occurring mark by the weighted value for that mark and then summing all the products for that location. The corresponding data for the "Annie" script (i.e., Going to the dentist; Table 8.4) are shown as dark broken lines with dark filled dots (●) in Figure 8.3. The numbers on the right are the total punctuation weights.

As can be seen in Figure 8.3, the changes in the direction of the dark line (representing the changes in punctuation weight as a function of inter-propositional locations) were strongly correlated with the variations in height of the inverted tree branches (which correspond to variations in the degree of relatedness of adjacent propositional contents). These trends are consistent with the predictions. They suggest that the strength of the inter-propositional link is an essential determinant of the frequency and strength of punctuation. The weighted punctuation pattern was very close to the proposition classification pattern, i.e., the more two propositions were related, the rarer and weaker were the punctuation marks between them.

In the second experiment, 20 sixth graders were asked to write texts from the same two script-like lists. The data were analyzed using the same method as that employed with the adults' texts, i.e., for each inter-propositional location, a weighted value was computed by combining the types of marks, their number, and their values (using the adult standards). The results are shown in Figure 8.3 as a gray line with empty dots (○). Here again, as expected, the grey line follows the variations in the height of the tree branches. A series of regression analyses confirmed that the strength of the interpropositional link was the most powerful determining factor of the frequency and type of punctuation. For both of these script-like texts, the r value varied between .80 and .90 for sixth graders as well as for adults.

A MODEL OF PUNCTUATION USAGE

One of the consequences of the linearization process required for oral or written language production is the disappearance of the multiple relationships among the elements in the mental model of the information to be related. Several devices are available in a language for indicating such relationships and helping the addressee re-construct a mental representation that is as close as possible to the speaker's or writer's. Among these devices are anaphoric marks, verb forms, and, above all, connectives and punctuation marks. Punctuation marks segment texts by linking pieces of information that go together and separating ones that do not. They also serve to indicate varying degrees of linkage between information. Connectives, at least those considered so far, fulfill a discourse segmentation–cohesion function comparable to that ensured by punctuation. They also indicate the nature of the links between propositional contents.

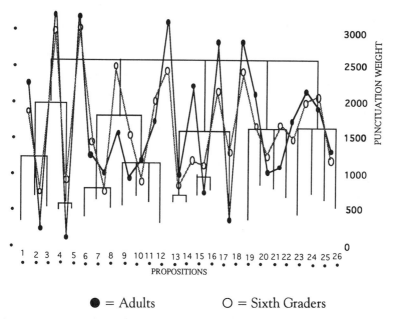

● = Adults   O = Sixth Graders

FIG. 8.3. Annie script: Degree of separation of the punctuation given for each interproposition. Results are plotted on the tree describing the script. (Adapted from Fayol & Abdi, 1988).

Clear evidence of children's use of punctuation marks and connectives in their productions has been found as early as second grade. Indeed, even when only a few marks are available, some forms of punctuation marks are used to separate blocks of unrelated information (Heurley, 1994). Such blocks sometimes contain a single sentence, in which case, the texts are juxtaposed announcements of news (Table 8.2), while at other times they group together several propositions to form one or more episodes. Propositions included in the same episode are rarely delimited by punctuation marks, but are sometimes linked by connectives, usually *et*. Simulated production experiments have confirmed the hypotheses suggested by corpus analysis.

Thus, for second graders, punctuation marks and connectives are employed to delimit blocks of related information, even if the marks do not appear in their conventional form and/or are not used in the conventional way. In the course of development, these marks become increasingly standardized and diversified. This diversification opens up new possibilities at the same time as it creates new problems. The appearance of new marks allows for the expression of finer shades of meaning in the links between adjacent propositions, but requires subjects to come to some degree of agreement on the respective values of the marks. Experiments with adults have shown that the same hierarchy is established among the various marks. However, the rare studies on how these marks are actually used by adults have revealed substantial variations. Some adults only employ a limited number of marks (Racine, for example, appears to have relied solely on the period and capitalization, and the comma; Ménétra, 1982, uses only the period and capitalization). Others, particularly authors of scientific articles, use a much larger set of marks. Any model of punctuation usage should be capable of accounting for the regularities as well as the exceptions in the use of punctuation, in both children and adults.

Table 8.5 presents a series of (numbered) propositions that correspond to the beginning of a short story involving several characters. Each proposition can be represented as a node in a semantic network (Figure 8.4, top). The network illustrates the strength of the links between the propositions, such that the strength of the link between two propositions increases as the length of the line connecting them decreases (e.g., there is a strong link between P2 and P3 and between P4 and P5, whereas the link between P3 and P4 and, even more so, between P5 and P6, is weak). A linear organization containing embedded parentheses can be used to represent these same hierarchical relationships in the form of a sequence of propositions (Figure 8.4, middle: Linearization). This format may correspond to the output of the linearization process.

The next step after the linearization process is the insertion of punctuation. This step depends, first of all, on the set of marks available to the individual.

Table 8.5
Series of Propositions Used to Begin a Story, for the
Semantic Network Displayed in Figure 8.4

1. Paul was coming to get Mary.

2. Mary was sleeping.

3. She got ready quickly.

4. Alan was waiting with Paul in the car.

5. He was reading the newspaper.

6. Ann and John were preparing dinner.

7. They had set the table.

8. In the next room their baby was sleeping.

9. The two groups of friends were going to have dinner together.

Several examples are considered in Figure 8.4. The simplest is characteristic of children aged 6 to 7 years, who only use one mark (noted X due to the diversity of forms). Two cases are presented: (a) the child employs one mark at one location only to separate the main episodes in the story (see Table 8.2, Samples 2 and 4) the same mark is used to separate a series of brief announcements of news (Table 8.2, Samples 2 and 3).

Figure 8.4 presents various patterns for cases where the subject disposes of at least two ranked marks (denoted A and B, where the two letters might represent the period, capitalization, and comma pattern of adults or the indentation and period or capitalization pattern of 8- and 9-year-olds). These patterns all follow the same rule: Whenever two ranked marks exist (e.g., period, capitalization, and comma) and both linkage strengths must be indicated, the higher mark in the hierarchy expresses the weaker link, and so on. All of the adult patterns illustrated in Figure 8.4 follow this rule, as do all of the characteristic fourth-grade patterns. These patterns account for all possible forms that can be derived from one simple rule and a variable size paradigm. Other patterns are possible and equally acceptable, depending on whether the number of marks is increased or decreased and whether or not each interpropositional location is instantiated. The last pattern is the only invalid one, because it violates the rule of correspondence between mark hierarchies and linkage strengths. Thus far, no other patterns have been reported in the corpus studies.

The patterns in Figure 8.4 illustrate the potential creativity of a procedure that assigns punctuation marks to interpropositional locations by simultaneously taking into account the strength of the perceived link between the contents of two adjacent propositions and the set of marks available to a given subject. This procedure works for children using a single punctuation mark, as

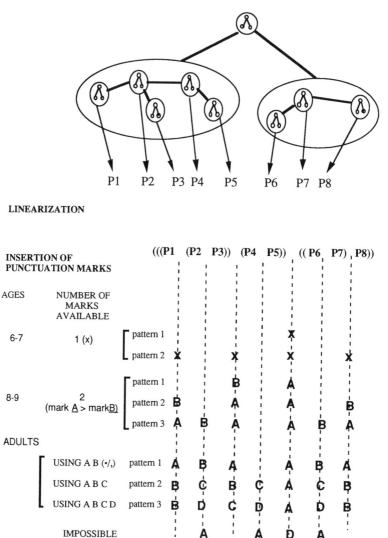

FIG. 8.4. From a semantic network to the insertion of punctuation marks: some hypothetical patterns as a function of available marks.

well as for adults using a set of several marks for which the only constraint is their hierarchical organization. Indeed, the production system needs only be capable of determining, for each interpropositional location, which mark is the most appropriate for indicating the strength of the link between the two successive states and/or events.

This hypothetical procedure for assigning a mark to an interpropositional location as a function of the available paradigm and the strength of the link to express, can account for two paradoxical phenomena. The first is that while punctuation rules seem to be used, they are applied in very diverse fashions. Between one writer and the next, or between one task and the next, the differences are so great that some investigators have given up studying punctuation usage. However, in spite of these variations, the distribution of punctuation marks generally follows the organization principles stated above. The reasons for this paradox lie not only in the differences between the paradigms elicited by each individual subject, but also in their decision-making criteria, that vary across individuals and across tasks in the same individual. Indeed, while in oral production, a speaker continuously changes inter-propositional pause duration (Foulin, Chanquoy, & Fayol, 1989), a writer has to make a choice as to where to place a period, capitalization, a comma, and an indentation.

The criteria on which decisions to use such and such a mark are based probably vary from one writer to the next (due to paradigm differences) and from one theme to the next (due to the fact that the estimated strength of the link between states and/or events is highly dependent upon previously acquired knowledge in the domain; Gobbo & Chi, 1986). It is not surprising that researchers have not been able to propose a clear account of punctuation usage, even for marks like indentation. Indeed, many subjects do not rely on this mark (see Heurley's (1994) observations concerning procedural text writing), and, when they do, they must feel that the information items being announced in succession are highly unrelated. The only texts in which individual punctuation mark oppositions can effectively be studied and the hypothesized usage regularities observed, are script-based texts, which everyone understands (all adults in any case), because the range of interpretations is limited.

The second paradox pertains to how punctuation marks and connectives are understood in text comprehension tasks. Many studies have found that modifications in marking by means of punctuation marks does not affect comprehension. Here again, the fact that no effects have been observed may be due both to an excessively simple conception of the role played by punctuation marks (in some studies, the punctuation marks are either left completely intact or are removed entirely, as if all punctuation marks were equivalent!) and to the unrefined methodologies used (for example, reading time is measured for the text as a whole). Recently, several more precise studies have shown that connectives (Mouchon, 1992; Mouchon, Fayol, & Gaonac'h, 1995), like punctuation marks (Bestgen & Vonk, 1993), do in fact modify information intake time during reading. The data can be easily interpreted in regards to Gernsbacher's (1990) structure building framework.

An additional problem is how the choice of punctuation marks and connectives is influenced by the writer's consideration of the addressee. Authors, who study the potential impact of punctuation marks and connectives on variables assumed to measure comprehension, have often found no impact of changes in the distribution of marks (Segal, Duchan, & Scott, 1991; Stark, 1988; for a review, see Fayol, 1989). This lack of an effect might be accounted for by the methods used and the fact that the marks are taken as a whole. Later studies that have considered specific marks (such as the comma/indentation opposition and the *et/soudain/mais/après* ('and/suddenly/but/afterwards') opposition in Mouchon, Fayol, & Gaonac'h, 1995) and/or used more refined methods (such as, reading time measures and probe recognition tasks in Bestgen & Vonk, 1993; Millis & Just, 1994) have shown that the presence and modification of punctuation marks and/or connectives do induce changes in both the online processing of texts and the organization of subjects' mental representations (Gernsbacher, 1990).

The question of whether, and to what extent, the use of punctuation marks (and connectives) is affected by message comprehension, and, in particular, the writer's assessment of how well the potential addressee might understand the information being conveyed remains unanswered. At the present time, it appears likely that initial punctuation usage depends essentially on the organization of knowledge in memory; punctuation marks delimit blocks of related information (Heurley, 1994; Heurley & Bestgen, 1993), but does not reflect consideration of the addressee. It is also likely that professional writers have a strategic way of using punctuation marks to achieve certain effects in readers, although no empirical evidence is available to support this hypothesis. Apparently, no one has studied the potential changes in usage resulting from the observation of the addressee's reactions and their integration into the production process. Once the roles of punctuation in production and in comprehension have been established, the study of the interactions between these two activities will be an essential step in gaining insight into how linguistic paradigms are acquired and enhanced to meet the demands of effective communication.

ACKNOWLEDGMENT

The author thanks L. Heurley for his helpful comments and L. Siegel for her help in revising the first draft of the English version of this paper.

REFERENCES

Bestgen, Y. (1992). *Deux approches du discours narratif : Marqueurs de la segmentation et profil émotionnel*. Unpublished doctoral disertation, Université de Louvain-la-Neuve, Louvain, Belgium.

Bestgen, Y., & Costermans, J. (1994). Time, space, and action: Exploring the narrative structure and its linguistic marking. *Discourse Processes, 17*, 421–446.

Bestgen, Y., & Vonk, W. (1993, May). *The role of segmentation marks in discourse processing*. Paper presented at the Journées d'étude of the Société Belge de Psychologie, Gent, Belgium.

Bloom, L. (1970). *Language Development*. Cambridge: MIT Press.

Bloom, L., Lahey, M., Hood, L. , Lifter, K., & Fiess, K. (1980). Complex sentences : Acquisition of syntactic connectives and the semantic relations they encode. *Journal of Child Language, 7*, 235–261.

Braunwald, S. R. (1985). The development of connectives. *Journal of Pragmatics, 9*, 513–525.

Bronckart, J. P. (1985). *Le fonctionnement des discours*. Neuchâtel, Paris: Delachaux & Niestlé.

Bruthiaux, P. (1993). Knowing when to stop: Investigating the nature of punctuation. *Language & Communication, 13*, 27–43.

Catach, N. (1994) *Le ponctuation*. Presses Universitaires de France.

Chanquoy, L. (1989). La description de l'emploi du temps d'une semaine par des enfants de CE1. *Etudes de Linguistique Appliquée, 73*, 47–56.

Corblin, F. (1987). Sur la notion de connexion. *Le Français Moderne, 55*, 147–157.

Costermans, J., & Bestgen, Y. (1991). The role of temporal markers in the segmentation of narrative discourse. *C.P.C./European Bulletin of Cognitive Psychology, 11*, 349–370.

Damourette, J. (1939). *Traité moderne de ponctuation*. Paris: Larousse.

De Saussure, F. (1916). *Cours de linguistique générale*. Paris: Payot.

Drillon, G. (1991). *Traité de la ponctuation française*. Paris: Gallimard.

Fayol, M. (1981).*L'acquisition du récit écrit chez l'enfant. Son évolution de 6 à 10 ans*. Unpublished doctoral dissertation, Université de Bordeaux 2, France.

Fayol, M. (1985). *Le récit et sa construction*. Neuchâtel, Paris: Delachaux & Niestlé.

Fayol, M. (1986). Les connecteurs dans les récits écrits. *Pratiques, 49*, 101–114.

Fayol, M. (1987). Vers une psycholinguistique textuelle génétique. L'acquisition du récit. In G. Pieraut-le-Bonniec & M. Dolitsky (Eds.), *Connaître et le dire* . Bruxelles: Mardaga.

Fayol, M. (1989). Une approche psycholinguistique de la ponctuation. Etudes en production et compréhension. *Langue Française, 81*, 21–39.

Fayol, M. (1991). Stories. A psycholinguistic and ontogenetic approach to the acquisition of narrative abilities. In G. Pieraut-le-Bonniec & M. Dolitsky (Eds.), *Language bases ... discourse bases* (pp. 229–263). Amsterdam: John Benjamins.

Fayol, M., & Abdi, H. (1988). Influence of script structure on punctuation. *C.P.C./European Bulletin of Cognitive Psychology, 8*, 265–279.

Fayol, M., & Abdi, H. (1990). Ponctuation et connecteurs. In M. Charolles, S. Fisher, & J. Jayez (Eds.), *Le discours* (pp. 167–180). Nancy: Presses Universitaires de Nancy.

Fayol, M., & Lété, B. (1987). Ponctuation et connecteurs. Une approche textuelle et génétique. *European Journal of Psychology of Education, 2*, 57–71.

Fayol, M. & Monteil, J. M. (1988). The notion of script. *C.P.C./European Bulletin of Cognitive Psychology, 8*, 335–361.

Foulin, J. N., Chanquoy, L., & Fayol, M. (1989). Approche en temps réel de la production des connecteurs et de la ponctuation. *Langue Française, 81*, 5–20.

Gernsbacher, M. A. (1990). *Language comprehension as structure building*. Hillsdale, NJ: Lawrence Erlbaum Associates.

Gobbo, C., & Chi, M. (1986). How knowledge is structured and used by expert and novice children. *Cognitive Development, 1*, 221–237.

Grimes, J. E. (1975). *The thread of discourse*. The Hague: Mouton.

Heurley, L. (1994). *Traitement de textes procéduraux. Etude de psychologie cognitive des processus de production et de compréhension chez des adultes non experts*. Unpublished doctoral dissertation, Université de Bourgogne, France.

Heurley, L. & Bestgen, Y (1993, September). *Effect of prior knowledge organization on text composition*. Paper presented at the European Association for Research on Learning and Instruction (EALI) Congress, Aix en Provence (France).

Jeruchimowicz, R. J. (1978). Use of coordinate sentences with the conjunction "and" for describing temporal and locative relations between events. *Journal of Psycholinguistic Research, 7*, 135–142.

Johnson-Laird, P. N. (1983). *Mental models*. Cambridge: Cambridge University Press.

Kress, C. (1982). *Learning to write*. London: Routledge & Kegan.

Levelt, W. J. M. (1981). The speaker's linearization problem. *Phonological Transactions of the Royal Society of London, B 295*, 305–315.

Levelt, W. J. M. (1982). Linearization in describing spatial networks. In S. Peters & E. Saarinen (Eds.), *Processes, beliefs, and questions* (pp. 199–220). Dordrecht: Reidel.

Levelt, W. J. M. (1989). *Speaking: From intention to articulation*. Cambridge, MA: Cambridge University Press.

Linde, C., & Labov, W. (1975). Spatial network as a site for the study of language and thought. *Language, 51*, 924–939.

Lurçat, L. (1972). L'acquisition de la ponctuation. *Revue Française de Pédagogie, 25*, 14–27.

Mandler, J. M. (1987). On the psychological reality of story structure. *Discourse Processes, 10*, 1–29.

Mandler, J. M., & Johnson, N. S. (1977). Remembrance of things parsed: Story structure and recall. *Cognitive Psychology, 9*, 111–151.

Menetra, J. L. (1982). *Journal de ma vie*. Paris: Montalba.

Millis, K. K., & Just, M. A. (1994). The influence of connectives on sentences comprehension. *Journal of Memory and Language, 33*, 128–147.

Mouchon, S. (1992). *Les marqueurs de liaison inter-événementielle dans les récits*. Unpublished doctoral dissertation, Université de Bourgogne, France.

Mouchon, S., Fayol, M., & Gaonac'h, D. (1995). The on-line processing of inter-event relationships in narratives. *C.P.C./ Current Psychology of Cognition*, 171–193.

Nunberg, G. (1990). *The linguistics of punctuation*. Stanford, CA: Center for the Study of Language.

Ochs, E. (1979). Planned and unplanned discourse. In T. Givon (Ed.), *Syntax and Semantics (XII) : Discourse and Syntax* (pp. 51–80). New-York : Academic Press.

Peterson, C., & Mc Cabe, A. (1987). The connective "and": Do older children use it less as they learn other connectives? *Journal of Child Language, 14*, 375–381.

Pollard-Gott, L., Mc Closkey, M., & Todres, A. K. (1979). Subjective story structure. *Discourse Processes, 2*, 251–281.

Rotondo, J. A. (1984). Clustering analysis of subjective partitions of text. *Discourse Processes, 7*, 69–88.

Schank, R. C., & Abelson, R. P. (1977). *Scripts, plans, goals, and understanding*. Hillsdale, NJ: Lawrence Erlbaum Associates.

Schneuwly, B. (1988). Le *langage écrit chez l'enfant*. Neuchâtel, Paris: Delachaux & Niestlé.

Segal, E. M., Duchan, J. F., & Scott, P. T. (1991). The role of interclausal connectives in narrative structuring: Evidence from adults' interpretations of simple stories. *Discourse Processes, 14*, 27–54.

Shaughnessy, M. P. (1977). *Errors and expectations*. New York: Oxford University Press.

Simon, J. (1973). *La langue écrite de l'enfant*. Paris: Presses Universitaires de France.

Stark, H. A. (1988). What do paragraph markings do? *Discourse Processes, 11*, 275–303.

Van, De Water, D. A. & O' Connel, X. X. (1986).From page to program: Some typographical and temporal variables in radio homilies. *Journal of Psycholinguistic Research, 15*.

van Dijk, T. A., & Kintsch, W. (1983). *Strategies of discourse comprehension*. New-York: Academic Press.

Chapter 9

Processing Units in Written Texts: Paragraphs or Information Blocks?

Laurent Heurley
McGill University & Université de Bourgogne

One of the major concerns of linguistic and psycholinguistic studies has been to establish that some language units are relevant units of processing. Levelt (1989) for instance, estimated that about 50 different units have been identified and studied in speech production. The same concern can be seen in researches on writing (see Foulin, 1993; Hunt, 1983; Matsuhashi, 1981). In writing, most of the units that have been analyzed correspond to four levels: the clause, the sentence, the text and an intermediate level between the sentence and the text that could be referred to as the suprasentential level. The suprasentential level is distinguishable from the others in that no consistent terminology exists to designate it (Mann & Thompson, 1992). This lack of unique terminology is well-illustrated by studies on the paragraph. During the last 30 years much has been done to define the notion of paragraph, but one is still forced to acknowledge, as did Linde (1981), that "there is currently no theory of paragraphs and their parts which is nearly as elaborate as a theory of sentences" (p. 85). Researchers seem to agree only on one point. *Paragraphs* are organized chunks composed of one or several sentences, and, therefore, of one or several clauses.

In this chapter, I will argue that the ambiguity, which has so long embarrassed linguists and psycholinguists concerning the use of the word "paragraph," may be due to the fact that this term refers to different concepts according to whether writers' or readers' perspectives are being considered. My aim in this chapter is to show that studying both sides of the written communication process in an integrated manner may lead to different interpretations for text organization as opposed to focusing on only one side of this process at a time. In the first section, I will present an overview of the written communication process that will serve as a framework for the more specific points discussed later. In the second section, I will review some findings about paragraph structure and functions, and I will argue in favor of integrated studies, that is, studies examining text organization from both the writer's and the reader's perspective. This position is illustrated by the presentation of the main results of a study conducted on procedural text processing. Finally, I will distinguish paragraphs (i.e., visual text units) from information blocks (i.e., structural or semantic organized text units).

THE WRITTEN COMMUNICATION PROCESS

The basic written communication process may be described as a text mediated two-step matching/transformation process that takes place between a writer and a reader (Frederiksen & Emond, 1993).

Step 1, text composition, is a goal-directed process during which a multidimensional informational structure is transformed into a linear sequence of linguistic units: the text. This process implies that relevant information is selected in memory and then organized and that writing plans are elaborated and executed (Fayol, 1991; Fayol & Heurley, 1995; Hayes & Flower, 1980). All these micro-transformations are assumed to be performed in a limited capacity working memory (Fayol, Largy, & Lemaire, 1994) by a planning, a textualization, a reviewing, and a control process.[1] In working memory, information comes from three different sources: the writer's prior knowledge, the perceived situation in which the text is produced (particularly in procedural text composition), and the perceived text.

In contrast, Step 2, that is reading/comprehension, refers to the building of a multidimensional structure, the situation model, from a text (van Dijk & Kintsch, 1983). Many studies on comprehension have established that this transformation is accomplished through multiple operations (i.e., lexical access, syntactic parsing, resolution of anaphora, etc.) that are assumed to take place in a limited capacity working memory (Just & Carpenter, 1992).

In a process such as this, the text may be considered as having a double status since, as a mediator, it is both the output (i.e., the "product") of Step 1 and the input (i.e., the "stimulus") of Step 2.

However, the use of such a mediator causes a *linearization problem* (Costermans, 1980; Levelt, 1981). This problem is mainly due to a double lack of isomorphism between what must be communicated and how it is communicated. First, there is

---

[1]Because text production implies not only the translation of a conceptual structure into a textual structure, but also the marking of the hierarchical organization of the content in the surface structure of the text, the use of the term "textualization" is preferable to the use of the term "translating" (Fayol & Schneuwly, 1987; C. H. Frederiksen, personal communication, November 25, 1994).

a lack of isomorphism between the structure of the information to communicate, which is generally multidimensional and hierarchical, and the composing process, which is strictly sequential in its output, since two words cannot be written at the same time. Second, there is an absence of isomorphism between the informational structure to convey and the product of this process: the text. Indeed, to produce a text, a writer has to transform some parts of his or her multidimensional mental model into a strictly linear organized word sequence (Fayol, 1993). Even if, in some cases, it presents spatial nonlinear characteristics (e.g., concrete poetry as in Crystal, 1987), a written text must be described as a meaningful sequence of propositions that are typically represented in language as a sequence of interrelated clauses (Mann & Thompson, 1992). Because of this double lack of isomorphism, text composition appears to be a very complex task. Writers must not only encode a linearized sequence of linguistic units without losing the hierarchical structure of the information they want to communicate but also ensure that their text will enable future readers to "perceive" the underlying hierarchical informational structure conveyed (Dressler, 1992). For readers, the problem is different. It consists of building a coherent representation (Gernsbacher, 1995). To do so, readers have to "capture" (Dressler, 1992) or to "follow" (Meyer, 1987) a hierarchical organization "within the rhythmic structuring of sequential linearization of text" (Dressler, 1992, p. 14). Such a result can be reached on only one condition: that readers correctly interpret the interclausal relationships (Fayol & Abdi, 1990). In other words, whereas writers must solve a linearization problem, readers, conversely, have to deal with a *delinearization problem*.

However, readers' tasks may be facilitated by the presence of cohesive ties (anaphora, tense, etc.) and connection or segmentation markers (punctuation marks, connectives, and textual organizers) in the surface structure of texts (see Fayol and Schneuwly, this volume). Moreover, it is assumed that some organizational principles play a role in reading. Paragraphing as a partitioning/chunking principle is one of them (Meyer & Rice, 1984). The next section examines the status and the role of paragraphing in the written communication process.

STRUCTURE(S) AND FUNCTION(S) OF THE PARAGRAPH

A paragraph can be examined either as a linguistic unit or as a processing unit.

The Paragraph as a Linguistic Unit

Depending on the investigator, a paragraph can be considered as an orthographic, as a structural, or as a mixed unit.

Considered as an orthographic unit, a paragraph is a typographic visible suprasentential unit of which the boundaries are marked by paragraph breaks such as indentation, margin symbols, new lines, extra blank spaces or lines, and so on (Bessonat, 1988; Ducrot & Todorov, 1972; Hofmann, 1989; Mitterand, 1985; Stark, 1988). The authors who adopt such a definition are generally aware of the fact that other features are involved in paragraphing. But they argue that without an adequate definition of the paragraph, the use of paragraph markers constitutes the most objective way to form an operational definition of this notion.

For researchers who support the thesis of the paragraph as a structural unit, a paragraph must first be defined on the basis of its formal and semantic features. This position is best illustrated in Longacre's (1979) theory of the paragraph. In this theory, the paragraph is described as a *grammatical unit* characterized by four main characteristics (see also Hinds, 1977, 1980; Hwang, 1989). The first characteristic is *closure*: a sentence introduces the paragraph (i.e., the "setting" or the "introduction") and a sentence ends it (i.e., the "terminus"). The second characteristic is *thematic unity*: a paragraph is built around a unique main topic (i.e., "participant," "theme," see also Grimes, 1975; Hinds, 1977; van Dijk, 1982). In most cases, the main topic is located at the beginning of the paragraph (Hinds, 1980). The third characteristic of the paragraph is *hierarchical organization*: the topic is assumed to be at the top of the hierarchy whereas the other statements are considered to be occupying a subordinate position. The fourth characteristic which is postulated in Longacre's theory is *recursivity*: Because one must postulate a finite number of paragraph types, a paragraph that does not correspond to a paragraph type must be analyzed as "embedding of paragraph within paragraph" (Longacre, 1979, p. 131).

For a last category of researchers, the paragraph is a mixed unit. The typical paragraph is characterized by an overlapping of structural and orthographic features (Brown & Yule, 1983; Christensen, 1965).

This brief review reveals the lack of consensus with regard to the definition of the paragraph as a linguistic unit. We can wonder if the same conclusion may be drawn with respect to the paragraph when it is considered as a processing unit.

The Paragraph as a Processing Unit

A review of the literature indicates that the identified functional properties of paragraphs depend to some extent on which step of the written communication process has been studied. Traditionally, two main approaches have been adopted.

According to many investigators who generally consider a text as an input or a "macrostimulus" for Step 2 of the written communication process (i.e., reading/comprehension), the paragraph's main function would be to facilitate the reader's activity by signaling and thereby making explicit text structure. This first approach, which is reader oriented, leads to a *reader-centered explanation* for paragraphing. For others who consider the text as the output of Step 1 (i.e., composing), and who examine text structure determination from the point of view of the writer, text structure, and, therefore, text paragraphing, depend on factors related to the composing process, to the writing task, and to the writer's characteristics. In such a perspective, paragraphs would constitute the visible trace of text encoding that takes place during the composing process. This second approach, which is centered on the writer, leads to a *writer-centered explanation*. The next two sections present in details these two explanations.

Reader-Centered Explanation for Paragraphing

Comprehending a text supposes that the reader is able to perceive the under-lying hierarchical structure (Bestgen, 1992; Meyer, 1975). Aggregating clauses or sentences into larger units seems particularly adapted to facilitate the elaboration of the successive "blocks of information" that are required for a good comprehension (Fayol, 1987). In this respect, text paragraphing (and more generally text organization) is considered by many linguists and psycholinguists to be determined by *reader design* considerations.[2] According to such a reader-centered explanation, writers would organize their texts into paragraphs to facilitate the reader's text processing (e.g., by making the thematic changes explicit). Text structure would be considered to be a complex set of signals or processing instructions provided by the author of a text to facilitate reader's comprehension (Bessonat, 1988; Britton, 1994; Brown & Yule, 1983; Denhière, 1985; Le Ny, 1985; Stark, 1988). For instance, according to Le Ny (1985), the instruction conveyed by a paragraph may be paraphrased as a shifting instruc-tion that tells the reader to close the current representational substructure and to open a new one. Such an approach is particularly well-illustrated in articles by Britton (1994), Hinds (1980), and Hofmann (1989) in which writers are considered as taking into account readers' limited processing capacity by organizing their texts into manageable units signaled by paragraph breaks. For instance, Hofmann (1989) stated his interpretation for paragraphing as follows:

---

[2]The term *reader design* has obvious roots in Clark and Murphy's (1983) and Clark's (1992) use of "audience design." Reader design here refers to the fact that writers design their texts for the people they believe will or could be reading their texts.

Thus, I believe that we can adequately account for the paragraph as a unit of writing, or speaking, which is intended to be held in mind, "on a mental blackboard" so to speak. The paragraph break, whether signaled visually by a white space, or by introductory elements, or by a change in voice or body stance, is an indication to clear this temporary memory (saving what is wanted) & to prepare for more information. (p. 248)

Consequently, if paragraph internal structure and paragraph boundaries are processing instructions, then reading failures would result from the fact that readers do not detect, perceive, or voluntarily "ignore" the instructions given by the authors (Britton, 1994, p. 644).

Such a concept implies that writers have the intention and are able to adapt the structure of their texts to the readers' needs. Among other things, it supposes, at least, high metacognitive and metalinguistic skills (cf. Gombert, 1992), a nonegocentric definition of the writing task (Kroll, 1978), an accurate model of the reader (Traxler & Gernsbacher, 1992), a high capacity to use the relevant linguistic devices available during the textualization phase (Fayol, 1993), and, above all, that writers be able to manage the multiple demands of writing (McCutchen, 1994). As no study directly addresses these questions with respect to paragraphing, and because it has been shown that even for expert writers words do not "flow effortlessly onto the page" while they are composing a text (McCutchen, 1994, p. 7), one may wonder if the "average person" is able to manage such a complex set of activities.

In fact, it seems, as Chafe (1994) and Stark (1988) pointed out, many prescriptive or descriptive accounts about paragraphs rely on investigators' general experience of texts rather than on empirical observations of writers' or readers' behavior. The analysis of data collected in psycholinguistic studies, both with online (i.e., reading times as indicators) and with offline methods, seems to confirm this interpretation, as it unexpectedly provides only weak support for the reader-centered explanation.

With respect to data collected with online methods, some effects of paragraph marking have been observed in experiments measuring local reading times. For instance, an increase of adults' reading times on the segment preceding a paragraph boundary marked by an indentation has been found during the reading of descriptive (Passerault & Chesnet, 1991) and script-based texts (Fayol, Gaonac'h, & Mouchon, 1992). But studies using global measures (i.e., global reading times) have failed to find significant facilitating effects of paragraph marks on reading (Fayol et al., 1992; Hyönä, 1994; Stark, 1988). Similarly, data collected with offline methods have not provided clear evidence for the reader-centered explanation.

For instance, using recall or metacognitive tasks, Fayol et al. (1992) and Stark (1988) have found facilitating effects of paragraphing on reading and comprehension, whereas Hyönä (1994) and Lorch and Lorch (1985) have not. Moreover, linguistic corpus analyses and psycholinguistic studies using segmenting paradigms have indicated that, in many cases, paragraph marking do not correspond to readers' needs nor to their expectancies.[3] For instance, these researches have shown that (a) paragraph markers frequently occur at locations other than paragraph boundaries (i.e., thematic boundaries) and (b) the criteria used by readers when segmenting texts do not exactly fit those that have been used by their authors when paragraphing them.

With respect to the first point, corpus analyses have revealed in a number of cases that paragraphs considered as visual units do not correspond to paragraphs considered as structural units (Braddock, 1974; Halliday & Hasan, 1976; Longacre, 1979). According to Longacre (1979), such a dissociation is due to the fact that the "paragraph indentations of a given writer are often partially dictated by eye appeal; that is, it may be deemed inelegant or heavy to go along too far on a page or a series of pages without an indentation or section break" (p. 116). Results obtained by Bond and Hayes (1984) partly support such an interpretation. According to these authors, people avoid one-sentence paragraphs. The "good" paragraph length depends on at least three spatial factors: the number of sentences in a paragraph, sentence length, and text length. In the same way, Halliday and Hasan (1976) have observed that, even if most of the time one can generally find a greater degree of cohesion ties within paragraphs than between paragraphs, some texts are characterized by a dissociation between paragraph structure and cohesive structure: "the writer extends a dense cluster of cohesive ties across the paragraph boundary and leaves the texture within the paragraph relatively loose" (p. 297). Similarly, Hofmann (1989) acknowledged that even if paragraph breaks are generally "barriers to anaphora," it is not uncommon to find "holes" in these barriers. Some pronouns act like "bridges" between paragraphs. Generally, these pronouns: "(1) occur in the first or occasionally the second sentence of a paragraph, (2) lack any potential antecedent in that paragraph, and (3) their antecedents appear to be something like the topics of their preceding paragraphs" (Hofmann, 1989, p. 245). Such exceptions led Halliday and Hasan (1976) to consider that paragraphing is a "pattern maker" rather than a "pattern marker." By this, they

---

[3]In experiments using the segmenting paradigms, subjects were typically asked to read unparagraphed texts (i.e., texts in which paragraph markers have been previously deleted) and to "place paragraph markers at the places that seemed right to them without regard to where the author may have put them" (Koen, Becker, & Young, 1969, p. 50).

meant that the main function of paragraphs would be to create or to suggest periodic rhythms in texts (i.e., alternation between tight and loose texture). If such an interpretation was correct, readers who systematically interpret paragraph features as *laying, mapping, shifting,* or *wrapping-up* instructions (see Gernsbacher, 1985; Just & Carpenter, 1980), would be misled, just as hearers are when speakers use *turn-yielding cues* at inappropriate points in a conversation (Beattie, Cutler, & Pearson, 1982).

With respect to the second point, psycholinguistic studies have shown that criteria used by authors to indent their texts do not completely overlap with segmentation criteria used by readers in segmenting tasks. For instance, Bond and Hayes (1984) reported the data of a study in which subjects had to reinstate paragraph markers in a 17-sentence unparagraphed text on the basis of their own definition of the paragraph. Results indicated that subjects' segmentation differed in many points from the initial author segmentation. Indeed, all subjects introduced a break where the author had put the first indentation, but only 8 (out of 21) did so for the second author's indentation, and, respectively, 5, 11, and 7 readers introduced a paragraph break in three sites that had not been initially indented by the author. Stark (1988) found similar results in a study in which university students had to reinstate paragraph boundaries into three unparagraphed texts. A mean score of accuracy was computed for each text to find out if subjects identified the same paragraph boundaries as authors. The accuracy values that were obtained for the three texts were respectively .22, .40 and .60 (a value of 1 would have indicated that no subjects ever failed to identify authors' boundaries). Only 9 author's breaks (out of 17) were identified as such by more than 50% of subjects. Obviously, these values are relatively low and text-dependent. Such results are surprising if one considers first, that subjects agreed with each other above the chance level (Bond & Hayes, 1984; Koen, Becker, & Young, 1969), and, second, that to paragraph the texts, readers reported having responded "to topic changes or to the introduction of new topics" (Stark, 1988, p. 284).

Examined as a whole, these results show that the effect of paragraphing on readers' behavior is far from being as clear-cut as expected by the supporters of the reader-centered explanation. To account for the lack of clear effects of paragraphs on readers' behavior, one can hypothesize that if a grammar of the paragraph does really exist as Longacre (1979) believed, its rules are neither shared nor used in the same way by all the members of the same linguistic community. One can imagine that expert and nonexpert writers do not have the same definition of the paragraph. For instance, some evidence has been found that professional writers' paragraphing is governed by complex and nonlogical criteria (see Braddock, 1974; Rodgers, 1966). This could explain why according to Stark (1988), some texts contain unpredictable paragraph breaks. More generally, a second explanation would emerge if text structure was not only considered from the reader's but from the writer's point of view. After all, as Chafe (1994) pointed out, the language producer "is by definition the person responsible for the form language takes" (p. 180).

Writer-Centered Explanation for Paragraphing

As we have seen in the preceding section, a text can be envisaged as an input if one only considers the reading process of written communication. However, if one considers the other side, the writer's side, the same text can be considered as the final visible output of the composing process (Step 1). With such a perspective, the features of the surface text structure can no longer be considered only as signals or instructions given by writers to readers. Instead, some features must be envisaged as "traces" of the writing process (Bestgen, 1992; Fayol, 1993; Frederiksen, Donin-Frederiksen, & Bracewell, 1987; Frederiksen & Emond, 1993; Schneuwly, 1988). Of course, these traces can be used by readers as cues to identify the structure of the text or to get some information on the way the composing process took place (cf. Frederiksen, 1986), but their presence and/or absence and their characteristics must not be systematically interpreted in terms of communicative functions. This writer-centered explanation for text structure can be illustrated by the following *snow footprints metaphor*. When someone is walking in the snow, he or she leaves footprints. But without knowing the exact intention of the walker, it is impossible to decide if footprints are signals, instructions to be followed, or only traces left by the walker. Only one thing is certain: Footprints exist and can eventually be used by someone else as cues to infer the itinerary that the walker has taken. In the same way, paragraph features may be provided intentionally or not by authors and thereby affect readers' activity.

The writer-centered explanation for paragraphing, in particular, and for text structure, in general, has been supported by speaking/writing studies that have been conducted during the last 20 years. These studies revealed that text organization depends on factors related either to writer/speaker characteristics, to referent structure, or to the production process. Four factors (among others) appear to play a central role in text structure elaboration.

The first factor is the structure of the referent to communicate. For instance, Ehrich and Koster (1983), and Levelt (1981), have shown that the organization of oral descriptions can be fairly well-predicted from the structure (or the visual appearance) of the configurations to describe. Similar results have been found in writing. For instance, when studying procedural text writing, Holland (1988) found important differences in the structure of instructions providing that they referred to procedures with continuous (i.e., tie tying) or discrete actions (i.e., Fischertechnik assembly). Typically, continuous procedures were conveyed by linear sequences of step-by-step instructions. In contrast, the instructions describing the discrete procedure were hierarchically structured around global and local goals.

The second factor, prior domain knowledge organization, has been shown to strongly influence both the speaking (Brown & Dell, 1987) and the composing process (Bereiter, Burtis, & Scardamalia, 1988; Caccamise, 1987; McCutchen, 1986). Such an influence is partly accounted for by Frederiksen's model of discourse production (see Frederiksen & Emond, 1993). In this model, the translation of conceptual knowledge into discourse is assumed to operate either indirectly or directly. In the indirect translation process, propositions play the role of mediator between knowledge structure and text structure. In contrast, in the direct process, discourse features directly reflect the writing process and conceptual knowledge organization (i.e., frame structure). This conception is clearly stated in the following excerpt from Frederiksen, Donin-Frederiksen, and Bracewell (1987): "text production is 'frame-driven', that is, propositional, clause, and text structures reflect frame structure through instantiating, encoding, staging, and frame-signalling relationships" (p. 284). In such a perspective, a text can be considered as a kind of "externalization" of a writer's mental models and database organization (Denis, 1992). This view has received some support by studies in which people were asked to punctuate text-based scripts (i.e., highly organized conceptual knowledge). For instance, Fayol and Abdi (1988) clearly showed that script structure determined punctuation in a 3-step study in which subjects had to punctuate two script-based texts (e. g., visiting the dentist). Regression analyses indicated that the interpropositional distances and the separating power of punctuation marks were inversely proportional. Similar results were found by Chanquoy (1989) in weekly timetable descriptions written by 8- and 9- year-old children.

The third factor is memory, both long-term and working memory. With respect to long-term memory, Kintsch and van Dijk (1978) have shown that in summarizing and recall tasks (summaries and recall must be considered as full texts), the probability that a macroproposition be reproduced is much higher than that it be a microproposition (see also Kintsch, 1987). Working memory also appears to be a very important factor for written text composition. Because writing supposes that several operations be performed simultaneously, the writer has been compared to a "busy switchboard operator" (McCutchen, 1994, p. 1). Some evidence has been found that an increasing memory load may produce a progressive reduction of both text structure and text content complexity (Kalsbeek, 1965). However, as functional aspects of writing have been neglected, very few data are available on this topic (Fayol, 1991; Fayol & Heurley, 1995).

The fourth factor determining text organization is speakers' (Linde & Labov, 1975) or writers' planning strategies (Bereiter et al., 1988; Schneuwly, 1988). For instance, Bereiter et al. (1988) found that texts can be composed either by using a knowledge-driven strategy (i.e., the *knowledge-telling strategy*) or a goal-driven strategy (i.e., the *knowledge-transforming strategy*). Both strategies can result in a coherent text organized around a main relevant topic, but what makes them different is that, in the first case, text coherence must be considered as a fortuitous consequence of the planning process, whereas, in the second case, it is a goal that has been intentionally pursued by the means of a problem solving activity.

All these results indicate that both global and local text organization do not depend uniquely on reader design considerations, but also on some factors related to writing processes and writers' characteristics. However, it must be pointed out that because most of the speaking/writing studies did not focus on the paragraph but on text structure, in general, most of the data provide only indirect support for the writer-centered explanation for paragraphing.

As a whole, the elements that have been reported in the two preceding sections suggest that taking into account both writers' and readers' perspective could avoid one-sided misleading interpretations for paragraphing. So, an approach that would address simultaneously both sides of the written communication process, that is, an *integrated approach*, would be particularly well-adapted to characterize the status of the paragraph as a functional unit.

Toward an Integrated Explanation for Paragraphing

Apart from the studies on oral face-to-face conversation (see Clark, 1992), studies having addressed both sides of the communication process both in the oral (see, e.g., Brown & Dell, 1987; Jarvella & Deutsch, 1987) and in the written modality (see, for instance, Frederiksen & Emond, 1993; Holland, 1988; Traxler & Gernsbacher, 1992) are fairly rare. To illustrate this kind of approach, with respect to the study of the paragraph, the main results are summarized of a series of experiments carried out to study both production and comprehension processes involved in the processing of procedural texts (i.e., texts instructing readers how to do something or how something can be done, e.g., assembly and operating instructions, etc.).

An Integrated Research: The Case of Procedural Text Processing. In this research, four experiments were conducted in order to examine the cognitive processes involved in the processing of procedural texts. Experiment 1 and Experiment 2 analyzed factors determining procedural text organization from writers' points of view, whereas Experiments 3 and 4 studied the effects of text characteristics on real readers' performances.

In Experiment 1, 16 adults had to write a text explaining to a reader how to draw an unfamiliar bidimensional geometric figure (five elementary shapes drawn on a squared cardboard) after they either drew or looked at it (for more details, see Heurley, 1994; Heurley, Gombert, & Fayol, 1995). Online (pause duration) and offline analyses (text analysis) revealed two important results.

The first result was that the mode of acquisition of prior knowledge affected the management of the subsequent writing task and the structure of texts both at a macro-level (i.e., the order used to explain the geometric's figure drawing) and at a micro-level (i.e., instruction's length). The second result was that each text was composed of several subparts, each being organized around a single topic, called *information blocks*.[4] Indeed, an informationally based segmentation procedure (see Ehrich & Koster, 1983) revealed that, overall, texts were composed of information blocks (i.e., *frame, goal, instructions* and *result*) that were characterized both by functional and structural properties. With respect to functional properties, online and offline analyses showed that block boundaries did correspond more to breaks in the writing process than to physical breaks on the page of paper. Thus, only 41.5% of information blocks were marked by at least one paragraph marker, and, therefore, fit the accepted orthographic definition of the paragraph. But block boundaries were marked by long pauses (for pause interpretation in writing, see Flower & Hayes, 1981; Foulin, 1993; Matsuhashi, 1981). The median duration of pauses occurring between two blocks (9.7 s) was more than twice as high as the median duration of pauses occurring between two sentences inside a block (4 s). Moreover, the analysis of revision activities indicated that block boundaries acted as "barriers" to revision episodes for 12 writers (out of 16) who never modified elements of the text located outside of the current block. This analysis revealed that 94% of the long-range episodes of revision (i.e., giving rise to modifications of a text element located outside the current block or across at least one block's boundary) present in the protocols of the 4 remaining writers "fired" outside of blocks, that is, immediately after a block was written or just before a new block was initiated. With respect to structural properties, text analysis revealed that

---

[4]Information blocks are larger units than Grimes' (1975) units. They are very similar to the instructions described by Terken (1984) and by Dixon (1987). The superordinate information corresponds to what Dixon (1987) called the "organizational information" and the subordinate information to the "component step information" (p. 24).

blocks conveying instructions (the only block category to be present in all the texts) could be characterized by a very specific hierarchical internal structure. Typically, these blocks were composed of at least one sentence (3% were composed of one clause) and conveyed two categories of information: (a) one superordinate main piece of information that stated the superordinate goal of the block (macro-action + information referring to one of the elements of the referent described, e.g., "Draw a circle.") and (b) one or more subordinate secondary pieces of information that indicated the sequence of micro-actions to accomplish so as to draw the element referred to in the instruction block (e.g., "The centre must be located at 10 squares from the left and at 7 squares from the red line."). The analysis of the ratings of 10 independent judges revealed that in 61.25% of the instruction blocks, the superordinate main information was stated at the beginning of the block; in 20%, at the end. In 18.75% of the cases, it either occurred in the middle of the block or else it was not possible for the judges to decide on its location in the block.

Initially, Experiment 2 was a pilot study, the objectives of which were of no interest with respect to the present chapter, although one unexpected finding justifies reporting it here. In this experiment, 17 university students were asked to do the same task that the subjects did in Experiment 1. The geometric figure used in this second experiment (Fig. 9.1) was similar to the figure used in Experiment 1 (i.e., it was composed of five elementary shapes drawn on a squared cardboard) except for one thing: whereas in Experiment 1 only one element could be easily located on the cardboard by landmarks, in Experiment 2, each element of the figure could be located by several numbered red landmarks (represented as numbered circles in Fig. 9.1).

The analysis of the 17 collected texts revealed that contrary to what was found in Experiment 1, all the texts were not composed of information blocks. In fact, only 73.8% of the instructions did correspond to information blocks organized around a single main superordinate piece of information. When blocks were present, the main superordinate information was located at the beginning of the block in 58.1% of the instructions and at the end in 32.3%. When blocks were not present (26.2% of the instructions), the statements explaining how to draw a given element of the figure were not chunked in an instruction block and so were not subsumed by a superordinate main piece of information. Such an organization was found in 6 texts (out of 17). Typically, the drawing of an element was explained by using a "landmark-joining strategy" and instructions took the form: "Join points (14) and (6)." More interestingly, the analysis of instruction blocks revealed a relationship between writers' strategies and text organization. If one looks at the geometric figure (Fig. 9.1), one can see that for the three elements located in the lower part of the cardboard

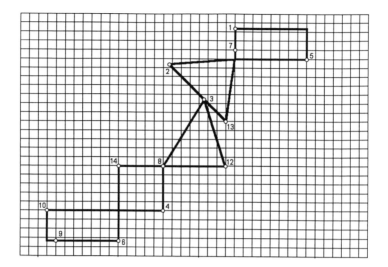

FIG. 9.1. Geometric figure used in Experiment 2.

(i.e., the rectangle, the square, and the triangle) adopting the joining strategy for segments 10–4, 6–14, and 14–12 leads to crossing the elements' boundaries. For instance, joining landmarks 10–4 results in the drawing of both the upper side of the rectangle and the lower side of the square. The analysis of the instructions explaining the drawing of these three elements revealed that when writers used the joining strategy, the probability that the main superordinate information was present in the instruction was weaker (.29) than when such a strategy was not used (.93). In addition, the analysis of the internal structure of the instructions containing a main superordinate piece of information indicated that this information was located at the beginning of the block in 40% of the instructions when the joining strategy was adopted and in 82% when it was not. As a whole, these results suggest that some decisions concerning local text organization are constrained by decisions the writer has taken formerly in the composing process.

Two other experiments were conducted to examine: (a) if information blocks identified in Experiments 1 and 2 constituted reading units for naive readers (as opposed to trained judges) and (b) the effect of the internal structure of these blocks on reading and carrying out instructions.

In Experiment 3, university students had to identify, according to their own criteria, the different parts of eight texts that had been previously collected in Experiment 1. Results showed that these "naive" readers were able to identify 66% of the blocks in nonmodified versions of the texts. When connectives and punctuation markers (except interword blanks) had been removed from the texts, readers were still able to identify a high proportion of blocks (62%) when the referent (i.e., the geometric figure) was available during the segmentation task, but not when it was not available (45%). These results showed that, as was expected, knowledge of the referent plays an important role in the identification of information blocks and neutralizes the effects of the deletion of connective and punctuation markers. These results also indicated that block identification relies more on semantic than on formal considerations.

Using material and a paradigm similar to Dixon (1987), Experiment 4 examined whether the structure of information blocks observed in Experiments 1 and 2 would affect reading processes. Results showed that, when the main superordinate information was stated at the beginning of instructions, the mean proportion of correct execution was significantly higher (+10.4%) and the mean reading time of sentences conveying subordinate information was significantly lower (-14.95%) than when the superordinate information was stated at the end. These results confirm Dixon's (1987) results, but not the appropriateness of the terminology he used since they indicate that the main superordinate information only plays an organizational role (for readers) when it occupies the initial mention in a block.

In summary, this study demonstrated that suprasentential textual organization partly depends on referent structure, writers' prior knowledge, and writers' strategies. Moreover, it showed that suprasentential units, that is information blocks, are units in the composing process as indicated by online analyses (see also Chafe, 1987; Flower & Hayes, 1981; Matsuashi, 1981). However, even if information block organization does generally correspond to readers' needs (i.e., by mentioning the superordinate information before the subordinate information, cf. Dixon, 1987; Kieras, 1980), results obtained in Experiment 2 suggest that this "adaptation" of production to comprehension is more fortuitous than intentional since it is determined by factors (i.e., writers' strategies and referents' structure) other than reader design consideration (see Brown & Dell, 1987).

Paragraphs or Information Blocks?   By taking into consideration all the elements that have been mentioned in the preceding sections, it becomes obvious that the ambiguity related to the term *paragraph* comes from the fact that it refers to at least two distinct dimensions that in some cases overlap and in others do not. The first dimension is reader oriented because some paragraph features may be perceived as having signaling functions, for instance, paragraph markers (e.g., indentation and extra blank spaces or lines). The second dimension is writer oriented. Indeed, some paragraph features must be considered as visible traces of how the composing process took place (e.g., superordinate and subordinate information location). To define more precisely these two dimensions, it is useful to refer again to Frederiksen's model of text production (Frederiksen, 1986; Frederiksen, Donin-Frederiksen, & Bracewell, 1987).

According to Frederiksen, conceptual knowledge translation into text (i.e., *textualization* in our terminology) supposes two distinct operations: encoding and signaling. Whereas *encoding* refers to the translation of propositions into clauses, *signaling* is the process by which "text-level linguistic structures are used by writers to signal high-level conceptual frame structures to a reader" (Frederiksen, 1986, p. 231). What is interesting in this model is that encoding and signaling are assumed to be partly independent processes. The ambiguity related to the term *paragraph* could be reduced if the same distinction was taken into consideration when characterizing suprasentential text units. One way to do it would be to use two distinct terms to refer to text units depending on whether they are assumed to result from encoding or from signaling operations. With such a perspective, I propose to keep the term, paragraph, for referring to visual text units resulting from the signaling process, that is: text segments marked by indentations, blank spaces, and/or extra-lines. These units are the only ones almost certainly produced according to reader design considerations (even if the readers are the writers themselves). Such a suggestion has already been made by Bessonat (1988). On the other hand, I propose to use the term *information block* to designate structural/semantic organized text units resulting from the encoding process regardless of any orthographic marking in the surface structure of the text (cf. Pitkin, 1969).

According to such a distinction, paragraphs should be identified only on the basis of orthographic features no matter whether they are characterized by a coherent and/or a cohesive internal structure or not. Conversely, information blocks should be characterized by their thematic unity, their hierarchical organization, and the presence of cohesive ties. Thus, it would be possible to find passages corresponding to information blocks but not to paragraphs, and vice versa, and passages corresponding both to paragraphs and to information blocks.

Adopting such a distinction would account for many textual phenomena. For instance, it could explain the presence of bridging anaphora at the beginning of new paragraphs (i.e., visual text units). Imagine two paragraphs, linked by a bridging anaphora, that were written during the same composing episode (Flower & Hayes, 1981) and that belonged to the same information block.[5] In

---

[5] According to Flower and Hayes (1981) composing episodes are "meaningful and verifiable units of concentration" (p. 234) whose boundaries are punctuated by long pauses. Although, to a great extent they vary in length, they are easily identified as meaningful episodes in the writers' thought. In most of the cases, composing episodes do not correspond to paragraphs (as visual units) and must be regarded as "goal-related planning units", that is "units in the process of the writer, rather than his or her written product" (p. 234) .

a case such as this, the presence of the bridging anaphora (i.e., and the absence of any antecedent to interpret it in the second paragraph) may be explained by the fact that because no shifting process occurred before the writer reached the end of the block (i.e., the end of the second paragraph), the antecedent was still highly active in the writer's working memory when the so called bridging anaphora was written (see Chafe, 1987, 1994; Gernsbacher, 1985). Similarly, the fact that most of information blocks are produced during the same composing episode (especially when composition takes place under time constraint) may explain why there are more cohesive ties within blocks than between them. However, it may happen that different parts of an information block are produced during different composing episodes. This is the case when some revision takes place. When revising a draft before writing the definite version of a text, one can add, delete, or modify some parts of an existing information block. In this case, the resulting information block must be considered as the trace of two or more successive encoding episodes.

CONCLUSION

In this chapter, focused on written text paragraphing, it is argued that integrated approaches focusing on both sides of the written communication process are particularly useful for analyzing the functional aspects of text suprasentential organization and may avoid misleading interpretations. As Chafe (1994) pointed out, when adopting a functionalist perspective, one must take into consideration each actor at either extremity of the information flow. With this in mind, one may wonder, and one should examine if (and when) a break in a written text, for instance, was designed by the author to create a shift in the reader's mind or if this break was simply the result of a shift in the mind of the author. In the first case, the break can be considered as a processing instruction for readers; in the second case, even if it is interpreted as a clue or as a signal by readers, it is primarily the trace of a mental processing that took place formerly in the author's mind. There is no doubt that text structure, in general, and text partitioning, in particular, play a role in written communication. However, it is one thing to show that a given aspect of the structure of a text may affect the readers' behavior (as measured with offline or online methods), but another to demonstrate that its function is to create such an effect. Consequently, for each aspect of a given text, one must ask and try to answer the following questions: What is its structure?; What is it function?; What is its functioning?; and What are the interactions between these three things?

ACKNOWLEDGMENTS

The writing of this chapter was supported in part by Contract No. 89721 from the French Ministère de l'Agriculture et de la Forêt, in part by Contract No. 268 from the French Ministère de l'Education Nationale et de la Recherche, and in part by a Lavoisier post-doctoral grant from the French Ministère des Affaires Etrangères.

I wrote this chapter while I was a post-doctoral fellow at McGill University. I thank all the members of the Laboratory of Applied Cognitive Science for their hospitality and their help. I am grateful to Robert J. Bracewell who accepted me at his laboratory and to Carl H. Frederiksen for his insightful comments and suggestions. I thank Anne-Marie Guenin, Sylvie Bosher, Robert Bouchard, George Carani, Paul Fournier, Litsa Papathanasopoulou, and Tom Patrick for their help and for their encouragements. I planned this chapter while I was a member of the LEAD (Laboratoire d'Etudes des Apprentissages et du Développement) at the University of Dijon. I thank the members of this laboratory for their help and, more specifically Patrick Bonin, Jean Emile Gombert, and Michel Fayol, without whom my research would have not been carried out. I thank Yves Bestgen for his relevant comments on a first version of this chapter.

Jean Costermans and Michel Fayol provided excellent editorial comments for which I am grateful.

REFERENCES

Beattie, G. W., Cutler, A., & Pearson, M. (1982). Why is Mrs. Thatcher interrupted so often? *Nature, 300,* 744–747

Bereiter, C., Burtis, P. J., & Scardamalia, M. (1988). Cognitive operations in constructive main points in written composition. *Journal of Memory and Language, 27,* 261–278.

Bessonat, D. (1988). Le découpage en paragraphe et ses fonctions. *Pratiques, 57,* 81–105.

Bestgen, Y. (1992). *Deux approches du discours narratif: Marqueurs de la segmentation et profil émotionnel.* Unpublished doctoral dissertation, Catholic University of Louvain-La-Neuve, Belgium.

Bond, S. J., & Hayes, J. R. (1984). Cues people use to paragraph text. *Research in the Teaching of English, 18,* 147–167.

Braddock, R. (1974). The frequency and placement of topic sentences in expository prose. *Research in the Teaching of English, 8,* 287–302.

Britton, B. K. (1994). Understanding expository text: Building mental structures to induce insights. In M. A. Gernsbacher (Ed.), *Handbook of psycholinguistics* (pp. 641–674). San Diego: Academic Press.

Brown, G., & Yule, G. (1983). *Discourse analysis.* Cambridge, England: Cambridge University Press.

Brown, P., & Dell, G. S. (1987). Adapting production to comprehension: The explicit mention of instruments. *Cognitive Psychology, 19,* 414–472.

Caccamise, D. J. (1987). Idea generation in writing. In A. Matsuhashi (Ed.), *Writing in real time* (pp. 224–253). Norwood, NJ: Ablex.

9. Processing Units in Written Texts   197

Chafe, W. (1987). Cognitive constraints on information flow. In R. S. Tomlin (Ed.), *Coherence and grounding in discourse* (pp. 21–51). Amsterdam and Philadelphia: John Benjamins Publishing Company.

Chafe, W. (1994). *Discourse, consciousness, and time: The flow and displacement of conscious experience in speaking and writing.* Chicago, IL: University of Chicago Press.

Chanquoy, L. (1989). La description de l'emploi du temps d'une semaine scolaire par des enfants de CE2: Etude de la ponctuation et des connecteurs. *Etudes de Linguistique Appliquée, 73,* 47–56.

Christensen, F. (1965). A generative rhetoric of the paragraph. *Composition and Communication, 16,* 144–157.

Clark, H. H. (1992). *Arenas of language use.* Chicago: University of Chicago Press and Center for the study of Language and Information.

Clark, H. H., & Murphy, G. L. (1983). Audience design in meaning and reference. In J.-F. Le Ny & W. Kintsch (Eds.), *Language and comprehension.* Amsterdam: North-Holland.

Costermans, J. (1980). *Psychologie du langage.* Bruxelles: Mardaga.

Crystal, D. (1987). *The cambridge encyclopedia of language.* Cambridge, England: Cambridge University Press.

Denhière, G. (1985). Statut psychologique du paragraphe et structure du récit. In J. Châtillon (Ed.), *La notion de paragraphe* (pp. 121–128). Paris: Editions du Centre National de la Recherche Scientifique.

Denis, M. (1992, July). Externalization of mental images. In A. Paivio (Chair), *New horizons in imagery research.* Symposium conducted at the XXV International Congress of Psychology, Brussels, Belgium.

Dixon, P. (1987). The processing of organizational and component step information in written directions. *Journal of Memory and Language, 26,* 24–35.

Dressler, W. (1992). Marked and unmarked text strategies within the semiotically based NATU-RAL texlinguistics. In S. J. J. Hwang & W. R. Merrifield (Eds.), *Language in context: Essays for Robert E. Longacre* (pp. 5–18). Arlington, TX: The Summer Institute of Linguistics and the University of Texas at Arlington.

Ducrot, O., & Todorov, T. (1972). *Dictionnaire encyclopédique des sciences du langage.* Paris: Editions du Seuil.

Ehrich, V., & Koster, C. (1983). Discourse organization and sentence form: The structure of room descriptions in Dutch. *Discourse Processes, 6,* 169–195.

Fayol, M. (1987, September). *Are there any surface cues that can help students select main points in texts? A tentative review.* Paper presented at the Second European Conference for Research on Learning and Instruction, Tuebingen, Germany.

Fayol, M. (1991). From sentence production to text production: Investigating fundamental processes. *European Journal of Psychology of Education, 6,* 101–119.

Fayol, M. (1993, October). *Ponctuation et connecteurs, fonctionnement et acquisition de quelques marqueurs de la structure textuelle.* Communication présentée au Workshop "Understanding early literacy in a developmental and cross-linguistic approach," Wassenaar, The Netherlands.

Fayol, M., & Abdi, H. (1988). Influence of script structure on punctuation. *Cahiers de Psychologie Cognitive, 8,* 265–279.

Fayol, M., & Abdi, H. (1990). Ponctuation et connecteurs: Etude expérimentale de leur fonction-nement dans des paires de propositions. In M. Charolles, S. Fisher & J. Jayez (Eds.), *Le discours* (pp. 167–180). Nancy, France: Presses Universitaires de Nancy.

Fayol, M., Gaonac'h, D., & Mouchon, S. (1992). L'utilisation des marques de surface lors de la lecture: L'exemple de la ponctuation. *Scientia Paedagogica Experimentalis, 29,* 83–98.

Fayol, M., & Heurley, L. (1995). Des modèles de production du langage à l'étude du fonctionne-ment du scripteur, enfant et adulte. In J.-Y. Boyer, J.-P. Dionne & P. Raymond (Eds.), *La production de textes: Vers un modèle d'enseignement de l'écriture* (pp. 17–48). Montréal: Les Editions Logiques.

Fayol, M., Largy, P., & Lemaire, P. (1994). When cognitive overload enhances subject-verb agreement errors. *Quarterly Journal of Experimental Psychology, 47A*, 437–464.

Fayol, M., & Schneuwly, B. (1987). La mise en texte et ses problèmes. In J. L. Chiss, J. P. Laurent, J. C. Meyer, H. Romian & B. Schneuwly (Eds.), *Apprendre/Enseigner à produire des textes écrits* (pp. 223–240). Bruxelles: De Broek.

Flower, L., & Hayes, J. R. (1981). The pregnant pause: an inquiry into the nature of planning. *Research in the Teaching of English, 15*, 229–243.

Foulin, J. N. (1993). *Pause et débit: Les indicateurs temporels de la production écrite. Etude comparative chez l'enfant et l'adulte*. Unpublished doctoral dissertation, Dijon, France.

Frederiksen, C. H. (1986). Cognitive models and discourse analysis. In C. R. Cooper & S. Greenbaum (Eds.), *Written communication annual: Vol. 1. Linguistic approaches to the study of written discourse* (pp. 227–267). Beverley Hills, CA: Sage.

Frederiksen, C. H., Donin-Frederiksen, J., & Bracewell, R. J. (1987). Discourse analysis of children's text production. In A. Matsuhashi (Ed.), *Writing in real time* (pp. 254–290). Norwood, NJ: Ablex.

Frederiksen, C. H., Emond, B. (1993). La représentation et le traitement cognitif du discours: Le rôle des modèles formels. In J.-F. Le Ny (Ed.), *Intelligence naturelle et intelligence artificielle* (pp. 165–195). Paris: Presses Universitaires de France.

Gernsbacher, M. A. (1985). Surface information loss in comprehension. *Cognitive psychology, 17*, 324–363.

Gernsbacher, M. A. (1995). The mechanisms of suppression and enhancement in comprehension. *Canadian Psychology/Psychologie Canadienne, 36*, 49–50.

Gombert, J. E. (1992). *Metalinguistic development*. Chicago, IL: University of Chicago Press.

Grimes, J. E. (1975). *The thread of discourse*. The Hague: Mouton.

Halliday, M. A. K., & Hasan, R. (1976). *Cohesion in English*. London: Longman.

Hayes, J. R., & Flower, L. S. (1980). Identifying the organization of writing processes. In L. W. Gregg & E. R. Steinberg (Eds.), *Cognitive processes in writing* (pp. 3–30). Hillsdale, NJ: Lawrence Erlbaum Associates.

Heurley, L. (1994). *Traitement de textes procéduraux: Etude de psycholinguistique cognitive des processus de production et de compréhension chez des adultes non experts*. Unpublished doctoral dissertation, Dijon, France.

Heurley, L., Gombert, J.E., & Fayol, M. (1995). *Writing procedural texts: Effect of prior knowledge mode of acquisition on linearization processes*. Manuscript submitted for publication.

Hinds, J. (1977). Paragraph structure and pronominalization. *Papers in Linguistics: International Journal of Human Communication, 10*, 77–99.

Hinds, J. (1980). Japanese expository prose. *Papers in Linguistics: International Journal of Human Communication, 13*, 117–158.

Hofmann, T. R. (1989). Paragraphs, & anaphora. *Journal of Pragmatics, 13*, 239–250.

Holland, V. M. (1988). Processes involved in writing procedural instructions (Doctoral dissertation, University of Pennsylvania, 1987). *Dissertation Abstracts International, 46*, 2124B–2125B.

Hunt, K. W. (1983). Sentence combining and the teaching of writing. In M. Martlew (Ed.), *The psychology of written language* (pp. 99–125). Chichester: John Wiley & Sons.

Hwang, S. J. J. (1989). Recursion in the paragraph as a unit of discourse development. *Discourse Processes, 12*, 461–477.

Hyönä, J. (1994). Processing of topic shifts by adults and children. *Reading Research Quarterly, 29*, 77–90.

Jarvella, R. J., & Deutsch, W. (1987). An asymetry in producing versus understanding descriptions of visual arrays. In A. Allport, D. G. Mackay, W. Prinz, & E. Sheerer (Eds.), *Language perception and production: Relationships between listening, speaking, reading and writing* (pp. 41–59). London: Academic Press.

Just, M. A., & Carpenter, P. A. (1980). A theory of reading: From eye fixations to comprehension. *Psychological Review, 87*, 329–354.

Just, M. A., & Carpenter, P. A. (1992). A capacity theory of comprehension: Individual differences in working memory. *Psychological Review, 99*, 122–149.

Kalsbeek, J. W. H. (1965). Mesure objective de la charge mentale: Nouvelles applications de la méthode des doubles tâches. *Le Travail Humain, 28*, 121–131.

Kieras, D.E. (1980). Initial mention as a signal to thematic content in technical passages. *Memory & Cognition, 8*, 345–353.

Kintsch, W. (1987). Psychological processes in discourse production. In H. W. Dechert & M. Raupach (Eds.), *Psycholinguistic models of production* (pp. 163–180). Norwood, NJ: Ablex Publishing Corporation.

Kintsch, W., & van Dijk, T. A. (1978). Toward a model of text comprehension and production. *Psychological Review, 85*, 363–394.

Koen, F., Becker, A., & Young, R. (1969). The psychological reality of the paragraph. *Journal of Verbal Learning and Verbal Behavior, 8*, 49–53.

Kroll, B. M. (1978). Cognitive egocentrism and the problem of audience awareness in written discourse. *Research in the Teaching of English, 12*, 269–281.

Le Ny, J. F. (1985). Texte, structure mentale, paragraphe. In J. Châtillon (Ed.), *La notion de paragraphe* (pp. 129–136). Paris: Editions du Centre National de la Recherche Scientifique.

Levelt, W. J. M. (1981). The speaker's linearization problem. *Philosophical Transactions Royal Society London, B295*, 305–315.

Levelt, W. J. M. (1989). *Speaking: From intention to articulation.* Cambridge, MA: The MIT Press.

Linde, C. (1981). The organization of discourse. In T. Shopet & J. M. Williams (Eds.), *Style and variables in English* (pp. 84–114). Cambridge, MA: Winthrop.

Linde, C., & Labov, W. (1975). Spatial networks as a site for the study of language and thought. *Language, 51*, 924–939.

Longacre, R. E. (1979). The paragraph as a grammatical unit. In T. Givón (Ed.) *Syntax and semantics: Vol. 12. Discourse and syntax* (pp. 115–134). New York: Academic Press.

Lorch, R. F., & Lorch, E. P. (1985). Topic structure representation and text recall. *Journal or Educational Psychology, 77*, 137–148.

Mann, W. C., & Thompson, S. A. (1992). Relational discourse structure: A comparison of approaches to structuring text by 'contrast'. In S. J. J. Hwang & W. R. Merrifield (Eds.), *Language in context: Essays for Robert E. Longacre.* (pp. 19–45). Arlington, TX: The Summer Institute of Linguistics and the University of Texas at Arlington.

Matsuhashi, A. (1981). Pausing and planning: The tempo of written discourse production. *Research in the Teaching of English, 15*, 113–134.

McCutchen, D. (1986). Domain knowledge and linguistic knowledge in the development of writing ability. *Journal of Memory and Language, 25*, 431–444.

McCutchen, D. (1994). The magical number three, plus or minus two: Working memory in writing. In E. C. Butterfield (Ed.), *Advances in cognition and educational practice: Vol. 2. Children's writing: Toward a process theory of the development of skilled writing* (pp. 1–30). Greenwich, CT: JAI.

Meyer, B. J. F. (1975). *The organization of prose and its effects on memory.* Amsterdam: North Holland.

Meyer, B. J. F. (1987). Following the author's top-level organization: An important skill for reading comprehension. In R. J. Tierney, P. L. Anders & J. N. Mitchell (Eds.), *Understanding readers' understanding: Theory and practice* (pp. 59–76). Hillsdale, NJ: Lawrence Erlbaum Associates.

Meyer, B. J. F., Rice, G. E. (1984). The structure of text. In P. D. Pearson (Ed.), *Handbook of reading research* (pp. 319–347). New York: Longman.

Mitterand, H. (1985). Le paragraphe est-il une unité linguistique? In J. Châtillon (Ed.), *La notion de paragraphe* (pp. 85–95). Paris: Editions du centre National de la Recherche Scientifique.

Passerault, J. M., & Chesnet, D. (1991). Le marquage des paragraphes: Son rôle dans la gestion des traitements pendant la lecture. *Psychologie Française, 36*, 159–165.

Pitkin, W. L. (1969). Discourse blocs. *College Composition and Communication, 20*, 138–148

Rodgers, P. C. (1966). A discourse-centered rhetoric of the paragraph. *College Composition and Communication, 17*, 2–11.

Schneuwly, B. (1988). *Le langage écrit chez l'enfant*. Neuchâtel: Delachaux & Niestlé.

Stark, H. A. (1988). What do paragraph markings do?. *Discourse Processes, 11*, 275–303.

Terken, J. M. B. (1984). The distribution of pitch accents in instructions as a function of discourse structure. *Language and Speech, 27*, 269–290.

Traxler, M. J., & Gernsbacher, M. A. (1992). Improving written communication through minimal feedback. *Language and Cognitive Processes, 7*, 1–22.

van Dijk, T. A. (1982). Episodes as units of discourse analysis. In D. Tannen (Ed.), *Analysing discourse: Text and talk* (pp. 177–195). Washington, DC: Georgetown University Round table on Language and Linguistics (1981).

van Dijk, T. A., & Kintsch, W. (1983). *Strategies of discourse comprehension*. London: Academic Press.

❋ Chapter 10

Temporal Markers
of Narrative Structure:
Studies in Production

Yves Bestgen
and Jean Costermans
Catholic University of Louvain

This chapter considers the role of temporal indicators in the segmentation of narratives. It reports on research that suggests that speakers and writers use certain temporal markers to highlight the most important shifts in their narratives, others to mark intermediate breaks, and still others to signal a locus of high continuity.

During the last 15 years, research on devices that help speakers and listeners in the difficult task of linearization and delinearization of discourse has increased. Early works concentrated on the different lexico–syntactic means that ensure cohesion and make the interlocutors' job of integration easier. More recently, it has been suggested that antagonist devices help listeners and readers too. By signaling discontinuities in discourse, these devices suspend the search for continuity when the latter is weak. This chapter reviews segmentation marker studies and contributes to the descripiton of these markers.

We first introduce the concept of *segmentation markers* and consider their discourse function. They seem to act as *signals*, indices introduced to indicate segmentation in a discourse. The main question we address here is whether speakers and writers have access to sets of lexical markers that allow them to signal discourse breaks of varying levels of importance. To answer this question, one needs to define, in detail, the importance of the thematic breaks in a text. For this purpose, a new tool has been developed that allows subject judges to indicate easily the subjective structure they discern in a text. This technique offers the opportunity to study the role of temporal indicators in marking the structure of narratives. Corpus analyses and experimental research are de-

201

scribed that show that speakers and writers use adverbial phrases, such as *around two o'clock*, to highlight the most important shifts in their narratives; they use connectives like *then* for the intermediate breaks and *and* to signal a locus of high continuity. The confirmation of these hypotheses allows consideration of the acquisition of the ability to organize discourse, both cognitively and linguistically.

SEGMENTATION MARKER

The idea of a *segmentation marker* was introduced in a study by Ehrich and Koster (1983). They asked subjects to describe, from memory, the model of a studio room they had previously seen. The furnishings of the studio were arranged in four distinct areas or blocks. All the descriptions mirrored this segmentation, because subjects mentioned all the pieces of furniture that belonged to a particular block before they described the next block. More importantly, Ehrich and Koster showed that their subjects used linguistic devices to highlight this segmentation in their discourse. The description of a block was systematically built in the following way: *Against the back wall*, there is a cupboard, and, *to the right of this cupboard*, there is a chair. The first-mentioned piece of furniture of each block was localized with reference to the studio space; in contrast, the following pieces mentioned within the same block were localized with reference to the previously introduced ones. The first spatial marker referred to the configuration of the room and occurred at the beginning of the block; it marked *discourse discontinuity*. The second spatial marker referred to an element already localized and occured within the block; it marked *discourse continuity*.

The Discourse Function of Segmentation Marker

Why do speakers and writers use segmentation markers? The answer can be found in a core characteristic of language: Its linear nature forces the message to be organized sequentially. Levelt (1981, 1989) discussed how this linearization problem is addressed by speakers through selection of the best order of mention. However, correctly ordering the information does not suffice to result in efficient communication. With their discourse, speakers enable the addressees to reconstruct the multidimensional or hierarchical organization of the discourse content. Even in narratives, the mere juxtaposition of statements cannot convey the greater or lesser proximity between items, in example, the existence of episodes that closely group connected elements into a block and separate them from other blocks (Bamberg & Marchman, 1991).

This segmentation problem, inherent in linearization, is even more obvious when considered from the addressee's point of view. Understanding a text is generally seen as an incremental process in which new sentences are integrated with the preceding sentences to construct a coherent mental representation of the text content. This strategy has been stated as a default principle of comprehension, called the *nextness principle* (Ochs, 1979) or the *principle of continuity* in which "readers assume, by default, that continuity is maintained" (Segal, Duchan, & Scott, 1991, p. 32). Following the *given-new contract* (Clark & Haviland, 1977), speakers or authors are expected to produce their discourse in such a way that addressees can apply the nextness principle. However, writers and speakers sometimes prevent readers and listeners from applying this principle directly, typically, when a new topic is introduced in the discourse. When there is a topic shift, the new sentence is, by definition, not directly connected to the previous sentences, and the nextness strategy is ill-advised. According to the Gricean maxims of communication (Grice, 1975), authors are expected to inform addressees that continuity with the preceding part of the discourse is not preserved. The lexicosyntactic devices that ensure cohesion (e.g., coreference, the use of definite vs. indefinite articles, and the use of pronouns) cannot perform this function, because it is only their lack that would signal a discontinuity. *Segmentation markers* that explicitly signal discontinuities in the content of the discourse, and thus establish negative connections, would solve this problem.

These kinds of devices belong to the general class of *discourse markers* (Redeker, 1991; Schiffrin, 1987) that include *cue phrases* such as *now* or *first* (Grosz, Pollack, & Sidner, 1989) and *text-signaling devices*, such as headings, pointer words, or typographical cues (Lorch, 1989). In general terms, discourse markers point out specific aspects of the content of a text or express the semantic and pragmatic connections between discourse segments. The term *segmentation markers* is used to refer more specifically to the second function of signaling discourse continuity or discourse discontinuity.

Punctuation marks are certainly the best prototype of segmentation markers (Fayol, this volume; Hofmann, 1989). They are organized along a continuum that corresponds to the strength of the link they signal: indentation, full-stop, comma, or space (no mark). However, the main question to be addressed here is whether speakers and writers have access, in addition to using these punctuation marks, to sets of *lexicosyntactic markers* that allow them to signal breaks of varying levels of importance.

The existence of such segmentation markers was suggested by the spatial description of Ehrich and Koster (1983). As just reported, they observed that sentences that introduced a description of a new area in the studio systematically started with spatial anchors while block-internal sentences were linked by sequential expressions. At the syntactic level, the initial sentences were very often independent main clauses, whereas the others were dependent constructions. Another device that speakers used to signal discontinuity was to explicitly break down the cohesion of their discourse. The best known device of this kind was the renominalization of an anaphor. In narratives, pronouns support thematic unity. They systematically refer to the main character (Karmiloff-Smith, 1981; Marslen-Wilson, Levy, & Tyler, 1982). However, this rule has an important exception. Authors may use nominal anaphora to refer to the main character when there is a topic shift (Clancy, 1980; Fox 1987; Vonk, Hustinx, & Simons, 1992).

These two instances of segmentation markers have the same limitation. They are all-or-none devices. They do not allow signaling at more than two different levels in the flow of discourse: continuity or discontinuity. But can speakers and writers not use sets of linguistic devices to highlight more than two different levels of continuity–discontinuity in a discourse? To examine this hypothesis, a set of linguistic devices must be defined that can function as segmentation markers, and the segmentation of a discourse in large as well as in small units must be determined.

Temporal Markers of Segmentation

The distribution of connectives and other lexical segmentation markers is determined by the discourse type (Bronckart, Bain, Schneuwly, Davaud, & Pasquier, 1985; Costermans & Bestgen, 1991). Empirical studies by Bestgen and Costermans (1994), focused on narratives, and, more precisely, on accounts of the events of a day. Bronckart (1985), in studying similar narratives, observed that these accounts were very rich in temporal expressions. Moreover, in this type of discourse, events are very often reported according to their real order of occurrence. Temporal expressions should, consequently, be highly relevant to the underlying structure of narratives.

Linguistic and psycholinguistic studies have shown that the simplest way for speakers or writers to express the temporal relation between successive actions or events is to put two subsequent actions in two, juxtaposed sentences as in, "I woke up. I had breakfast." Since Reichenbach's (1947) seminal work, a number of writers have named this strategy, the *default process*. This simple strategy indicates implicitly that the second event follows the first (Dowty, 1986; Hinrichs, 1986; Partee, 1984). It can be modulated to highlight the continuity or the discontinuity of actions or events by introducing a connective between the two sentences (Fayol, 1986; Segal et al., 1991). For continuity, the preferred connective is the asymmetrical *and* (Lakoff, 1971). For discontinuity, preferred connectives are *then, next,* or *afterwards.* These devices place the second (new) event in relation to the preceding one by using an *intrinsic time scale* that is internal to the narrative. However, the devices only give partial information about the temporal organization of the narrative; the amount of time spent in each action must be determined by the context (Moens & Steedman, 1988). Speakers and writers can improve on this organization by using an absolute reference framework that indicates, explicitly, the time of the day when an action started (e.g., "around 10 o'clock"). Following Ehrich and Koster's 1983 analysis of spatial markers in description, this kind of temporal expression can be called an *anchorage marker* as it anchors the starting time of an action in an absolute time scale external to the narrative. It is worth noting that, by considering anchorage markers, we deviate from the traditional definition of discourse markers that restricts them to devices that do not add to the content of the text (Lorch, 1989; Grosz et al., 1989).

DISCOURSE SEGMENTATION

To test the prediction that speakers and writers use the various temporal expressions described here to highlight the structure of their discourse, the structure must be examined independently. Moreover, this determination must be realized with great precision, because it is predicted that specific markers signal the most important discontinuities, whereas others signal less important discontinuities.

In specific types of discourse, such as description, certain physical parameters (e.g., the distance between the objects to be described) allow one to predict this conceptual structure, especially if the material is generated by the experimenter (Ehrich & Koster, 1983; Levelt, 1981). Outside the spatial field, however, the definition of the discourse structure becomes much more uncertain. One way to remedy this need is to ask subjects to define the structure they understand in a text or in an experimental material, already independently proposed by psycholinguists (Butterworth, 1975) and social psychologists (Dickman, 1963; Newtson, 1973). To gather this type of data, two options are available (see Bestgen, 1992b for a discussion on other procedures). Usually, researchers ask subjects to segment the materials according to their perceptions. The logic of this procedure is that some subjects take into account only the most important discontinuities, whereas other judges segment more often by taking into account the small discontinuities. Combining the data from several subjects allows one to determine the complete structure.

A more efficient way to gather such data is to use a task that permits the determination of the complete hierarchical structure perceived by each subject (Bestgen, 1992b). Instead of indicating the segments they perceive, subjects are asked to determine the importance of every possible break by physically spacing the sentences that make up the text (Bestgen, 1992b) or the pictures that form the experimental materials (Bestgen, 1992a). This technique allows the computation of an intersubject agreement coefficient and a comparison between groups of subjects based on age, for instance. It also permits study of the metacognitive knowledge that people have about the structure of a discourse or about its underlying content. Such knowledge is, at least partially, postulated by the view of segmentation markers as signals explicitly addressed to listeners and readers.

Finally, this second approach allows study of the principles that determine the structure of a narrative; it manipulates parameters that may affect the perceived structure. For instance, Bestgen & Costermans (1994) studied the effect of two principles (i.e., the similarity between the actions or events and the changes in location) on the structure of narratives. A first experiment showed that the similarity between the actions or events determined, to a large extent, the structure perceived. Subjects received ordered lists of statements that described a person's activities during an afternoon. One group rated the similarity of two activities described in consecutive statements, whereas the second group indicated the natural hierarchical divisions in the activities. Comparison of these two tasks showed that the similarity ratings were highly correlated ($r > 0.90$) with the hierarchical divisions. In a second experiment, major or minor changes in location were introduced into the statement lists before either an important break or a weak break. Subjects indicated the hierarchical divisions within the sequences. Results suggested that hierarchical judgments were affected by the place changes, and major changes of location systematically produced a perception of a deeper break. However, these changes did not globally modify the structure perceived by the subjects. The positions of the most important breaks, as identified in the first study, did not change.

TEMPORAL EXPRESSION
AS SEGMENTATION MARKERS

Once the set of possible markers have been selected and tools for the determination of the discourse segmentation are available, hypotheses on the use of temporal expressions by speakers and writers can be formulated. The first hypothesis states that temporal expressions highlight the structure of the discourse: anchorage and sequence expressions are inserted before a topic discontinuity in the narrative, whereas no temporal expression or the connective *and* is the rule in case of continuity. In other words, temporal expressions play the same function in narratives as spatial expressions in description (Ehrich & Koster, 1983) and renominalization in biographical texts. A second and more central hypothesis asserts that temporal expressions can be discriminated according to the importance of the continuity–discontinuity they signal: Anchorage markers highlight the most important discontinuity, sequence markers mark less important discontinuity, and the connective *and* signals a greater continuity than when no temporal expression is inserted.

These hypotheses were examined in a study (Costermans & Bestgen, 1991) in which two complementary approaches were used. A corpus analysis that tracked the existence of these phenomena in a relatively natural situation and a confirmatory experiment in which the structure of discourse was controlled. All the experiments reported used native, French-speaking subjects.

Corpus Analysis

The data for the corpus analysis were narratives gathered from 42 subjects who were recorded as they recounted what they had done on the previous day, a Sunday.

The first step of the analysis was to divide the narratives into statements, each of which set forth one event, and to localize the temporal expressions. To determine the structure of each narrative, 19 subjects were asked to judge and regroup the events to bring out the general organization of the day. The importance of break before each statement ranged from 0 (nobody splits this statement from the preceding one) to 19 (every judge localizes a break between this statement and the previous one).

The question to be answered was whether statements that included a temporal expression were preceded by a more important break than statements that did not include such an expression. It was also essential to compare the depth of the break before a statement that contained an anchor (e.g., *around two o'clock*) or a sequence marker (e.g., *then*).

Results are reported on Table 10.1. The mean depths of the break were significantly different following the presence or absence of a temporal expression. This observation agreed with the first hypothesis. The second hypothesis was not confirmed. First, even if the difference in the depth of the break between *and* statements and no-marker statements was statistically non significant, this difference was in the wrong direction. Second, there was no difference in favor of the anchorage marker, with a qualification. A more careful analysis of the

Bestgen and Costermans

TABLE 10.1
Mean Depth of the Breaks Before Sentences Including
the Temporal Markers (Corpus Analysis)

	And	*No Marker*	*Sequence*	*Anchorage*
Mean depth	4.65	3.40	7.79	7.68

anchorage expressions showed this class was not homogenous. Forty-two out of 120 anchors (35%) were observed in front of a statement such as, "around 4 o'clock, I read the newspaper," whereas others were at the end of statements, such as "I read the newspaper *around 4 o'clock*". As it is suggested that a linguistic device must appear in front of a sentence to behave as a discourse marker (Redeker, 1991; Schiffrin, 1987), only anchors in front of a sentence should signal a high discontinuity. The mean depth of the breaks that preceded statements was 10.57 if the anchor was at the beginning, and 5.87 if it was at the end of the statement. When the anchor was in front of the statement, it was far more powerful than sequence markers in signaling the most important discontinuities, as predicted by the second hypothesis.

Experimental Study

To control more efficiently the content and the complexity of the narratives produced by the subjects, 16 subjects received a list of statements that set out a prearranged sequence of activities. The activities were selected in such a way as to be easily grouped and organized hierarchically. As noted in Fig. 10.1, the breaks had four different levels: the first level corresponded to a shift between two closely linked sentences, the fourth level to those breaks that segmented the list into three main episodes.

The subjects' task was to write a short narrative based on these narratives. The texts produced by the subjects were broken up in such a way that the list of activities was recovered. The sentences that set out these activities now contained two particularly interesting cues: the temporal markers and the various punctuation marks. It was thus possible to determine the efficiency of temporal markers by comparing it to the efficiency of the punctuation marks.

Categories used for the examination of the punctuation included the paragraph, the full-stop, the comma, and the absence of any punctuation mark. Fig. 10.2 shows the distribution of these marks in relation to the depth of the breaks. It can be seen that the paragraph was reserved essentially for the most important breaks (i.e., the fourth level). The full-stop had a more general usage, but was evident in association with the intermediate breaks. The comma did not appear

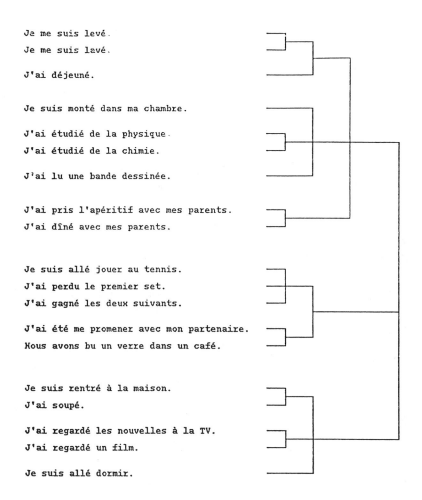

Je me suis levé.
Je me suis lavé.

J'ai déjeuné.

Je suis monté dans ma chambre.

J'ai étudié de la physique.
J'ai étudié de la chimie.

J'ai lu une bande dessinée.

J'ai pris l'apéritif avec mes parents.
J'ai dîné avec mes parents.

Je suis allé jouer au tennis.
J'ai perdu le premier set.
J'ai gagné les deux suivants.

J'ai été me promener avec mon partenaire.
Nous avons bu un verre dans un café.

Je suis rentré à la maison.
J'ai soupé.

J'ai regardé les nouvelles à la TV.
J'ai regardé un film.

Je suis allé dormir.

English translation : (1) I got up. (2) I washed myself. (3) I had breakfast. (4) I went up to my room. (5) I studied some physics. (6) I studied some chemistry. (7) I read a comic book. (8) I had an aperitif with my parents. (9) I had lunch with my parents. (10) I went to play tennis. (11) I lost the first set. (12) I won the following two. (13) I went for a walk with my partner. (14) We had a drink in a bar. (15) I went home. (16) I had supper. (17) I watched the news on the TV. (18) I watched a film. (19) I went to bed.

FIG. 10.1. Canvass used in the experimental study. From Costermans & Bestgen (1991). Reprinted with permission.

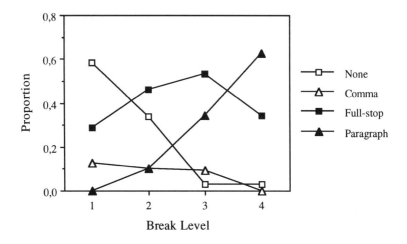

FIG. 10.2. Proportions of the punctuation marks as a function of the break level.

frequently in the material and was most often associated with the lowest level as was the case for the complete absence of punctuation marks.

Temporal expressions were coded by distinguishing four cases: anchorage marker, sequence marker, *and*, and sentences containing no marker at all. In Fig. 10.3, it can be seen that the anchorage markers were observed mainly in the sentences that followed the most important breaks, the sequence markers in the sentences that followed intermediate breaks, and the absence of temporal expression, as well as the connective *and*, in the locus of high continuity.

This experiment confirmed that temporal expressions were used by speakers and writers to highlight the structure of their narratives and that some expressions were used for the more important breaks, whereas others were used for intermediate breaks. These observations were replicated in a second study with two different lists of activities (Bestgen & Costermans, 1994). In that study also, temporal expressions were as efficient as punctuation marks as signals of the segmentation of discourse. The segmentation power of the markers that spans from the strongest segmentation markers (i.e., the anchors) to the continuity marker (i.e., *and*) via the sequence and the no-marker condition, was observed as well.

Segmentation Markers and Cognitive Structure: Developmental Aspects

Clearly, adults use temporal expressions to underline the structure of their discourse. Such competence rests on at least two abilities. Authors must take into account the structure of the content they want to express, and they must know the mapping between each marker of the set and its continuity–discontinuity power. But when are these two abilities acquired by children? Because the problems experienced by children in the management of the global organization of their discourse is well known (Fayol, 1986; Jisa, 1987; Karmiloff-Smith, 1981; Scardamalia & Bereiter, 1987), one should not expect a very early development of the use of segmentation markers to signal discourse structure.

To answer this question, the development of a child's capacity to organize discourse both cognitively and linguistically (Bestgen, 1992a) was examined. Children in first grade (N = 19, mean age 6;7), third grade (N = 19, mean age 8;6) and sixth grade (N = 17, mean age 11;6), as well as university students (N = 20, mean age 21) viewed a series of 19 pictures reporting the anthropomorphic activities of a little bear during one day and a half. First, they were asked to tell a narrative based on the pictures. They had to follow strictly the sequence of the pictures, but they could add other activities and mention where, when, and why things happened. Then, they were asked to indicate the structure they perceived in the sequence of activities. They had to localize the most important breaks between the pictures, then the less important breaks, and so on.

The intersubject agreement of the subjective structure (Siegel, 1956) was high for each of the four groups, but higher for the 12-years-olds (0.52) and for the adults (0.57) than for the 7- (0.41) and the 9-years-olds (0.43). The analysis of the depth of structure perceived by each subject was very informative in that subjects perceived a more or less fine-grained structure in the narratives. Some

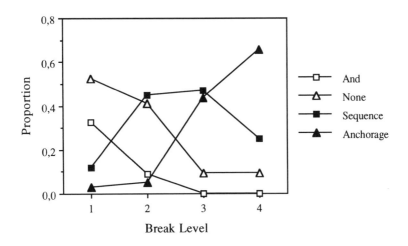

FIG. 10.3 Proportions of the temporal markers as a function of the break level.

of them proposed a structure that took into account only two levels: Between every pair of contiguous pictures, there was or was not a break, but all the breaks had the same importance. In this case, they perceived a structure with a depth of two. Other subjects considered that the breaks had unequal importance and so constructed three, four or more levels. The number of different levels discriminated by a subject was used as an index of the depth of the structure perceived.

Table 10.2 reports the distribution of the range of levels as a function of the age of the subjects. There was a highly significant monotone tendency; each group was different from the two contiguous ones (by a test for ranked data). The older the subjects were, the more fine-grained was the structure reported. More importantly, the majority of 7-year-old children perceived only a dichotomous structure.

What about temporal markers of segmentation? Would a similar evolution be observed? Before the subjects had to indicate the structure they perceived in the nonverbal material, they were asked to tell a narrative based on the pictures. They had to follow strictly the sequence of pictures, but they could add other activities, mention where, when, and why things happened.

The temporal expressions were analyzed as in the previous experiment. The hierarchical structure of the sequence of pictures as determined by the subjects in the segmentation task, was split into three break levels. Table 10.3 reports the distribution of the temporal markers as a function of the level of the break. It can be seen that adults used the temporal markers in a way very similar to the subjects of the previous studies, but this was clearly not the case for 7-year-old children. They functioned locally, processing each picture independently, inserting sometimes a *then*, sometimes an *and*, and sometimes nothing between two statements. The only use noted was the adequate use of the very few anchorage markers they introduced into their narratives. Nine-year-old children used a more global strategy. The anchor was used where the breaks were very important, at the sequence marker for the intermediate level,

TABLE 10.2
Distribution of the Range of Structural Level Discriminated
in the Picture Sequence as a Function of Age.

Number of levels used	First Grade	Third Grade	Sixth Grade	Adults
2	12	6	0	0
3	5	10	11	6
4	1	2	6	10
5	0	0	0	4

TABLE 10.3
Percentages of Temporal Markers as a Function of the Break Level
and the Age of Subjects

	Level	And	No marker	Sequence	Anchorage
	1	9	58	31	1
First Grade	2	5	62	32	1
	3	5	55	27	13
	1	16	54	30	0
Third Grade	2	9	33	49	10
	3	6	28	35	31
	1	13	67	19	1
Sixth Grade	2	7	34	47	12
	3	5	26	34	35
	1	16	54	29	1
Adults	2	15	20	37	28
	3	7	13	30	50

whereas an absence of temporal expressions was noted where the continuity was high. The same pattern was observed for the older children; their use of the temporal expressions was quite similar to their use by adult subjects.

CONCLUSION

This chapter reported on a series of studies that showed that speakers and writers, as young as 9 years old, used temporal expressions to highlight the structure of their narratives. The functional organization of the temporal markers (i.e., the anchorage markers, the sequence markers (*then* and other temporal adverbs), no temporal expression, and *and*) is summarized in Fig. 10.4. The vertical dimension displays the strength with which subjects highlighted the (dis)continuity in narratives. The horizontal dimension splits the devices after the framework used to express temporality: internal for the first three devices, external for the anchorage marker.

This organization was derived from the study of a specific type of narrative, although it can be generalized to other types of narratives and to other types of discourse. The opposition "and / no marker / then" seems very general; it has been observed in several types of narratives (Segal et al, 1991; Fayol, 1986) and in procedural and argumentative discourse (Caron-Pargue & Caron, 1989; Schiffrin, 1987; Schneuwly, 1988). The case for the anchorage marker is less

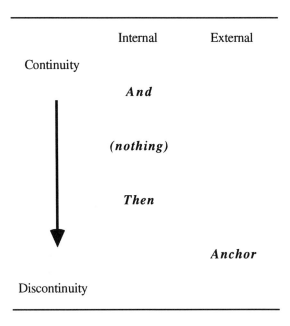

FIG. 10.4.   Functional organization of the four temporal devices. From Bestgen & Vonk (1995). Reprinted with permission.

clear-cut. On the one hand, the segmentation function of the time indicators is obviously limited to discourse in which such information is relevant (i.e., event narration). On the other hand, this category of anchorage markers has been observed in description (e.g., Ehrich and Koster's spatial anchor). In a more general point of view, anchorage markers correspond to the beaconing signals advocated by Schneuwly and by Fayol (this volume) that express the starting point of a text and mark the central step of its unfolding.

An important question not yet addressed is why temporal expressions are suited for playing the role of a segmentation marker. To propose an answer, two other lexicosyntactic devices as considered: spatial expression (Ehrich & Koster, 1983) and renominalizing of the main character (Vonk et al., 1992). What is common to these three devices is that they are the linguistic expressions of segmentation principles ruling narratives. Grimes (1975), for instance, proposed four segmentation principles based on the units of time, space, character, and theme; a change in one of these introduces a narrative break. The same idea can be found in the work of van Dijk on the episode (van Dijk, 1982). From a historical point a view, it has been suggested that these principles may go back to the three units of the classical tragedies originating in Aristotle's work (Bray, 1931).

A more psycholinguistic expression of these principles can be found in Gernsbacher's structure building framework (1990, see also Gernsbacher, this volume). In this framework model, comprehension rests on three processes that allow the construction of a mental structure based on the information being comprehended: the processes of *laying a foundation*, *mapping*, and *shifting*. The first words of a text are used to lay the foundation for the first substructure. Then new information is mapped onto this substructure providing that this new information is sufficiently coherent with the previous information. If this is not the case, readers shift and initiate a new substructure. The mapping process, which allows the size of the ongoing substructure to increase, is facilitated by referential, temporal, spatial, and causal coherence. Conversely, readers are expected to shift from the current substructure to a new substructure when there is a break in these sources of coherence or when the possibility of such a break is expressed in the discourse. For Gernsbacher's framework, the simple presence of *then* or *next* inserted at the beginning of a sentence triggers readers and listeners to shift and lay a foundation for a new substructure. *Adverbial leads*, as she calls these devices, are instances of the segmentation markers studied here, even if they are not the strongest ones.

Comprehension theories, which put the accent on the need to construct a mental model of what the text is about, also give the segmentation markers an important function. They suggest that readers build their mental model from a specific point of view that determines the "here-and-now" point of the narrative (Bower & Morrow, 1990; Segal et al., 1991). When reading, this here-and-now focus center interprets the new sentences, but also decides what information should be kept in the foreground. When there is an episode shift in the narratives, readers update the "here-and-now" pointer to facilitate the integration of the new information (Morrow, Bower, & Greenspan, 1989). By specifying the temporal, spatial, and casting setting, authors facilitate this updating (Chafe, 1979; Segal et al., 1991).

Thus, theoretical and empirical arguments support the idea that speakers and writers must use, and actually do use, a set of segmentation markers to signal discontinuity in their discourse. What is needed now is evidence that these segmentation markers are helpful for the comprehenders as postulated by the marker-as-signal view (Bestgen & Vonk, 1993). Recent data (Vonk et al., 1992) confirms this comprehension function of segmentation markers by investigating the discourse function of referential expressions that give more information than needed to identify the referent (such as a noun phrase when a pronominal anaphor is sufficient). Results confirmed that these overspecified expressions can act as segmentation markers. Next, the impact of these expressions on discourse processing was examined, using a probe recognition task that directly tapped the accessibility of words encountered in the preceding part of a text. Vonk et al., (1992), found that preceding words were less available to the reader after an overspecified expression; readers took more time to say that they had seen a given word after such an overspecified expression. Replication of these results by Bestgen and Vonk (1995) in three experiments in which temporal expressions, such as *around two o'clock* or *then*, were used as segmentation markers, illustrate the helpfulness of these markers, confirming the marker-as-signal concept, and the role of temporal markers in narrative structure.

This study showed that the role of temporal markers in comprehension parallels their role in production. Anchorage markers heavily reduced the availability of previous information while *and* had less effect.

REFERENCES

Bamberg, M., & Marchman, V. (1991). Binding and unfolding: Towards the linguistic construction of narrative discourse. *Discourse Processes, 14,* 277–305.

Bestgen, Y. (1992a). Structure cognitive et marquage linguistique de la narration: étude développementale. *Archives de Psychologie, 60,* 25–44.

Bestgen, Y. (1992b). Le textomètre : un outil pour l'étude de la structure du discours et de son marquage. *Psychologica Belgica, 32,* 141–167.

Bestgen, Y., & Costermans, J. (1994). Time, space, and action : Exploring the narrative structure and its linguistic marking. *Discourse Processes, 17,* 421–446.

Bestgen, Y., & Vonk, W. (1993, May). *The role of segmentation marks on discourse processing.* Poster session presented at the annual meeting of the Belgian Psychology Society, Ghent, Belgium.

Bestgen, Y., & Vonk, W. (1995) The role of temporal segmentation markers in discourse processing. *Discourse Processes, 19,* 385–406.

Bower, G. H., & Morrow, D. G. (1990) Mental models in narrative comprehension. *Science, 247,* 44–48.

Bray, R. (1931). *La doctrine classique en France.* Lausanne: Payot.

Bronckart, J. P. (1985). Les opérations temporelles dans deux types de textes d'enfant. *Bulletin de Psychologie, 38,* 653–666.

Bronckart, J. P., Bain, D., Schneuwly, B., Davaud, C., & Pasquier, A. (1985). *Le fonctionnement des discours.* Neuchâtel: Delachaux & Niestlé.

Butterworth, B. (1975). Hesitation and semantic planning in speech. *Journal of Psycholinguistic Research, 4,* 75–87.

Caron-Pargue, J., & Caron, J. (1989). Processus psycholinguistiques et analyse des verbalisations dans une tâche cognitive. *Archives de Psychologie, 57,* 3–32.

Chafe, W. (1979). The flow of thought and the flow of language. In T. Givón (Ed.), *Syntax and Semantics (XII): Discourse and Syntax* (pp. 9–50). New York: Academic Press.

Clancy, P. M. (1980). Referential choice in English and Japanese narrative discourse. In W. Chafe (Ed.), *The pear stories: Cognitive, cultural, and linguistic aspects of narrative production* (pp.127–198). Norwood: Ablex.

Clark, H. H., & Havilland, S. E. (1977). Comprehension and the given-new contract. In R. O. Freedle (ed.), *Discourse production and comprehension* (pp. 1–40). Norwood: Ablex.

Costermans, J., & Bestgen, Y. (1991). The role of temporal markers in the segmentation of narrative discourse. *CPC: European Bulletin of Cognitive Psychology*, 11, 349–370.

Dickman, H. G. (1963). The Perception of Behavioral Units. In Barker, R. G. (Ed.), *The stream of behavior* (pp. 23–41). New York: Appleton-Century-Crofts.

Dowty, D. (1986). The effect of aspectual class on the temporal structure of discourse. *Linguistics and Philosophy*, 9, 37–61.

Ehrich, V., & Koster, C. (1983). Discourse organisation and sentence form: the structure of room description in Dutch. *Discourse Processes*, 6, 169–195.

Fayol, M. (1986). Les connecteurs dans les récits écrits. *Pratiques*, 49, 101–114.

Fox, B. A. (1987). Morpho-syntactic markedness and discourse structure. *Journal of Pragmatics*, 11, 359–375.

Gernsbacher, M. A. (1990). *Language Comprehension as Structure Building*. Hillsdale: Lawrence Erlbaum Associates.

Grice, H. P. (1975). Logic and conversation. In P. Cole & J. L. Morgan (Eds.), Syntax on semantics, Vol. III: *Speech acts* (pp. 41–58). New York: Academic Press.

Grimes, J. E. (1975). *The Thread of Discourse*. The Hague: Mouton.

Grosz, B .J., Pollack, M. E., & Sidner, C. L. (1989). Discourse. In M. I. Posner (Ed.), *Foundations of cognitive science* (pp. 437–468). Cambridge: MIT press.

Hinrichs, E. (1986). Temporal Anaphora in discourses of English. *Linguistics and Philosophy*, 9, 63–82.

Hofmann, T. R. (1989). Paragraphs, and anaphora. *Journal of Pragmatics*, 13, 239–250.

Jisa, H. (1987). Sentence connectors in French children's monologue performance. *Journal of Pragmatics*, 11, 607–621.

Karmiloff-Smith, A. (1981). The grammatical marking of thematic structure in the development of language production. In W. Deutsch (Ed.), *The child's construction of language* (pp.123–147). New York: Academic Press.

Lakoff, R. (1971). If's, and's, and but's about conjunction. In C. J. Fillmore & D. T. Langendoen (Eds.), *Studies in linguistic semantics* (pp.114–149). New York: Holt, Rinehart, & Winston.

Levelt, W. J. M. (1981). The speaker's linearization problem. *Philosophical Transactions of the Royal Society of London*, B295, 305–315.

Levelt, W. J. M. (1989). *Speaking: From intention to articulation*. Cambridge: MIT Press.

Lorch, R. F. (1989). Text-signaling devices and their effects on reading and memory processes. *Educational Psychology Review*, 1, 209–234.

Marslen-Wilson, W. D., Levy, E., & Tyler, L. K. (1982). Producing interpretable discourse: The establishment and maintenance of reference. In R. J. Jarvella & W. Klein (Eds.), *Speech, place and action* (pp.339–378). New York: Wiley.

Moens, M. & Steedman, M. (1988). Temporal ontology in natural language. *Computational Linguistics*, 14, 15–28.

Morrow, D. G., Bower, G. H., & Greenspan, S. (1989). Updating situation models during narrative comprehension. *Journal of Memory and Language*, 27, 292–312.

Newtson, D. (1973). Attribution and the unit of perception of ongoing behavior. *Journal of Personality and Social Psychology*, 28, 28–38.

Ochs, E. (1979). Planned and unplanned discourse. In T. Givón (Ed.), *Syntax and Semantics (XII): Discourse and Syntax* (pp.51–80). New York: Academic Press.

Partee, H. B. (1984). Nominal and temporal anaphora. *Linguistics and Philosophy*, 7, 243–286.

Redeker, G. (1991). Linguistic markers of discourse structure. *Linguistics*, 29, 1139–1172.

Reichenbach, H. (1947). *Symbolic logic*. Berkeley: University of California.

Scardamalia, M., & Bereiter, C. (1987). Knowledge telling and knowledge transforming in written composition. In S. Rosenberg (Ed.), *Advances in applied Psycholinguistic (II): Reading, writing and language learning* (pp.142–175). Cambridge: Cambridge University Press.

Schiffrin, D. (1987). *Discourse markers*. Cambridge: Cambridge University Press.

Schneuwly, B. (1988). *Le langage écrit chez l'enfant*. Neuchâtel: Delachaux & Niestlé.

Segal, E.M., Duchan, J. F., & Scott, P. T. (1991). The role of interclausal connectives in narrative structuring: Evidence from adults' interpretations of simple stories. *Discourse Processes, 14,* 27–54.

Siegel, S. (1956) Nonparametric statistics for the behavioral sciences. New York: McGraw Hill.

van Dijk, T. A. (1982). Episodes as units of discourse analysis. In D. Tannen (Ed.), Analysing discourse: text and talk (pp. 177–195). Washington: Georgetown University Press.

Vonk, W., Hustinx, L. G. M. M., & Simons, W .H. G. (1992). The use of referential expressions in structuring discourse. *Language and Cognitive Processes, 7,* 301–333.

Part IV

BEYOND THE COHESION–SEGMENTATION DICHOTOMY

The last three chapters each develop an original global conception about the structuring of the discourse or text and the linguistic devices. The first one faces the problem of the relationship between the status of the textual information and the types of markers available to signal this status in different languages and at different levels of development. The second one examines the relationships between a limited set of markers, the textual organizers, and the social context of the text production. The third is an attempt to provide an assessment of the procedural conception of the use of connectives in comprehension.

In chapter 11, Hickmann recalls that a few general universal guidelines drive the information flow in discourse production/comprehension. One such guideline is to distinguish foreground and background information; another one is to distinguish given and new information in view of the mutual knowledge that the speakers may have. She also recalls that the languages differ as to the linguistic devices (local vs. global) available for these purposes. Thus, the relative contribution of the different markers can only be examined according to each language, which leads to a cross-linguistic approach. The developmental perspective is especially well suited to bring forward the way in which a particular language uses various linguistic tools to ensure various functions. In this perspective, Hickmann reports a series of results about the acquisition of the time and aspect of the verb and about the use of referring expressions and clause structure. The cross-linguistic studies show that, beyond the diversity of their marking systems, the various languages allow their users to discriminate the given from the new and the foreground from the background information.

In chapter 12, Schneuwly proposes a view on language production according to which a test, if it is a strongly organized linguistic unit, includes a set of cues indicating that it is the product of a speech action realized in a given social context. Thus, the textual organizers are traces of the linearization processes and of the connecting operations that organize the clauses into hierarchical structures. The class of textual organizers includes the coordinators, the conjunctions, part of the adverbial phrases and certain prepositional phrases. Their functions are the marking of structural levels (beaconing), the integration of strongly linked units (packaging), and the maintenance of the continuity of the production process (linking). Schneuwly backs up his views by studying the configuration of textual organizers as they appear in different types of texts (narratives and descriptions), at various ages and in various languages.

In chapter 13, Townsend draws up an assessment of the effect of connectives on comprehension. He considers that text comprehension implies several dimensions. First, the base unit of the treatment would be the proposition. Then, comprehension would require the accounting of associations that could be directly activated (between words, events, and sequences of facts), on the one hand, and of structural information-inducing computation bearing on the relations between the items activated by association, on the other. Finally, listeners/readers would have limited resources at their disposal, which would oblige them to draw their attention to the information either of the associative or of the structural type. In this general context, the connectives appear to belong to the structural treatment and to focus the comprehender's attention on the structural aspects in a more or less decisive way. To illustrate his views, Townsend reports on a series of experimental results. These show that different connectives (in particular, causal vs. adversative connectives) differently steer the online allocation of the cognitive resources. In other words, during comprehension, the previous knowledge (i.e., associations) interact with the structural treatment, as induced by the connectives. It follows that, according to what the subjects know and according to the interclause relations signaled by the connectives, the text representation built by the reader is more or less integrative.

�֎ Chapter 11

Information Status and Grounding in Children's Narratives: A Crosslinguistic Perspective

Maya Hickmann
CNRS, Université René Descartes, Paris

INTRODUCTION

During the course of language acquisition, children must learn to organize well-formed utterances according to syntactic and semantic rules, as well as to organize discourse according to pragmatic rules. This chapter focuses on the development of referential discourse cohesion with particular attention to two domains, temporal reference and reference to entities, and with a two-fold aim: to show how factors at both levels, the sentence and discourse, affect the acquisition of linguistic devices and to examine universal versus language-specific aspects of this development.

Discourse Cohesion

The production and comprehension of discourse requires that speakers rely on a number of organizing principles that go beyond isolated utterances. In particular, the well-formedness of utterances depends both on sentence-internal rules and on discourse rules governing the relations between utterances and their contexts of use. In all languages, a variety of devices are available and necessary to relate utterances to nonlinguistic and linguistic aspects of speech situations, for example, to indicate who speaks to whom, where, and when; about what focal information, and in relation to what shared knowledge.

Particular attention will be placed here on principles of organization that are necessary for discourse *cohesion*. Cohesive relations exist when the uses and interpretations of linguistic devices in a given utterance depend on linguistic devices in other utterances within the discourse (cf. Chafe, 1976; Halliday & Hasan, 1976). Discourse cohesion requires that speakers regulate information flow from utterance to utterance, following at least two general principles: they must mark the *status* of information in relation to mutual knowledge and *ground* information as a function of communicative focus. From each of these two principles follow various rules, either obligatory or optional in a given language, that partly determine how speakers use linguistic devices in different domains.

Although these principles apply to all speech situations, their relative importance in determining speakers' utterances varies as a function of whether the situation requires discourse-internal relations. For example, narratives produced in the absence of mutual knowledge illustrate situations that require a great deal of reliance on discourse-internal organization, that is, cases where a narrator talks about entities that are not known to interlocutors and recounts events they have not witnessed. In these cases, linguistic devices are necessary to regulate information in such a way that discourse becomes its own context, for example, referents that are not mutually known must be first introduced for subsequent discourse and the interlocutors' attention must be drawn to central information in relation to surrounding discourse. In contrast, situations that depend heavily on nonlinguistic context require less discourse-internal organization, for example, speech uttered in front of a counter of vegetables in a shopping situation. In these cases, reliance on linguistic or nonverbal deixis (e.g., demonstratives, labelings, and pointing) can be used efficiently, and interdependencies among utterances become less necessary. Note that reliance on discourse is a matter of degree (maximal in the former type of situation, minimal in the latter) and that it can be difficult to determine, with certainty, whether particular instances depend on linguistic or nonlinguistic context (Hickmann, 1987, 1991).

These general principles governing the regulation of information flow are universal. Regardless of their native language, all children must learn them to be able to communicate competently when maximal reliance on discourse is required. However, languages vary in the particular devices they make available to speakers for this regulation, presenting children with different problems to solve during the acquisition process. In this chapter, some relevant developmental crosslinguistic evidence is reviewed, following a brief summary of universal versus language-specific aspects of each principle (also see Hickmann, 1995).

Information Grounding in Discourse

All languages provide speakers with means of distinguishing the foreground and background of discourse. Roughly, the foreground corresponds to chronologically ordered events, such as those that constitute the main plot line that makes a narrative move forward, whereas the background corresponds to more secondary situations, that need not be chronologically ordered, that surround the foreground. Temporal-aspectual systems are central to this discourse distinction, particularly the linguistic category of *aspect*. Aspect allows speakers to take two perspectives on situations: imperfective aspect views situations from within their temporal structure and presents them as ongoing, whereas perfective aspect views them from outside as undifferentiated points. Example 1 shows an opposition between a past perfective (*arrived*), which presents Mary's arrival as a point in the foreground, and an imperfective one (*was reading*), which presents Peter's reading as an ongoing event in the background. From this example, it can be inferred that Mary arrived at some point after Peter began reading the book but before he finished it. In contrast, the two perfective inflections in Example 2 (*read, arrived*) present successive foregrounded points, while the two imperfective ones in Example 3 (*was reading/cooking*) present two ongoing and overlapping events. As shown in Example 4 through Example 7, additional explicit markers contribute to different interpretations (*as, while, then, after*), as well as allow different clause orders, for example, Example 7. In this respect, Example 2, by default, presents events in their order of appearance in the real world, that is, in the absence of other markers; the order of foregrounded clauses is assumed to correspond to chronological order.

1. Peter was reading a book. Mary arrived.
2. Peter read a book. Mary arrived.
3. Peter was reading a book. Mary was cooking dinner.
4. Peter was reading a book as Mary arrived.
5. Mary arrived while Peter was reading a book.
6. Peter read a book, then Mary arrived.
7. Mary arrived after Peter read a book.

The opposition between perfective and imperfective aspect is universal, contributing in all languages to the grounding of information in discourse in conjunction with connectives and adverbials (Hopper, 1979). However, crosslinguistic variations exist in the particular systems of devices available (Comrie, 1976, 1985; Dahl, 1985). For example, in some languages verbal inflections mark not only *aspect*, but also the deictic category of tense, which relates the time of denoted events to speech time or to some other reference point established in discourse, for example, the past tenses in Examples 1–7 indicate that events occurred before speech time. In contrast, a language such as Chinese has practically no morphology, including no grammaticalized tense forms; it optionally marks the time of events by means of adverbials and aspect by means of particles or adverbials (e.g., the perfective particle, *le*, and the imperfective particle, *zhe*). In addition, whereas English provides an imperfective progressive (*-ing*) with all tenses (*he is/ was/ will be running*, etc.), French and German provide aspectual oppositions only in the past, that is, perfective versus imperfective in French (*il courut or il a couru* ['he ran/has run'] versus *il courait* ['he was running']) or perfective versus aspectually unmarked in German (*er ist gelaufen* ['he has run'] versus *er lief* ['he ran/was running']). Both languages neutralize aspect in the present (*il court/er läuft* ['he runs/is running']), except for optional periphrastic constructions explicitly marking the imperfective progressive (*il est en train de courir* ['he is in the course of running'] and *er is dabei zu laufen* ['he is at this moment running']).

Finally, aspect is also related to the predicate with which it is combined within the clause. In particular, aspectual markings partly depend on universal cognitive categories of situations encoded by predicates. These predicates vary along several semantic dimensions, such as durativity, that is, whether they represent situations as *punctual* (e.g., *explode*) or as *nonpunctual* (e.g., *be big, read a book*), and *boundedness*, that is, whether they denote situations as having an intrinsic terminal point (e.g., *run a mile, read a book, go to school*) or not (*run around, be big, know*) (Comrie, 1976; Cziko, 1986a; Smith, 1983; Vendler, 1967). These properties partly constrain the uses and interpretations of aspectual markers, for example, some inflections are impossible or odd with some verb types (**I'm knowing*), and the past perfective has a different meaning depending on predicate type: Completion with bounded predicates (the sentence *John ran a mile and left* implies that John ran an entire mile before leaving), but not with unbounded ones (*John ran around and left* merely implies that he stopped his activity of running before leaving). The uses of temporal-aspectual markings, then, depend both on clause-internal factors (predicate types) and on inter-clausal ones (relations among situations denoted in discourse).

Information Status in Discourse

The other principle governing the regulation of information flow in discourse concerns the status of denoted information in relation to mutual knowledge. In particular, speakers must mark whether the entities to which they refer are relatively new or given for their interlocutors at any given point in discourse

(Chafe, 1976; Clark & Haviland, 1976; Halliday & Hasan, 1976). For example, when speakers first mention referents that are not known to their interlocutors, they cannot use linguistic devices that presuppose their existence and identity. All languages provide two types of devices for this purpose: local devices, consisting typically of different types of noun phrases (NPs), and global ones affecting the entire utterance (word order and other aspects of clause structure). Thus, many languages provide an opposition between indefinite and definite noun phrases (NPs) marking the distinction between new and given information (among other functions), for example, English indefinite forms (*a man*) introduce new referents, whereas definite nominals (*the man*), pronouns (*he*), and zero elements (e.g., *he came in and ø greeted her*) maintain reference, thereafter. In addition, the marking of information status follows a universal principle, according to which new information is preferred toward the end of the utterance. As a result, speakers typically use various clause structures in which indefinite NPs occur after the verb, for example, objects in subject–verb–object (SVO) structures (Example 8), existentials (Example 9), or subject–verb inversions (Example 10).

    8. He saw a man behind the door.
    9. There was a man behind the door.
  10. Behind the door stood a man.

Although both types of devices are universally available to mark information status, languages rely on them differentially. The opposition between indefinite and definite nominal determiners is obligatory in English to distinguish new from given, whereas clause structure is entirely optional, e.g., new information can be preverbal (*A man stood behind the door*) as a function of verb–argument structure (preverbal subjects and postverbal objects). French is similar to English in this respect, providing an obligatory distinction between indefinite and definite determiners (un/une/des vs. le/la/les) and optional clause-structure variations similar to Example 8 through Example 10 to mark information status. However, in contrast to English, French partially grammaticalizes the given/new distinction because all clitic pronouns (subject or not) must be preverbal, while the position of nominals in the clause partially depends on verb-argument structure, for example, Example 11 versus Example 12. Furthermore, discourse factors frequently result in the dislocation of nominals to the left (Example 13) or to the right (Example 14). Analyses of such constructions (Lambrecht, 1981) show that they serve a number of functions, for example, left-dislocations typically promote NPs to the status of "topic," and they are constrained by information status; when reference is specific, only definite nominals (given information) can be dislocated, not indefinite ones (new information) as in Examples 15 and 16.[1]

11. Il l'a mangé. ('He[Sub] him[Obj] ate' —> 'He ate him').
12. Le chat a mangé le rat. ('The cat ate the rat').
13. Le chat, il a mangé le rat. ('The cat, he ate the rat').
14. Il a mangé le rat, le chat. ('He ate the rat, the cat').
15. *Un chat, il a mangé le rat. ('*A cat, he ate the rat').
16. *Il a mangé le rat, un chat. ('*He ate the rat, a cat').

An even more striking crosslinguistic variation is shown by the fact that nominal determiners are entirely optional in some languages. For example, although some nominal determiners exist in Chinese, potentially differentiating the new (numerals) from the given (demonstratives), these devices are optional and position in the clause is the only obligatory marking of information status; new information must be postverbal, whereas given information can be either preverbal or postverbal as a function of both verb-argument structure and discourse factors. Thus, both Example 17 and Example 18 constitute appropriate introductions by virtue of postverbal position, regardless of whether the NP is marked locally (numeral yi1 'one' in Example 17) or not (bare noun in Example 18), whereas the NP in Example 19 denotes given information (preverbal bare noun) and the utterance in Example 20 is ungrammatical, because it combines markings for new information (numeral) and for given information (preverbal) (see Li & Thompson, 1981).[2]

17. Lai2 le yi1-zhi1 mao3.
    come APCL NUM-CL cat.
    '(There) came a cat.'
18. Lai2 le mao3 le.
    come APCL cat APCL
    '(There) came a cat/cats.'
19. Mao3 lai2 le.
    cat come APCL

---

[1] With nonspecific reference, dislocations require a demonstrative coreferential pronoun in the clause, for example, *Un chat, ấa mange les rats* ('A cat, that(DEM) eats rats', i.e., 'Cats eat rats').

[2] All examples concern Mandarin Chinese (notwithstanding dialectal variations) and are translated both literally and freely with the following conventions: numbers show tones (1 to 4), APCL aspect particles, CL classifiers, NUM numeral determiners, and DISC discontinuous elements. Chinese nominal determiners require classifiers, among which specific ones are most frequent for newness (e.g., zhi1 in Example 17).

'The cat(s) came.'
20. *Yi1-ge mao3 lai2 le.
    NUM-CL cat come APCL
    'A cat came.'

Within a crosslinguistic perspective, the relative contribution of different markings to information status must be examined in light of all of their functions in a given language. Determiners also serve to express nonspecific reference and to label referents (English, French, and German); to count (French, German, and Chinese); and to carry morphological distinctions, such as number (English, French, and German), gender (German and French), and case (German).[3] Clause structure expresses syntactic and semantic relations within the clause, for example, partly differentiating subjects and/or agents (sentence-initial NP in SVO languages) from other roles. Studies focusing on sentence comprehension show that local and global markings play different roles across languages, depending on their availability and reliability (MacWhinney & Bates, 1989). Thus, when processing sentences, English-speaking adults and children rely on word order, Italian speakers on local lexical or morphological cues. In French and Chinese, however, only young children rely on word order, as expected (MacWhinney & Bates, 1989; Miao & Zhu, 1992), whereas adults often rely on local cues, presumably because of frequent structural variations. In a given language, then, the relative contribution of different marking to the discourse level partly depends on their contribution to the sentence level. Therefore, speakers' reliance on different devices depends on both levels.

DEVELOPMENTAL STUDIES

Such crosslinguistic differences raise the question of how children learn to regulate information flow in discourse. Among the relevant developmental studies, some have focused on children's developing ability to "displace reference," in example, to represent entities and events that are not in the here-and-now, typically inferring this ability anecdotally on the basis of various linguistic devices. Other studies have examined the acquisition of these devices, but they have typically focused on sentence-internal factors, rather than on discourse factors.

Displaced Reference

Different strands of research have made the following observation: After an initial period, during which children mostly talk about the here-and-now, they

---

[3]In Chinese, bare nouns can be nonspecific or label referents, and there is no morphology (on verbs or nouns). English singular numerical and indefinite NPs are distinct (*one/a* N).

begin to talk about the there-and-then, at first with some difficulty, then more efficiently. Psychologists focusing on cognitive development have interpreted displaced reference as part of a larger development involving children's ability to decontextualize all mental processes from immediate perception. Thus, "decentering" has been invoked in the Piagetian tradition to account for child development across several domains, for example, children's ability to produce comprehensible narratives or explanations is seen as reflecting their ability to take the interlocutor's viewpoint (Piaget, 1923/1959; also see a discussion in Hickmann, 1987).

Other researchers have examined the emergence of specific linguistic de-vices in children's spontaneous productions. Observations show that, toward the middle of the second year, displaced reference is accompanied by the uses of temporal-aspectual markings (connectives, adverbials, verbal inflections) and by means of denoting entities (nominal determiners, pronouns) that show some concern for discourse organization. These uses, however, are at first limited, for example, occurring mostly in familiar scripted events and/or in small stretches of speech that require adult scaffolding and providing little informa-tion that situates past events in time or introduces protagonists, despite some spatial information (French & Nelson, 1985; Peterson, 1990; Sachs, 1983; see a review in Hickmann, 1995).

More detailed evidence is available concerning how children learn to use temporal-aspectual markings to ground information, as well as to use referring expressions and clause structures to mark information status. Both discourse factors and clause-internal ones affect development, and this development follows both universal and language-specific patterns. In each domain, the main issues are first reviewed; here, results are presented from a crosslinguistic project carried out with collaborators on the development of discourse cohesion (Hendriks, Hickmann, & Liang, in press; Hickmann, 1991; Hickmann, Kaiser, & Roland, 1991; Hickmann & Liang, 1990). The database consists of narratives produced by adults and children of approximately 4 to 5 years, 7 years, and 10 years in English, French, German, and Mandarin Chinese on the basis of two picture sequences in the absence of mutual knowledge.[4]

---

[4]The method in this project can be summarized as follows. Subjects were seen individually with two adults (E1 and E2). E1 asked them to blindfold E2, look at picture sequence showing one story, and tell it to E2, in such a way, that E2 could retell it. The procedure was repeated for the other story. Half of the subjects began with one story, half with the other. The materials can be described as follows:

Story 1: A horse is running in a meadow (Picture 1), gets to a fence, sees a cow and bird (Picture 2), jumps over the fence (Picture 3), and falls down (Picture 4); the cow and bird bandage his leg (Picture 5).

Story 2: One sees a nest in a tree with a mother and baby birds (Picture 1); the mother leaves as a cat arrives (Picture 2); the cat looks up (Picture 3) and climbs up as a dog arrives (Picture 4); the mother returns, while the dog pulls the cat down (Picture 5) and chases it away (Picture 6).

The Acquisition of Tense and Aspect

A large number of studies have examined the acquisition of verbal inflections. A first set of studies has focused mostly on cognitive determinants of how these devices are used within the utterance, arguing that the uses of these devices are mainly dependent on particular predicate or situation types, for example, past perfective inflections occur with predicates that are inherently bounded and/or denote situations with immediately perceptible results. Such a finding has been reported in a considerable number of languages, including English, Italian, Greek, French, German, and Turkish (Aksu-Koç, 1988; Antinucci & Miller, 1976; Bloom, Lifter, & Hafitz, 1980; Bronckart & Sinclair, 1973; Cziko, 1986b; Harner, 1981; Meisel, 1985; Rispoli, 1990; Stephany, 1981). Findings have led to a *defective tense hypothesis*, according to which children use inflections at first exclusively to mark viewpoint (perfectivity) or situation type (e.g., results) and only later to mark tense. This hypothesis, however, has been disputed, for example, young children mark tense with all verb types in Polish (a highly inflected language), suggesting that it should be at least qualified (Weist, Wysocka, Witkoska-Stadnik, Buczowska, & Konieczna, 1984).

A second set of studies has focused on discourse factors affecting the acquisition of tense and aspect. Analyses of interpersonal interactions suggest that children's uses of such markings may either have other functions, for example, to mark modal distinctions (Gerhardt & Savasir, 1986) or be influenced by adults, who use them to draw children's attention to the results of events (De Lemos, 1981). Analyses of narrative productions suggest that children gradually learn to use these markings to ground information in discourse. For example, Bamberg (1987) shows that older German children (9 to 10-year-olds) and adults use the German Perfekt (perfective past) to mark episodic "chunks" and to ground information, whereas younger children (3 years) use it to mark completion. Further analyses are necessary to determine the relative impact of verb semantics and of discourse factors on all these uses. In this respect, an experimental study (Fayol, Hickmann, Gombert, & Bonnotte, 1993) suggests that verb semantics can even override discourse factors. French 10-year-olds and adults were asked to inflect verbs in the past (by verb completion in the written modality) either in isolated sentences or in sentences inserted at different points in narratives (beginning, middle, and end). Bounded predicates were more often inflected with past perfective inflections and unbounded ones with past imperfective ones, regardless of presentation condition. However, 10-year-olds, in contrast to adults, also overgeneralized the past imperfective in the narrative condition; they used this inflection type with all verb types (sometimes inappropriately).

Researchers have begun to examine children's uses of tense and aspect markings in narratives across languages. A number of analyses (Berman & Slobin, 1994) show that narrative organization varies as a function of language–specific factors and that young children first use the morphosyntactic devices that are obligatory in their language, for example, they rely on different anchoring strategies (past vs. nonpast), focus on different aspects of the narratives (states vs. processes), and express simultaneity differently in English, Spanish, Hebrew, German, and Turkish, depending on the verbal morphology available.

Other crosslinguistic analyses (Hendriks et al., in press; Hickmann et al., 1991) examined the impact of semantic and discourse factors on temporal-aspectual markings in English, French, German, and Chinese narratives (see footnote 4), yielding the following main findings. First, at all ages, children rely more on the past in English (49% to 61%) than in German (20% to 24%) or French (13% to 26%), but this difference decreases in adults (English 24%, French 16%, and German, 12%). As a result, more English narratives are anchored in the past (exclusive use of the past or a majority of past inflections), while more French and German ones are anchored in the present (exclusive use of the present or a majority of present inflections). At all ages, Chinese particles are more frequently perfective than imperfective (overall 30% vs. 6%), but the majority of utterances contain no aspect particle at all (64%).

Second, temporal-aspectual markings are related to predicate types, for example, perfective markers (past perfective, perfective particle) are more frequent overall with bounded predicates than with unbounded ones. However, as shown in Figure 11.1, the strength of this relation varies across ages and languages: the attraction between perfective markings and boundedness is strongest in Chinese at all ages and among young English-speaking children, while French and German speakers of all ages (as well as English-speaking adults) anchor their narratives mostly in the present with all predicate types. Chinese aspect particles might be all the more tightly related to predicates that they are not frequently used and that tense is not grammaticalized. In addition, the present might be easiest and most unmarked in French and German, since it neutralizes aspect, whereas it is stylistically marked in English (the historical present), since tense and aspect are more symmetrical. This hypothesis must be tested with a broader set of languages.

Third, discourse factors have a strong impact on children's uses in all languages, particularly on their tense/aspect shifts. Among the functions of such tense/aspect shifts, the most striking one consisted of marking *situational over-laps*, that is, total or partial simultaneity among situations in discourse. Example 21 (7-year-old), Example 22, and Example 23 (10-year-olds) are extracted from

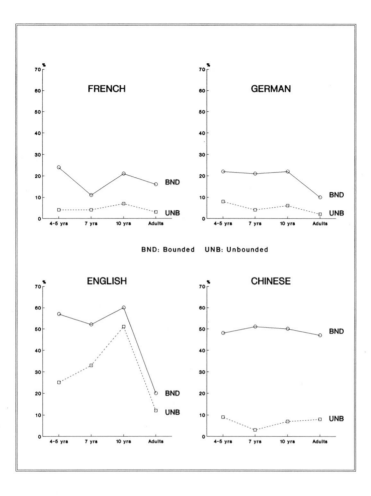

FIG. 11.1. Proportions of perfective markings as a function of boundedness.

English, German, and French narratives that were anchored in the present, illustrating shifts from the present to the (perfective or imperfective) past (underlined) and back to the present.

21. ...The cat comes to the tree, sits down and starts to climb. And the dog's just walking along and the dog bites the cat's tail when the cat just about *got up* there and the bird's coming. ...

22. ...aber im Hintergrund ist ein Hund, der beißt sie so in en Schwanz und zieht sie wieder runter. Und inzwischen ist die Vogelmutter *wiedergekommen* und bringt den Kleinen was zu fressen....

'...but in the background is a dog, he bites him in the tail and pulls him down again. And in the meantime the mother bird *has returned* and brings something to eat to the little ones...'

23. [...] Elle va chercher à manger pour ses petits mais en dessous y'a un chat et pendant qu'elle *est partie* le chat i regarde le nid [...], au moment où il atteint la branche pour attraper les trois petits oiseaux, y'a un chien qui arrive par derrière qui lui mord la queue et même à ce moment–là y'*avait* la mère qui *arrivait* et après le chat i retombe [...]
'... She goes to get food for her little ones but underneath there's a cat and while she *has left* the cat he looks at the nest...just as he reaches the branch to catch the three little birds, there's a dog that comes from behind that bites him in the tail and even at this moment there *was* the mother that *was* coming and then the cat he falls down...'

Similarly, Example 24 (adult) and Example 25 (7–year–old), show aspect shifts marking situational overlaps in Chinese, that is, a shift from an imperfective particle (*zhe*) to a perfective one (*le*) in Example 24 and another one from no particle, Example 25a, to a perfective particle, Example 25b.

24. *Dao4-ZHE shu4-shang4, yi4-zhi1 da4 huang2gou3 lai2-LE*
    arrive-APCL top-tree, NUM-CL big dog come-APCL
    '(When) he was getting to the top of the tree, a dog came.'

25. a. *Dang1 niao3 ma1ma gang1 fei1 zou3 de shi1hou4,*
       DISC-while bird mother just fly leave DISC-while
       'While the mother bird was leaving,'
    b. *jiu4 lai2-LE yi1-zhi1 loa3 mao1.*
       then come-APCL NUM-CL old cat
       '(there) came an old cat.'

As shown in Figure 11.2 (based on story 2), a striking increase occurs at 7 years of age in the uses of tense/aspect shifts for the marking of overlaps in all languages. This increase is either followed by a further increase up to 10 years of age and by a decrease at the adult age (French), or it is followed by a decrease up to 10 years of age and no change thereafter (English, German, Chinese). In all cases, decreases with age result from other functions served by temporal-aspectual shifts, for example, marking the setting, explanatory comments, restrospective comments, and so forth. Some differences can also be observed across languages. Thus, at 4–5 years of age, German children mark more overlaps than other children, perhaps as a result of the fact that the German past differentiates the perfective versus nonperfective, rather than the perfective versus imperfective. In addition, the marking of overlaps by means of aspect particles in Chinese is less frequent than the corresponding markings in the other languages (especially from 7 years of age onward), because these particles are optional and, therefore, overlaps are often marked by means of other devices (adverbials, connectives). In this respect, although connectives and adverbials are most frequent in Chinese, they mark overlaps in all languages, either instead of tense/aspect shifts (*au moment où* in Example 23) or in conjunction with them, e.g., *when* and *just about* in Example 21; *inzwischen* ('in the meantime') in Example 22; *pendant que* ('while'), *au moment où* ('at the moment when'), and *même à ce moment-là* ('even at this moment') in Example 23, *dang1/de shi1hou4* ('while'), *gang1* ('just'), and *jiu4* ('then') in Example 25.

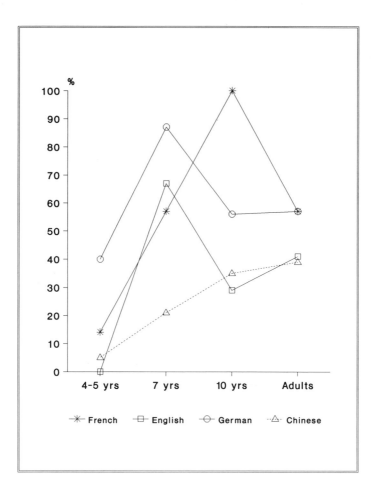

FIG. 11.2.   Proportions of tense/aspect shifts marking situational overlaps.

By age 7 years, children have learned some discourse functions of tense/aspect markings in all languages, despite differences in the rate of this progression and, notwithstanding, semantic determinants of these markings that can also be observed at the sentence level to different degrees across languages. The results presented clearly show that both types of factors affect how children use temporal-aspectual markings. Further analyses show that discourse factors and sentence-internal semantic ones interact, for example, some overlaps involve foregrounded bounded predicates in the past perfective or override them. Example 26 (adult) contains two overlaps (*at the same moment* + *has reached/grabbed; just at that moment*), one of which presents the same bounded event (reaching the nest) twice, first in the foreground, then in the background.

26. . . . the cat reaches the nest, but at the same moment that *it's reached* the nest, the dog *has grabbed* a hold of its tail. Just at that moment the mother bird is flying back with a worm in her mouth. . . .

Finally, as shown in Example 21 to Example 26, tense/aspect shifts often coincide with the introduction or reintroduction of referents (e.g., arrival of dog or cat, return of mother bird). More generally, temporal-aspectual markings interact with other devices, such as different types of referring expressions and clause-structure variations marking information status in discourse.

Referring Expressions and Clause Structure

A number of developmental studies have focused on the acquisition of referring expressions and have reported divergent results concerning the age at which these devices are acquired: either as early as ages 3–4 years (e.g., Cziko, 1986b; MacWhinney & Bates, 1978; Maratsos, 1976) or after 7 years (e.g., De Weck, 1991; Emslie & Stevenson, 1981; Hickmann, 1987, 1991; Kail & Hickmann, 1992; Karmiloff-Smith, 1979, 1981; Power & Dal Martello, 1986; Vion & Colas, 1987; Warden, 1981; Wigglesworth, 1990). This divergence in results comes partly from the different goals and methodologies of these studies, all of which have not focused on the same functions and situations, for example, specific versus nonspecific reference, discourse cohesion versus picture descriptions, spontaneous productions versus experimental situations, mutual knowledge, and/or prior familiarity with stories on the part of the child.

Studies focusing on discourse cohesion in children's narratives have observed the uses of various organizational strategies in reference maintenance. A recurrent finding is that children at some point organize discourse around the *thematic subject* (main protagonist), for which they systematically reserve subject pronouns. Studies have disagreed with respect to whether this strategy occurs early (Bamberg, 1987) or late (Kamiloff-Smith, 1981), presumably because of different methodologies, for example, children were either quite familiar with the story (Bamberg, 1987) or not at all (Karmiloff-Smith, 1981). However, researchers agree that it demonstrates children's reliance on top–down cognitive processes, rather than on more primitive *bottom–up* ones, allowing global discourse-internal organization, rather than dependance on external stimuli.

The results concerning nominal determiners suggest that some functions of these devices are mastered early, such as the uses of indefinite NPs for nonspecific reference and for labelings (Cziko, 1986b; Karmiloff-Smith, 1979; Maratsos, 1976). In contrast, the discourse-internal uses of determiners are a later development, particularly to mark newness in situations requiring that children organize discourse in the absence of mutual knowledge, for example, narratives elicited with films or picture sequences and produced for a naïve interlocutor (blindfolded, in another room, separated by a screen etc.). In such situations, children do not use indefinite NPs systematically for referent introductions until around 7 years of age or they use them deictically to label referents in English (Emslie & Stevenson, 1981; Hickmann, 1987, 1991; Warden, 1981), Italian (Power & Dal Martello, 1986), and French (De Weck, 1991; Kail & Hickmann, 1992; Vion & Colas, 1987).

Some evidence is also available concerning children's uses of clause structure to mark newness in discourse. MacWhinney & Bates (1978) compared productions in languages where nominal determiners are either obligatory (English, Italian) or optional (Hungarian). Findings show that 4-year-olds differentiate new information from given information with indefinite versus definite NPs in English and Italian, but that word order and information status are not related in any language. However, as suggested by a replication study in French (Vion & Colas, 1987), young children use expressions deictically in a task of descriptions of jointly perceived pictures that did not form stories. Longitudinal studies indicate that very young children tend to place new information at the beginning of their utterances, rather than at the end (see a review in Slobin, 1985). From 3 years on, they use subject–verb inversions or existential relatives to mark newness more often in Italian, Hebrew, and Spanish than in English, German, or Turkish (e.g., Bates & Devescovi, 1989; Dasinger & Toupin, 1994). A comparative study of adult productions (Sridhar, 1989) shows that English is most resistant to such clause structure variations in comparison to several other SVO languages (Chinese, Finnish, Hebrew, Slovenian, and Spanish).

Other crosslinguistic studies (Hickmann, 1991; Hickmann et al., in press; Hickmann & Liang, 1990) compared the uses of local (nominal determiners)

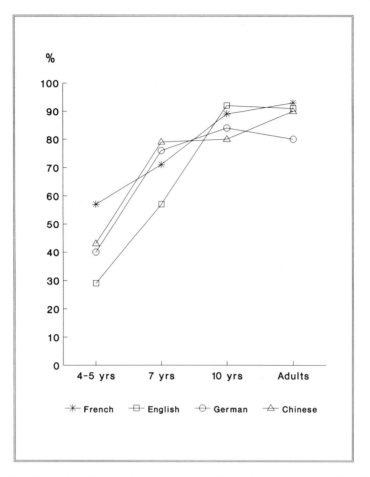

FIG. 11.3.   Proportions of referent introductions containing local newness markings. From Hickmann, Hendriks, Roland & Liang (in press). Reprinted with permission from Cambridge University
Press.

and global markings (clause structure) to introduce referents in English, French,
German, and Chinese narratives. Figure 11.3 shows the proportions of first
mentions containing local newness markings and Figure 11.4, the proportions
of postverbal first mentions in comparison to subsequent ones.

These results show the late mastery of obligatory newness markings in all
languages; indefinite determiners at around 7 years in the Indo-European
languages (Fig. 11.3) and postverbal position at around 10 years in Chinese (Fig.
11.4). In addition, Chinese children use determiners systematically to mark
newness from 7 years on (Fig. 11.3), despite the fact that these devices are
optional. Thus, regardless of the optional versus obligatory nature of different
newness markings, local markings are less complex than global ones, as is also

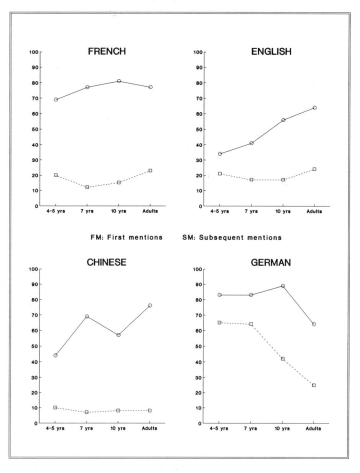

FIG. 11.4. Proportions of postverbal first and subsequent mentions. From Hickmann, Hendriks, Roland & Liang (in press). Reprinted with permission from Cambridge University Press.

the case in sentence comprehension (Ammon & Slobin, 1979; Slobin & Bever, 1982; Slobin, 1982, 1985). Indeed, the main function of Chinese determiners is to mark information status (in addition to their numerical function), whereas position marks both information status in discourse and grammatical relations in the clause. In this respect, children do not use global newness markings to the same degree across languages (Fig. 11.4), using them the least in English and the most in French (at all ages) with Chinese as intermediary. Note that young French children who do not introduce referents appropriately frequently use definite left–dislocated forms (e.g., *le chien il arrive* 'the dog it comes'), whereas older children use these constructions in conjunction with appropriate introductions, thereby promoting NPs to topic status before pronominalization, as in Example 27. As for German, position is irrelevant to information status in children's narratives, because of their frequent uses of sentence-initial temporal and/or spatial elements to structure discourse, resulting in obligatory subject–verb inversions with both first and subsequent mentions, such as Example 28.

27. Et y'a un chat qui arrive. Alors le chat i regarde le nid, i voit les oiseaux, alors i commence à grimper.
   'And there's a cat that comes. Then the cat it looks at the nest, it sees the birds, so it starts to climb.'
28. Und da kommt ein Hund, und dann zieht er die Katze runter.
   (lit: 'then comes a dog, then pulls he the cat down.')

Finally, local and global markings of newness are strongly related in all languages. Figure 11.5 shows the distribution of the following types of introductions in each language (collapsing age): postverbal locally marked (e.g., *He saw a dog, There was/came a dog*), preverbal locally marked (*A dog came*), postverbal locally unmarked (*He saw the dog*), and preverbal locally unmarked (*The dog came*). In all languages, most locally marked introductions are postverbal and most postverbal ones are locally marked. This strong relation between local and

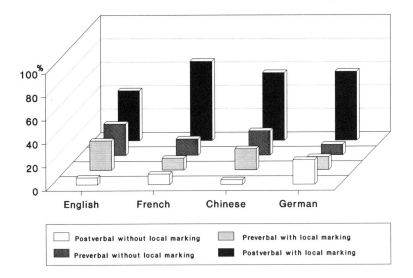

FIG. 11.5.   Referent introductions as a function of local and global newness markings. From Hickmann, Hendriks, Roland & Liang (in press). Reprinted with permission from Cambridge University Press.

global markings is predicted by the universal tendency for new information to occur towards the end of the sentence (a relation which is obligatory in Chinese, but optional in the other languages). It might partially account for previous developmental findings that show either an inverse relation (new information first) or no relation at all, since these studies focused on very young children (aged 2 years on), who do not use local markings systematically or use them deictically (MacWhinney & Bates, 1978; Slobin, 1985).

CONCLUSIONS

In this chapter, children's acquisition of linguistic devices in two domains of child language was examined: tense-aspect systems, which play a central role in the grounding of information in discourse, and the conjoined uses of referring expressions and of clause structure for the marking of information status. Findings suggest the gradual development of discourse-internal functions, showing that children from about 7 years on begin to regulate information flow within discourse. This evidence further shows that both discourse-internal and clause-internal principles play a role in acquisition and that both universal and language-specific factors affect the rate and course of this development.

Functional Determinants of Language Acquisiton

Evidence shows the impact of two main determinants in discourse: factors operating within and across utterances. In the domain of tense-aspect systems, both verb semantics within the utterance (boundedness) and discourse factors (relations among events, foreground vs. background) affect children's uses of verbal inflections or of aspect particles in conjunction with connectives and adverbials. In the domain of reference to entities, both clause-internal relations (subject vs. object, agent vs. patient) and interclausal ones (thematic status, new vs. given information) affect children's uses of referring expressions (nominal determiners, pronouns) and clause structure (word order, clause types). Therefore, an adequate model of acquisition must take into account two levels of organization in language, the sentence and discourse, particularly to explain results within a crosslinguistic perspective. The particular functional factors that were considered in this chapter concerned discourse-internal principles governing the regulation of information flow across utterances, in example, information grounding and information status. A more complete account of functional determinants should consider also other functional aspects of linguistic devices, including a variety of dependence relations between language and nonlinguistic context.

Universal Versus Language-Specific
Aspects of Development

Both universal and language-specific factors are necessary to accounts for these results. At least two types of universal cognitive factors have been invoked by previous studies on the basis of different theoretical frameworks: some that might apply to all of child development (general, language-independent processes), some that might be exclusively specific to the domain of language development (e.g., innate universal grammar or cognitive processes specialized for the construction of language). Further independent evidence is necessary to determine which of these universal processes best account for specific results.

It is likely that some general cognitive process akin to decentering might play a role in children's ability to regulate information flow in the absence of mutual knowledge, enabling them, for example, to take the perspective of others when it differs from their own and to organize information in discourse accordingly. However, it remains to be seen whether such processes are sufficient and/or entirely domain-independent or whether the particular type of perspective-taking necessary for discourse organization might be highly constrained by the acquisition of linguistic devices. Other types of universal determinants have been proposed, such as syntatic and semantic categories, e.g., concepts of specific vs. nonspecific reference, agency, subjecthood, and/or factors affecting cognitive complexity, for example, the greater functional complexity of global markings that contribute heavily to both the sentence and discourse levels. Thus, local newness markings are more easily acquired than global ones across many languages, a result that may be difficult to explain only on the basis of general language-independent processes, requiring processes that may be very predominant and partially specialized for language development.

Whatever the case may be, language-specific factors also affect the rate and course of development; in this review, different developmental patterns were found in several domains across languages. In the domain of tense-aspect systems, language-specific patterns have led some researchers to qualify or reject the claim that acquisition should be determined exclusively by universal cognitive factors. Thus, predicate types have a different impact on tense/aspect markings across languages and the discourse uses of these markings develop at a different rate. Similarly, results concerning referring expressions and clause structure show that these devices do not mark information status at the same rate across languages, for example, global ones appear earlier in some languages than in others, depending on how sentence-internal and discourse-internal functions interact.

In conclusion, two types of factors affect acquisition in different domains, both of which require a consideration of acquisition at the sentence and discourse levels of organization: (a) universal determinants (e.g., discourse principles regulating information flow, the categorization of situation types, the relative cognitive complexity of different markings; and (b) language-specific factors that result from the different systems of devices available and from the different ways in which languages map sentential and discourse functions onto these devices. These two types of factors may account for why the course of development for particular devices is similar across different languages, while the rate of development differs from language to language.

REFERENCES

Aksu-KoÁ, A. (1988). *The acquisition of aspect and modality: the case of past reference in Turkish.* Cambridge: Cambridge University Press.

Ammon, M., & Slobin, D. I. (1979). A cross-linguistic study of the processing of causative sentences. *Cognition, 7*, 3–17.

Antinucci, F. and Miller, R. (1976). How children talk about what happened. *Journal of Child Language, 9*, 627–43.

Bamberg, M. G. W. (1987). *The acquisition of narratives: Learning to use language.* Berlin: Mouton de Gruyter.

Bates, E., & Devescovi, A. (1989). Cross linguistic studies of sentence production. In B. MacWhinney & E. Bates (Eds.), *The cross-linguistic study of sentence processing* (pp. 225–253). New York: Cambridge University Press.

Berman, R. A., & Slobin, D. I. (Eds.) (1994). *Different ways of relating events in narrative: a crosslinguistic developmental study.* Hillsdale, NJ: Lawrence Erlbaum Associates.

Bloom, L., Lifter, K., and Hafitz, J. (1980). Semantics of verbs and the development of verb inflection in child language. *Language, 56*, 386–412.

Bronckart, J. P., & Sinclair, H. (1973). Time, tense, and aspect. *Cognition, 2*, 107–30.

Chafe, W. (1976). Givenness, contrastiveness, definiteness, subjects, topics and point of view. In C. N. Li (Ed.), *Subject and topic* (pp. 25–55). New York: Academic Press.

Clark, H. H. and Haviland, S. E. (1976). Comprehension and the given-new contract. In R. Freedle (Ed.), *Discourse production and comprehension* (pp. 1–40). Hillsdale, NJ: Lawrence Erlbaum Associates.

Comrie, B. (1976). *Aspect: An introduction to the study of verbal aspect and related problems.* Cambridge: Cambridge University Press.

Comrie, B. (1985). *Tense.* Cambridge: Cambridge University Press.

Cziko, G. A. (1986a). A review of the state-process and punctual-nonpunctual distinctions in children's acquisitions of verbs. *First Language, 9*, 1–31.

Cziko, G. A. (1986b). Testing the Language Bioprogram Hypothesis: a review of children's acquisition of articles. *Language, 62*, 878–98.

Dahl, O. (1985). *Tense and aspect systems.* Oxford, England: Basil Blackwell Ltd.

Dasinger, L., & Toupin, C. (1994). The development of relative clause functions in narrative. In R. A. Berman & D. I. Slobin (Eds.), *Different ways of relating events in narrative: A crosslinguistic developmental study* (pp.457–514). Hillsdale, NJ: Lawrence Erlbaum Associates.

De Lemos, C. (1981). Interactional processes in the child's construction of language. In W. Deutsch (Ed.), *The child's construction of language* (pp. 57–76). New York: Academic Press.

De Weck, G. (1991). La cohésion dans les narrations d'enfants. Neuchâtel, France: Delachaux and Niestlé.

Emslie, H. C., & Stevenson, R. J. (1981). Pre-school children's use of the articles in definite and indefinite referring expressions. *Journal of Child Language*, 8, 313–28.

Fayol, M., Hickmann, M., Bonnotte, I. and Gombert, J.E. (1993). The effects of narrative context on French verbal inflections: a developmental perspective. *Journal of Psycholinguistic Research*, 22(4), 453–478.

French, L. A., & Nelson, K. (1985). *Children's acquisition of relational terms: some ifs, ors, and buts*. New York: Springer Verlag.

Gerhardt, J. B., & Savasir Iskender (1986). The use of the simple present in the speech of two three-year-olds: normativity not subjectivity. *Language and Society*, 15, 501–36.

Halliday, M. A. K., & Hasan, R. (1976). *Cohesion in English*. London: Longman.

Harner, L. (1981). Children talk about the time and aspect of actions. *Child Development*, 52, 498–506.

Hendriks, H., Hickmann, M., & Liang, J. (in press, July). *The uses of temporal-aspectual devices by Chinese children: semantic and discourse determinants*. Proceedings from the Third Meeting of the International Conference on Chinese Linguistics, July 14–17, 1994. Hong Kong: Studia Linguistica Serila.

Hickmann, M. (1987). The pragmatics of reference in child language: Some issues in developmental theory. In M. Hickmann (Ed.), *Social and functional approaches to language and thought* (pp. 165–184). Orlando, FL: Academic Press.

Hickmann, M. (1991). The development of discourse cohesion: some functional and cross-linguistic issues. In G. Piéraut-Le Bonniec and M. Dolitsky (Eds.), *Language bases... discourse bases* (pp. 157–185). Amsterdam: John Benjamins B.V.

Hickmann, M. (1995). The development of reference to person, time, and space. In P. Fletcher & B. MacWhinney (Eds.), *Handbook of child language* (pp. 194–218). Oxford, England: Blackwell.

Hickmann, M., Hendriks, H., Roland, F., & Liang, J. (in press). The marking of new information in children's narratives: A comparison of English, French, German, and Mandarin Chinese. *Journal of Child Language*.

Hickmann, M., Kaiser, B., & Roland, F. (1991, July). Semantics and pragmatics in the development of tense and aspect: a crosslinguistic study. Paper presented at the Second European Congress of Psychology, Budapest, Hungary.

Hickmann, M., & Liang, J. (1990). Clause-structure variation in Chinese narrative discourse: a developmental analysis. *Linguistics*, 28, 1167–200.

Hopper, P.J. (1979). Aspect and foregrounding in discourse. In T. Givón (Ed.), *Syntax and semantics; Vol. 12, discourse and syntax* (pp. 213–241). New York: Academic Press.

Kail, M., & Hickmann, M. (1992). French children's ability to introduce referents in narratives as a function of mutual knowledge. *First Language*, 12, 73–94.

Karmiloff-Smith, A. (1979). *A functional approach to child language: a study of determiners and reference*. Cambridge: Cambridge University Press.

Karmiloff-Smith, A. (1981). The grammatical marking of thematic structure in the development of language production. In W. Deutsch (Ed.) *The child's construction of language* (pp. 121–47). New York: Academic Press.

Lambrecht, K. (1981). Topic, antitopic, and verb agreement in non-standard French.. *Pragmatics and Beyond*, II:6. Amsterdam: John Benjamins B.V.

Li, C.N., & Thompson, S. (1981). *Mandarin Chinese: a functional reference grammar*. Berkeley: University of California Press.

MacWhinney, B., & Bates E. (1978). Sentential devices for conveying givenness and newness: a cross-cultural developmental study. *Journal of Verbal Learning and Verbal Behavior*, 17, 539–58.

MacWhinney, B., & Bates, E. (Eds.) (1989). *The cross-linguistic study of sentence processing*. Cambridge, MA: Cambridge University Press.

Maratsos, M. P. (1976). *The use of definite and indefinite reference in young children.* Cambridge, MA: Cambridge University Press.

Meisel, J. M. (1985). Les phases initiales du développement des notions temporelles, aspectuelles et de modes d'action. *Lingua, 66,* 321–74.

Miao, X. C. & Zhu, M. S. (1992). Language development in Chinese children. In H. C. Chen and O. J. L. Tzeng (Eds.), *Language processing in Chinese* (pp. 277–311). New York: Elsevier.

Peterson, C (1990) The who, when and where of early narratives. *Journal of Child Language, 17,* 433–55.

Piaget, J. (1959). *The language and thought of the child.* London: Routledge & Kegan Paul. (Original work published 1923).

Power, R. J. D., & Dal Martello, M. F. (1986). The use of the definite and indefinite articles by Italian preschool children. *Journal of Child Language, 13,* 145–54.

Rispoli, M. (1990). Lexical assignability and perspective switch: the acquisition of verb subcategorization for aspectual inflections. *Journal of Child Language, 17,* 375–92.

Sachs, J. (1983). Talking about the there and then: the emergence of displaced reference in parent-child discourse. In K. Nelson (Ed.), *Children's language, Vol. 4 (pp. 1–28).* Hillsdale, NJ: Lawrence Erlbaum Associates.

Slobin, D. I. (1982). Universal and particular in the acquisition of language. In E. Wanner & L. Gleitman (Eds.), *Language acquisition: the state of the art* (pp. 128–170). New York: Cambridge University Press.

Slobin, D. I. (1985). Crosslinguistic evidence for the language-making capacity. In D.I. Slobin (Ed.), *The crosslinguistic study of language acquisition* (pp. 1157–1257). Hillsdale, NJ: Lawrence Erlbaum Associates.

Slobin, D. I., & Bever, T. (1982). Children's use of canonical sentence schemas: a cross-linguistic study of word order and inflections. *Cognition, 12,* 229.

Smith, C. (1983). A theory of aspectual choice. *Language, 59,* 479–501.

Sridhar, S. N. (1989). Cognitive structures in language production: A cross-linguistic study. In B. MacWhinney & E. Bates (Eds.), *The cross-linguistic study of sentence processing* (pp. 209–224). Cambridge, MA: Cambridge University Press.

Stephany, U. (1981). Verbal grammar in Modern Greek child language. In S. Dale & D. Ingram (Eds.), *Child language: an international perspective* (pp. 361–377). Baltimore, M.D.: University Park Press.

Vendler, Z. (1967). *Linguistics in philosophy,* Ithaca, New York: Cornell University Press.

Vion, M., & Colas, A. (1987). La présentation du caractère ancien ou nouveau d'une information en Français. *Archives de Psychologie, 55,* 243–64.

Warden, D. (1981). Learning to identify referents. *British Journal of Psychology, 72,* 93–99.

Weist, R. M., Wysocka, H., Witkowska-Stadnik, K., Buczowska, E., & Konieczna, E. (1984). The defective tense hypothesis: On the emergence of tense and aspect in child Polish. *Journal of Child Language, 11,* 347–74.

Wigglesworth, G. (1990). Children's narrative acquisition: a study of some aspects of reference and anaphora. *First Language, 10,* 105–25.

Chapter 12

Textual Organizers and Text Types: Ontogenetic Aspects in Writing

Bernard Schneuwly
University of Geneva

This chapter reviews those units of language that function as textual organizers and the psychological operations underlying their production. The experimental studies that are reported on are characterized by an interactionist and differential approach that reveals the relationships of interdependence between certain configurations of linguistic units and certain configurations of contextual parameters. Such an approach implies the description of types of texts, including specific linguistic characteristics, and the formulation of linguistic operations that represent the different forms of interdependence between text and context.

THE PLACE OF TEXTUAL ORGANIZERS IN A LANGUAGE PRODUCTION MODEL

Our general point of view can be stated as follows (see also Bronckart, Bain, Schneuwly, Davaud, & Pasquier, 1985; Schneuwly, 1988a; Bronckart 1994): the aim of the psychology of language is to place the speech action in a social context that is always its origin and its endpoint. The speech action is materialized in texts, sets of strongly organized linguistic units that are the traces of linguistic operations realizing the action. This general definition has important theoretical and methodological implications.

From a theoretical point of view, three areas have to be incorporated into the theory: the extralinguistic area or the context of the speech action; the mechanisms that treat the extralingistic areas and whose traces are the linguistic units; and the linguistic units that constitute the text.

Every human action takes place in a space of cooperation that takes the form of a social place in which specific forms of social practices function; they determine what can be said, by whom, how, and by what means. Every actor is defined as enunciator by the role he or she takes and the specific nature of the relationship with the addressee. In acting, he or she pursues aims in relation to the role the social place in which he or she is acting. At the same time, every speech action is also a physical act defining a material situation with, on the one hand, an emitter and a receiver, and, on the other, a physical space and a moment in which language is produced. These parameters function as points of reference on which to anchor texts from an enunciative point of view.

Three levels of linguistic operations can be distinguished. The first is the elaboration of an *orientation base* for the speech action by the representation of the social interaction (social place, enunciator, adressee, goal) and of the material situation. On each of these parameters of the extralinguistic context, choices have to be made that define the mode of the speech action, that is, the text type (or genre) most efficient to act in the situation given. The second is the *discursive planning* of the text that includes two main dimensions: the planning of the text on the basis of more or less stereotyped models (genres) related to the context and the anchoring of the text, that is, archetypical ways of language functioning that determine, to a certain degree, the envelope of certain linguistic units. The third is the *linearization* process with, on the one hand, the propositional structuration resulting in predicative units and, on the other, the processes of textualization that integrate these predicative units into a web of relations. Two main aspects can be distinguished in the process of textualization: operations of *cohesion* that guarantee the progression of the text on the level of the noun phrase (anaphora, phenomena of topicalization; De Weck, 1991) or of the verb phrase (continuity and change of tenses; Bronckart & Fayol, 1988) and operations of *connection* that act on the level of clauses, and structure them into hierarchically organized units. *Textual organizers* are the most important traces of the operations of connecting.

TEXTUAL ORGANIZERS: A DEFINITION

Except for Antoine's monograph devoted to *La Coordination en Français* (Antonie, 1958/1962), very few linguists belonging to the structuralist school studied textual organizers. Indeed, Brunot (1926), Sechehaye (1950), and Bally (1932) investigated textual organizers, but their main concern was to introduce some order and consistency into a rather vague classification of this unit category. On the other hand, for the proponents of generative grammar, connectives were used mainly as preferred criteria for validating some hypotheses on syntactic description (see, in particular, the synthesis proposed by Grunig, 1977).

For the last 20 years, however, as an extension of the studies performed by logicians and philosophers, connectives and organizers have been analyzed in numerous, often stimulating, studies. Dealing with the logic of language from a pragmatic perspective, Ducrot and his collaborators (Ducrot, 1980) analyzed the conditions of use in French of such units as *mais* ('but'), *eh bien* ('well'), *décidément* ('indeed'), *d'ailleurs* ('moreover'), etc. They demonstrated that the functioning of these units was highly dependent on the characteristics of the situation in which they were used. Within the framework of textual linguistics, Van Dijk (1979) and, above all, Biasci (1982) proposed a distinction between the *semantic functioning* (chaining of clauses) and the *pragmatic functioning* (chaining of speech acts) of various connectives in English, German, and Italian. A more exhaustive study of textual organizers was proposed by Gülich (1970), who demonstrated that the distribution of units is dependent on the type of text and what it contributes to the structuration of episodic units in narratives. Quasthoff (1979) expanded this idea for narratives by distinguishing marks of segmentation (metanarrative sentences, abstraction, orientation) that indicate primarily macrosemantic cæsuras and connection marks that have a twofold status: They can be the trace of general planning as well as the trace of means used for connecting events within a temporal or causal sequence to orient the adressee's attention. Both authors also analyzed a number of units that seem to be involuntary traces of an intense activity of cognitive planning and that signal that one is going to continue to speak. These functional analyses led to a definition of a class of linguistic units that expands the traditional class of connectors or conjunctions to what the authors call *Verknüpfungs- und Gliederungssignale*, or signals of connection and segmenting. They include certain adverbs, some prepositional phrases, and other expressions like "well," "so," ad so forth.

The functions of textual organizers are analyzed in the same vein in the research of Adam (1990) and Adam and Revaz (1989) who studied a corpus of descriptive texts. More precisely, they showed that these units mark, on the local level, the intra- and interpropositional chaining and, on the global level, the structure of textual sequences. In descriptive texts, three categories of textual organizers are used: *enumerative* units, which give no other information than the fact that the discursive segment which they introduce has to be integrated in a linear fashion into a series (Coltier & Turco, 1988); *temporal* units, which orient the addressee toward a chronological interpretation of the elements, as the description of a series of actions; and *spatial* units, which also segment and organize the text into different parts. These studies lead to the conclusion that to study the problem of connecting in text, it is necessary to define a relatively large class of linguistic units, that is, textual organizers including conjunctions, prepositional phrases, adverbs, and so forth. These units constitute configurations whose form depends on the type of text analyzed. These results lead to a definition of a class of linguistic units in the framework just defined.

What are Textual Organizers ?

As stated earlier, the operations of connecting act on the level of clauses and structure them into hierarchically organized units. The formal characteristic of these operations is to act *on* the clauses. The linguistic units that are the main traces of these operations are distributed on the interpropositionnel level or, in some cases, on the predicative level between utterances (Bronckart, et al., 1985). In French, three classes of linguistic units perform the connecting and segmenting function in the text:

1. Coordinate conjunctions (for instance: *et* ('and'), *mais* ('but'), *car* ('for'), and subordinate conjunctions (*lorsque* ('when'), *parce que* ('because')).
2. A subset of adverbs or adverbial locutions that function independently of the syntax of sentences, that do not have any clear grammatical function in the utterance in which they appear; for example, (*tout à coup* ('at once'), *soudain* ('suddenly'), *premièrement* ('first'), *finalement* ('finally'), *plus tard* ('later on'), *d'une part* ('on the one hand'), *c'est pourquoi* ('that is why'). Often, these units appear at the beginning of utterances. 3. A subset of prepositional phrases that can be simple; for example, *à sept heures* ('at 7 o'clock'), *pendant huit jours* ('for a week'), *au sud* ('in the south'), or more complex structures such as *après la tombée de la nuit* ('after nightfall'), *lors du passage de Luc à Berlin* ('during Luc's stay in Berlin'), etc. The subset also includes nominal groups that function as prepositional phrases, such as, *un jour* ('one day'), *le lendemain* ('the next day'), and so forth.

These units may be called *textual organizers.*

The Functions of Textual Organizers

On the basis of the existing literature, it seems possible to distinguish three groups of operations of connecting and segmenting:

1. *Beaconing* operations mark the different structural levels of a text, be they the semantic macrostructure or the conventional superstructure of a text type. They create the origin of a text and relay it through the text by temporal, spatial, or logicoargumentative expressions; they specify also the transitions between the different phases of a conventional text plan. In French, a set of entities seems to constitute more specifically the traces of these processes: nominal groups, prepositional groups, and some adverbs such as *premièrement* ('firstly'), *deuxièmement* ('secondly'), *tout d'abord* ('first of all').

2. *Packaging* operations create strongly connected textual entities by forming packages of clauses (as defined by Adam, 1984) and, where necessary, by defining the type of linkage between the different components of the entities created. According to Smith and Frawley (1983), who analyzed the influence of situation and type of text on the use of organizers, it is possible to distinguish integrative packaging (one clause is embedded in another, essentially, by pro-cedures of subordination) and additive packaging (one clause is added to another by procedures of coordination). 3. *Linking* operations, as, Quasthoff (1979), Gülich (1970), and others have shown, guarantee the material conti-nuity of the language production process. They are important in oral produc-tion, but only rarely leave traces in written texts. In an ontogenetic perspective, they also seem, nonetheless, to be important in writing.

How Can Textual Organizers Be Studied ?

On the basis of these theoretical proposals, an experimental method was derived that aimed to bring out the relationships of dependence existing between certain types of contexts and certain configurations of surface units in a corpus. More precisely, the types of text production conditions that constitute the independent variables in the experiments are defined by controlling the pa-rameters of social interaction and by their relations with the parameters of the act of production (Bronckart & Schneuwly, 1991). This chapter demonstrates the crucial importance of considering text types in describing the deep restruc-turing of the configuration of textual organizers during the ontogenesis of writing. This is done by presenting the main results of several studies with a common methodology.

1. Types of text production conditions are defined by controlling the main parameters of social interaction (enunciator, addressee, goal, social place) that result, generally, in a given text type. The referential content is the same for the text produced in the same conditions.

2. Texts collected were produced in these conditions by children of different age groups.

3. The textual organizers are categorized in accordance with the main categories introduced previously: formal (coordinate vs. subordinate), functional (beaconing, packaging, linking) or lexical (mainly temporal vs. nontemporal organizers). The categorization depends largely on the specific text type analyzed. 4. The configurations of textual organizers are analyzed as a function of the text types and of the age groups.

THE USE OF TEXTUAL ORGANIZERS: AN ONTOGENETIC VIEW AND SOME GENERAL HYPOTHESES

There have been many studies on the use of connectives at different ages. Kail and Weissenborn (1991) gave a critical overview, which shows that in these studies, connectors are never analyzed as a system of oppositions. Moreover, the studies are generally devoted to the comprehension or the production of connectors by very young children in situations of communication that are very different from the production of more complex, monologic texts. Fayol's pioneering studies (Fayol, 1981, 1986; see also Mouchon, Fayol, & Gombert, 1991) on written narratives describe three systems of textual organizers in children ages 7 to 10: connection versus absence of connection marked by the presence or absence of *et* ('and'); strong versus weak connections marked by a system of opposing units like *puis* ('then') to *et* ('and'); and, finally, a more complex system where the degree of connexion, the antecedent/consequence relation, and other chronological relationships are marked. Chanquoy (1991) varied the types of written text (descriptive vs. narrative) and observed the connectors used at different ages (children in second and third grade of primary school). The results of her study demonstrate that the use of these units is not defined by the level of the sentence, but depends on, besides the age of the subjects, the type of texts and the topic of the texts (for similar results, see Rosat, 1989a).

These studies on the development of some textual organizers in written texts show two essential aspects that are in accordance with the general framework developed so far. First, textual organizers have to be analyzed as wholes functioning together, as configurations marking essential aspects of a text or, to put it in another way, as traces of operations on different levels of the production of a text. Second, these configurations differ strongly across different text types; this also means that their acquisition can only be studied by taking into account the dimensions of communication situation and text type. What a student masters is not the use of a particular textual organizer, but a certain way of acting verbally, of using a text type that is likely to be efficient in certain communication situations. In this way, the student acquires the subsystems of linguistic units that function in these text types. This theoretical position is illustrated by analysis of the use of textual organizers at different ages in different types of written texts. Aspects to be discussed include how, at the early stages of learning to write texts, textual organizers and, more particularly, the unit *et*, play an important role in the external control of the ongoing activity of writing (linking operations). Further, the learning of writing can be described as a process of differentiation of text types. This includes the building of different configurations of textual organizers in accordance with different text types. But, this process of differentiation cannot be conceived of as a homogeneous process, rather it is a process of unequal development of different units and configurations. In addition, one path across which development takes place can be described as new functions enacted by old forms before the functions are stabilized by new and differentiated forms.

EMPIRICAL ILLUSTRATIONS

The Tendency for Textual Organizers to be Used with Decreasing Frequency

To acquire a first general idea about the use of textual organizers in different text types produced by students of different age groups, it is interesting to know the overall frequencies of these linguistic units. Two hypotheses are plausible regarding these frequencies. First, because mastery of organizers and of texts increases with age, one might suppose that the frequency of organizers increases in all text types. Second, because the mastery of organizers and of texts is incomplete in younger students, they tend to use the units very frequently and in an undifferentiated way to compensate for a less-than-perfect internal structure of the texts.

Observation of the overall frequencies of textual organizers in different text types produces a very regular pattern. Although they may vary from one type to another, there is one clear ontogenetic tendency:[1] textual organizers, as defined by the ratio between these linguistic units and finite verbs, are used with

---

[1]The same observation has not been made for oral texts; see Rosat 1989b and 1991 for a comparison between oral and written texts in the same conditions of production (explanation and argumentation). It is interesting to note here that in two studies, the observation has been made that there is an inverse relationship between the density of textual organizers and anaphora (Schneuwly, & Bronckart, 1986; De Weck, 1991). Fairy tales for instance, where textual organizers are not very frequent, are quite dense in anaphora.

TABLE 12.1
The Global Decrease of the Rate of Textual Organizers Defined by the Ratio
Between Number of Organizers and 100 Finite Verbs in Texts

	Age				
Text Types	8	10	12	14	AD
Letter to the editor[a]		73	64	58	
Rules of a game[a]		52	53	47	48
Construction of an object[b]	65	60	59		31
Report of a museum visit[c]	72	44	42		
Fairy tale[d]		54	49	41	
Short news item[d]		58	49	43	
Explanation[d]		47	45	41	
Letter relating story[d]		52	47	43	

Notes. [a]Schneuwly, 1988; [b]Schneuwly, & Rosat, 1986; [c]Schwinn Lang, & Rieben, 1992; [d]Dolz, 1990.

decreasing frequency, as demonstrated in Table 12.1.

This decrease is due to two main factors. First, there is a decline in the use of units like *et* ('and') or *et puis* ('and then'), but also of *puis* ('then') for enumeration or narration, *après* ('after') for narration and *aussi* ('also') for enumeration of arguments. Second, this tendency is only partly compensated for by the use of other organizers that can take the place of the units no longer used. The second hypothesis mentioned before is thus confirmed. To understand more exactly what is the function of the high frequency of units *et* ('and'), *puis* ('then'), *après* ('after'), it is necessary to proceed to a more qualitative analysis of the functions of *et*.

The unit *et* ('and'), although becoming less frequent, does not disappear, but rather, changes its function. This can be demonstrated, for instance, in informative texts (for explanations of the rules of a game, see Schneuwly, 1988a; for similar results on narrations and reports, see also Schwinn Lang & Rieben, 1992; and, on argumentative and injunctive texts, Rosat, 1991 and 1989b). From a formal and functional point of view, three ways of using the unit *et* can be distinguished.

1. *Et* can be used beween clauses referring to actions or events that are necessarily related. In particular, this strong relationship concerns the case where the same person executes several related actions. Syntactically, the grammatical subject can be mentioned only once. For example, *He runs to the tree, claps <u>and</u> calls out the name of the hidden person.*

2. *Et* can also be used between clauses that refer to actions or events that happen together (with the possible substitution by *pendant que* ['while']) or where the one is the consequence of the other (with the possible addition of *par conséquent* ['consequently']). For example, *He calls out <u>and</u> (consequently) is set free.* 3. *Et* between clauses without apparent relationship or accompanying other textual organizers. For example, *He has to look for them <u>and</u> the others have to set themselves free <u>and</u> the last one can set all others free. <u>And</u> if he has not been set free.*

Use of *et* of the first category corresponds to an integrative; use of the second to an additive packaging. The *et* of the third category has, essentially, the function of ensuring the material continuity of the production of the text (linking operation). Table 12.2 provides the results of the use of *et* in 120 texts written by 30 students in 4 age groups.

This table reveals a clear decline in the percentage of the *et* of the third category in favor of the first one, with the second category being more or less stable across the age groups. In other words, whereas in the younger students' texts the *et* functions as a way of linking superficially, in a undifferentiated way, the utterances of a text, it specializes more and more in the function of creating packages of utterances, forming clearly marked textual units. The following examples illustrate the results (Schneuwly, 1988a, p. 130):

1. *Il faut coller et compter jusqu'à 100 et les autres doivent se cacher. Après il doit aller les chercher et les autres doivent se délivrer et le dernier a le droit de délivrer tous les autres. Et s'il n'a pas attrapé personne, il doit recompter.* (*Fabien, age 10*) 'One of you has to cover his eyes and count up to hundred **and** the others have to hide. Afterwards he has to look for them **and** the others have to

Table 12.2
Three Types of *AND* in Explanatory Texts

| | Age | | | | | | | |
| | 10 years | | 12 years | | 14 years | | Adults | |
Types of *AND*	N	%	N	%	N	%	N	%
Strong relationship	3	4	28	30	42	49	66	67
Concomitance	19	25	24	26	24	28	20	20
No relationship	51	68	38	40	15	18	6	6
Not categorized	2	3	4	4	4	5	6	6
Total	75	100	94	100	85	100	98	100

set themselves free **and** the last one has the right to set all the others free. **And** if he has not caught anybody, he has to count again.'

*...A la fin du jeu, quand chacun est soit délivré ou attrapé **et** qu'il ne reste qu'une personne cachée, celle-ci peut délivrer tout le monde. Dans ce cas, le jeu recommence **et** la personne collée reste la même. Si ce n'est pas le cas, la première personne attrapée doit coller au tour suivant. **Et** le jeu recommence. (Xavier, adult)*

...At the end of the game, when everybody is set free or captured **and** there is only one person still hiding, this one can set everybody free. If this happens, the game begins again **and** the person covering his eyes is still the same one. If not, the first person captured has to cover his eyes the next time. **And** the game begins again.

For the 10-year-olds, most *ets* are units that ensure the continuity of the activity of text production. As can be seen in the example, the *ets* do not so much connect the clauses of the text as guarantee the continuation of the process of enunciation itself. This is what it means to be the trace of operations of linking. The high proportion of *ets* of the first category (50 and 67%, respectively) in the 14-year-olds' and adults' texts is the result of a more and more precise definition of the function of *et* as a means of creating strongly homogeneous units in the text, that is, integrative and additive packaging.

The Increasing Differentiation of Text Types by Textual Organizers

As stated above, the fundamental assumption about development underlying these studies is that this development must be conceived of as a progressive mastery of text types (or genres) adapted to different communication situations; a process of increasing differentiation. This viewpoint has two consequences for the analysis of textual organizers. First, the increasing mastery of text types or genres appears, when one observes textual organizers, as a change of the global configurations of these units or, more accurately, as an ongoing process of the restructuring of configurations of textual organizers corresponding to text types. Second, one and the same textual organizer in different text types, and, consequently, in different configurations, is unequally mastered. In other words, the development of textual organizers has necessarily to be analyzed as part of the ongoing mastery of text types in given communication situations.

The decreasing rate of poorly differentiated textual organizers like *et* ('and'), *puis* ('then'), and *après* ('after') allows specification of text types more and more by characteristic configurations of textual organizers. This ontogenetic tendency is well documented in most of the studies on the relationship between text types and textual organizers, and can be illustrated by three text types (for other text types, see Schneuwly & Rosat, 1986, 1995).

In the first text type, 28 students ages 10, 12, and 14 see contradictory points of view on the ecological problems of car use in a video film. They discuss this as a group, analyze the different arguments, and watch the film again. Afterward, they write a short text on the topic for the school magazine giving arguments for and against (Rosat, 1990, 1991). The categories of textual organizers in Table 12.3 show a clear change in the configuration.

A more qualitative analysis reveals the underlying reasons for the change. In the texts of the youngest students, the *ets* ('ands'), but also the other organizers (mainly expressions like *puis* ['then']), mark the material continuity of the text in juxtaposing different arguments. The nontemporal subordinates are essentially *parce que* ('because'), which introduces a justification. The few other nontemporal organizers are mainly *mais* ('but'), which locally contrasts two opposite utterances. The texts of the 12-year-olds, although still containing a large number of *ets* simply juxtaposing utterances, also exhibit organizers with more specific semantic values. Among them, the nontemporal subordinate *parce que* is still frequent, but other units appear to be marking an opposition (*tandis que* ['whereas']) or a possibility (*si* ['if']). The other nontemporal organizers are still mainly *mais*, but units of enumeration (*soit ... soit* ['either ... or']), opposition (*par contre* ['on the other hand']) and illustration (*par exemple* ['for instance']) appear. The system changes much more radically in the texts of the 14-year-olds. Generally, organizers become relatively rare and mainly specific units are used with the following functions: many non-temporal organizers have a clear beaconing function (marking the different arguments and counterarguments like *en outre* ['furthermore'], *en revanche* ['on the other hand']; they are

TABLE 12.3
Textual Organizers in Argumentative Texts

Categories of textual organizers	Age		
	10	12	14
AND	19.3	16.1	10.5
Subordinate nontemporal	25.4	18.0	9.6
Other nontemporal organizers	7.3	10.0	17.8
Other organizers	5.0	9.1	8.9
Total	57.0	53.2	46.8

introducing reformulations in the text like *en fait* ['in fact'], and *en bref* ['in brief']). The subordinate nontemporal units, and also most of the remaining *ets*, create integrated packages of utterances in the different parts of the text. Textual organizers thus serve the hierarchizing of the text in specifying, at the same time, the relationships between the arguments in the different parts and subparts of the text.

In the second text type, 30 Catalan students ages 10, 12, and 14 produce a short news item for a newspaper (Dolz, 1990) after observation of the following event: a car driver without number plate is stopped by a policeman who wants to check his driving license; the car driver escapes and he is arrested later despite resistance, by a group of policemen.

The text to be produced can be broken down in three main parts. The first part, an introductory paragraph in the form of a preliminary abstract of the events and situation, is typical for short news items. The event itself is composed of two clearly distinct parts: the check by the policeman and the arrest. For the analysis of organizers, the following categories are distinguished: *et* as a form of archiconnector; *mais*, which often marks a change of perspective in stories written by young students; temporal expressions, which essentially mark the chronological dimensions; deictic expressions, which play a particular role for situating events; and nontemporal expressions, namely, spatial expressions situating the events.

In the texts of the 10-year-olds, there is the usual high frequency of *et* that guarantees the continuity of the text. In the texts of the 12-year-olds, the frequency of *et* diminishes sharply, and there is a large increase of organizers that mark the two parts of the text corresponding to the two parts of the event. *Pero* ('but') appears particularly often in this position, but also *llavors* ('then') and some temporal subordinates. *Pero* almost disappears in the texts of the 14-year-olds where the parts are marked mainly by spatial organizers (*en uns carrers* ['in a street']) and temporal subordinates. The texts generally contain an introductory paragraph where the events are precisely located by temporal deictics and spatial expressions. Many temporal expressions like *a cap d'uns minuts* ('one minute later') and temporal subordinates (*com que* ['while']) locating events at a precise moment, on an absolute scale, or in relation to other events become frequent. In accordance with the general aim of this text type, the older children no longer interpret it as narrating events, but mainly as informing or relating that and how things happened and how they happened in a quite straightforward way.

Three aspects of the system of textual organizers thus seem to appear: units specifically situating the events in the present time (deictic expressions); precise temporal units describing events as accurately as possible on a chronological axis; in this way, these units demonstrate the essentially informative value of the text. The communicative aim influences the construction of an efficient configuration of textual organizers.

The third text type was obtained from explanations of how a canal lock functions as produced by students ages 10, 12, and 14 in French (Schneuwly, Rosat, & Dolz, 1989), German (Schneuwly, 1988b), and Catalan (Dolz, 1990). The content of the text was constant because it was elaborated through a teaching sequence including silent video film, diagrams, discussion, and a summary using key words.

The analysis of the texts of all the students shows that there is no difficulty concerning the understanding of the functioning of a canal lock. Important differences appear, however, in the structure of the text. An explanatory text of the type intended is generally made up of two parts: an introduction that situates the problem and an explanation; it can be followed by a conclusion that generalizes the explanation. This structure is normally marked by a particular configuration of textual organizers.

In the younger students' texts (the 10-year-olds), a very different structure of the text appears with a completely different system of organizers. The explanations are organized as a script or as a list of events. The addition of events is mainly marked by *et*, by *puis*, and by marks like temporal subordinate clauses introduced by *quand* ('when'). The 12-year-olds' texts generally contain a short introduction where the general function of the canal lock is described by expressions like *car* ('for'), *parce que* ('because'), and *si* ('if'). The list of actions is less clearcut. In the older students' texts, a large number of nontemporal textual organizers appear, that give the chronological, step-by-step explanation a new perspective. Whereas the explanation, generally given in the second part of the text, continues to be mainly segmented by temporal organizers marking important phases of the process (beaconing function) and by *et* (packaging function), nontemporal organizers appear in the introduction and the conclusion, namely, final expressions (*pour que* ['so that']), *pour* +*inf.* ['in order to' + inf.]), causal expressions (*c'est pourquoi* ['that is why'], *car* ['for']) and expressions like *par exemple* ('for instance'), and *c'est-à-dire* ('in other words') that mark the explanatory intervention of the enunciator in his own text. The conclusion is clearly introduced by specific expressions like *finalement* ('finally'), and *en conclusion* ('in conclusion').

It is as if the simple chronological content is articulated to the specific goal that text type is aimed at, namely, the explanation. The text becomes more interactive, the structure of the text is clearly marked by textual organizers, and metalinguistic expressions are introduced that allow the enunciator to comment its own text. Again, the textual organizers form a particular configuration in accordance with the specific structure of the particular genre.

The Unequal Development of Textual Organizers as a Function of Text Types

We have seen that textual organizers can be looked upon as configurations that function in accordance with the overall structure of a text and that the mastery of such a text type implies a complete restructuring of the configuration of textual organizers in a text. This point of view, which considers the functioning of textual organizers as configurations, has an important implication. Even if a particular textual organizer is used in a certain function in a given text type, this does not mean that it can automatically be used in the same way in another text type whose system of textual organizers is not yet established and mastered by the student. In other words, development is unequal. What is already mature in some contexts must still mature in others. This observation can be illustrated by two studies.

Schwinn Lang, and Rieben (1992) compared two text types; an invented story of a child meeting an extraterrestrial and a report on a museum visit made the day before. These texts are produced by the same children who are about 8, 10, and 12 years old (2nd, 4th, and 6th grades of primary school). The main results are presented in condensed form in Table 12.4.

The total density of textual organizers shows a very different pattern between the report and the short story. Whereas in the former, the density declines sharply only in the text produced by the 12-year-olds; in the latter, this is already happening at the age of 10 with no significant change observed between ages 10 and 12. This difference is due to two factors. In the case of the report, the density of *et* decreases less than in the short story and the density of temporal organizers remains roughly the same; a strong decrease takes place for both categories in the case of the short story. Obviously, ontogenetic change does not take place in the same way and at the same time in both text types.

A more qualitative analysis allows a more precise understanding of the observed phenomena. In the report, the temporal organizers are predominantly *après* ('after'), *ensuite* ('then'), and *puis* ('then'), which essentially mark the chronology of events. Generally, only one of these organizers appears in one text, which means that there is no real hierarchy between linguistic units that could be used to mark different levels of the texts. The texts are thus organized as a simple concatenation of events, almost every one being linked to the preceding one in the same way as the others; these events are not structured into more coherent phases with packages of clauses. Packaging appears only in the texts of the 12-year-olds, where the lower density and the simultaneous presence of different temporal organizers, marking different levels in the text,

TABLE 12.4
Number and Density (in % of Number of Verbs) of Textual Organizers
in Reports and Short Stories

	Age					
	8 years		*10 years*		*12 years*	
	N	%	N	%	N	%
	Report					
ET	113	40	149	26	95	11
Temporal organizers	74	28	153	29	213	24
Nontemporal organizers.	3	0	28	5	113	12
Total	190	68	330	60	421	47
	Short Story					
ET	100	35	99	19	99	14
Temporal Organizers	60	27	64	15	99	13
Nontemporal organizers	27	9	59	11	139	15
Total	187	72	222	45	337	42

make it possible to structure the text according to these levels. In the short stories, this is already happening in the texts produced by the 10-year-olds. These students leave behind a stereotypical marking of the chronology of all (or most) events and mark, by differentiated temporal organizers, the main parts of the text, such as the complicating event or the resolution, using organizers like *un jour* ('one day'), and *tout à coup* ('suddenly') or by using nontemporal coordinating organizers like *mais* ('but') or *alors* ('so'). The change that is observable between the texts of the 10- and 12-year-olds consists exclusively in a larger variety of temporal organizers that have the same kind of beaconing function as those used by the 10-year-olds. The textual organizers are thus not acquired all at once and used in different text types, rather they are acquired more specifically for a given text type.

Another example illustrates this phenomenon, namely, the comparison of the uses of *et* ('and') in explanatory texts (see Table 12.2) and in argumentative texts (see Table 12.5), namely, a letter to the editor written by the same pupils.

The differences noted are striking. In the argumentative texts, the majority of the uses of *et*, at the age of 14, are still of the type "without relationship" (41% compared to 33% for the first category), whereas in explaining the game most ets are clearly of Category 1 (49% compared to 18%). These results seem to indicate that producing texts by writing is not a skill acquired all at once, in a homogeneous way, but that it follows very different paths depending on the text type concerned. Textual patterns, in this case the textual organizers, that are abandoned in a given text type by children of a specific age are still in use at the same time in other text types.

How Do New Textual Organizers Appear in a Text Type?

From an ontogenetic perspective, it is most interesting to observe precisely how new textual organizers appear in a text type. One way of answering this question is to analyze, very closely, for which textual functions the same textual organizer is used at different ages in the same text type and to compare by which means the textual parts it marks at a certain age are marked at other stages. By observing the use of *mais* ('but') in explanatory texts, this analysis can be demonstrated.

In texts explaining games, *mais* ('but') is used essentially in two different ways (Schneuwly, 1988a). It introduces a new situation. The intervention of a player can change the whole direction of the game or the writer can explain the game from the point of view of one player and then from the point of view of the others, for example, *The one looking finds somebody, runs over and says: 1, 2, 3 and the name. But the others…*

It also has a more local use; it limits the expectation that a word, expression, or clause creates on the part of the reader (*exterior, but also interior; he looks, but remains close to the tree; do the same, but by calling out*). The distribution of the use of *mais* as a function of these two categories is given in Table 12.6.

An important tendancy appears at the age of 14, which is confirmed in adult texts. *Mais*, which has an important function of changing perspective in the texts of the younger students (100% of the occurrences), is used increasingly in

TABLE 12.5
Three Types of *AND* in Argumentative Texts

	Age					
	10 years		12 years		14 years	
Types of AND	N	%	N	%	N	%
Strong relationship	7	15	16	27	26	33
Concomitance	10	21	10	17	20	26
No relationship	31	65	34	57	32	41
Total	48	100	60	100	78	100

TABLE 12.6
Number and percentage of Two Categories of BUT in Explanatory Texts

	Age							
	10 years		12 years		14 years		Adults	
Types of BUT	N	%	N	%	N	%	N	%
Change of perspective	8	100	17	100	11	69	5	33
Local use	0	0	0	0	5	31	10	67
Total	8	100	17	100	16	100	15	100

a more local context (31% of the occurrences in the 14-year-olds' texts and 67% in the adults' texts). This change of perspective is marked, by other means, which can also be combined with rhetorical questions (*What do the others have to do ?*); exclamations (*Watch out !*); paragraphs and numbers; thematization (*The role of the others is to* ...); and other nontemporal organizers (*par contre* ['on the other hand'], and *toutefois* ['however']).

In the texts of the adults, almost all important changes of perspective are marked by one or another of these means, although generally not by *mais*. In the texts of the 14-year-olds, this is the case for a majority of texts and passages.

The change observable in the texts seems to indicate that *mais* plays an important role in the acquisition of textual competence in this text type. It signals, for the writer and the reader, an important change of perspective in the text, change which, on a higher level of mastery, can be indicated by other means. *Mais* is a first, primitive means that children use to structure their texts. A new function—the structuring of a text—is first expressed by a former means. In the course of development, this new function, that has been stabilized by the former means, will find new, more adequate forms of expression.

CONCLUSIONS

The studies presented here yield the following conclusions for further ontogenetic research on textual organizers: (a) Certain aspects of their functioning can only be understood from a textual point of view (b) Their functions can change profoundly with age (c) They form configurations that function as systems in text types, and (d) These systems are acquired at different rates in the different text types.

These findings indicate that the careful interpretation of any single textual organizer has to take into account its textual use, that is, the system it forms with others in a text as well as the text type in which it is used.

REFERENCES

Adam, J. M. (1984). *Le récit* [The Story]. Paris: P.U.F.

Adam, J. M. (1990). *Eléments de linguistique textuelle. Théorie et pratique de l'analyse textuelle* [Elements of textual linguistics. Theory and practice of textual analysis]. Bruxelles: Mardaga.

Adam, J. M., & Revaz, F. (1989). Aspects de la structuration du texte descriptif: les marqueurs d'énumération et de reformulation [Aspects of the structuration of descriptive texts: the makers of enumeration and reformulation]. *Langue Française, 81*, 59–98.

Antoine, G. (1962). *La coordination en français* (Vol. 1 and 2). Paris: D'Artrey. (Original work published 1958).

Bally, C. (1932). *Linguistique générale et linguistique française* [General Linguistics and French Linguistics]. Berne: Francke.

Biasci, C. (1982). *Konnektive in Sätzen und Texten* [Connectors in sentences and texts]. Hamburg: Buske.

Bronckart, J. P. (1994). Action, langage et discours. Les fondements d'une psychologie du langage [Action, language and discourse. Foundations of a psychology of language]. *Bulletin Suisse de Linguistique Appliquée, 59*, 7–64.

Bronckart, J. P., Bain, D., Schneuwly, B., Davaud, C., & Pasquier, A. (1985). *Le fonctionnement des discours. Un modèle psychologique et une méthode d'analyse* [The functioning of discourse. A psychological model and a method analysis]. Neuchâtel: Delachaux et Niestlé.

Bronckart, J. P., & Fayol, M. (1988). Temps et texte: un modèle psychologique et quelques illustrations [Tense and text; a psychological model and some illustrations]. In N. Tersis & A. Kihm (Eds.), *Temps et Aspects* [Tense and Aspects] (pp. 255–263). Paris: Peeters/SELAF.

Bronckart, J. P., & Schneuwly, B. (1991). Children's production of textual organizers. In G. Piéraut-Le-Bonniec & M. Dolitsky (Eds.), *Language Bases...Discourse Bases* (pp. 143–156). Amsterdam: John Benjamins.

Brunot, F. (1926). *La pensée et la Langue* [The thinking and the language]. Paris: Masson.

Chanquoy, L. (1991). *Ponctuation et connecteurs: Acquisition et fonctionnement* [Puncutation and connectors; acquisition and functioning]. Unpublished doctoral thesis, University of Bourgogne, Dijon, France.

Coltier, D., & Turco, G. (1988). Des agents doubles de l'organisation textuelle: les marqueurs d'intégration linéaire [The double agents of text organization: the markers of linear integration]. *Pratiques, 57*, 21–37.

De Weck, G. (1991). *La cohésion dans les textes d'enfants: étude du développement des processus anaphoriques* [The cohesion in children's texts; study of the development of anaphoric processes]. Neuchâtel: Delachaux et Niestlé.

Dolz, J. (1990). *Catégorie verbale et activité langagière. Le fonctionnement du verbe dans les textes écrits des enfants catalans* [Verbal category and verbal activity. The functioning of the verb in texts written by catalan children]. Unpublished doctoral thesis, University of Geneva, Switzerland.

Ducrot, O., Bourcier, D., Bruxelles, S., Diller, A.-M., Guoazé, J., Maury, L., Nguyen, T. B., Nunes, G., de Saint-Alban, L. R., Rémis, A., Sirdar-Iskander, C. (1980). *Les Mots du Discours* [The words of the discourse]. Paris: Minuit.

Fayol, M. (1986). *L'organisation du récit écrit chez l'enfant. Son évolution de 6 à 10 ans.* [The organization of the written story. Its evaluation from six to ten]. Unpublished doctoral thesis, University of Bordeaux II, Bordeaux.

Fayol, M. (1986). Les connecteurs dans les récits écrits. Etude chez l'enfant de 6 à 10 ans [The connectors in written sotries. Study of children from six to ten]. *Pratiques, 49*, 101–131.

Grunig, B. N. (1977). Bilan sur le statut de la coordination. [Results of studies on the status of the coordination]. *Documents de recherche en linguistique appliquée de Versailles, 15*, 46–77.

Gülich, E. (1970). *Makrosyntax der Gliederungssignale im gesprochenen Französisch* [Macrosyntax of signals of segmenting in spoken French]. München, Germany: Fink.

Kail, M., & Weissenborn, J. (1991). Conjunctions: Developmental issues. In: G. Piéraut-Le-Bonniec, & M. Dolitsky (Eds.), *Language Bases...Discourse Bases: Some Aspects of Contemporary French-language Psycholinguistics Research* (pp. 125–142). Amsterdam: Benjamins.

Mouchon, S., Fayol, M., & Gombert, J.-E. (1991). L'emploi de quelques connecteurs dans les récits [The use of some connectors in the stories]. *Repères, 3,* 87–98.

Quasthoff, U. (1979). Verzögerungsphänomene, Verknüpfungs- und Gliedrungssignale in Alltagsargumentationen und Alltagserzählungen. In H. Weidt (Ed.), *Die Partikeln der deutschen sprache* [Phenomenons of retardation, signals of connection and segmentting in daily argumentations and stories] (pp. 39–57). Berlin: de Gruyter.

Rosat, M.-C. (1989a). Notes relatives au fonctionnement des organisateurs dans quatre types de textes. In: Rubattel, C. (Ed.) *Modèles du Discours. Recherches actuelles en Suisse romande* [Notes relative to the functioning of organizers in four text types] (pp. 423–436). Berne: Lang.

Rosat, M.-C. (1989b). Texte injonctif chez l'élève. Organisateurs textuels et conditions de production [Injunctive texts of students. Textual organizers and production conditions]. *Le Français Aujourd'hui, 86,* 40–50.

Rosat, M.-C. (1990). Pour ou contre une analyse de formes textuelles argumentatives. *Travaux neuchatelois de linguistique* [For or against an analysis of argumentative textual forms] *16,* 99–112.

Rosat, M.-C. (1991). A propos de réalisations orale et écrite d'un texte argumentatif [Concerning the oral and written realization of an argumentative text]. *Etudes de Linguistique Appliquée, 81,* 119–130.

Schneuwly, B. (1988a). *Le langage écrit chez l'enfant. La production des textes informatifs et argumentatifs* [The written language of the child. The production of informative and argumentative texts]. Neuchâtel: Delachaux et Niestlé.

Schneuwly, B. (1988b, June). *"How does a canal lock work?" Explanations written by pupils aged 10 and 14.* Paper given at the Third European Conference on Developmental Psychology. Budapest, Hungary.

Schneuwly, B., & Bronckart, J.-P. (1986). Connexion et cohésion dans quatre types de textes d'enfants [Connection and cohesion in four text types of children]. *Cahiers de Linguistique Française, 7,* 279–294.

Schneuwly, B., & Rosat, M.-C. (1986). Analyse ontogénétique des organisateurs textuels dans deux textes informatifs écrits [Ontogenetic analysis of textual organizers in two written informative texts]. *Pratiques, 51,* 39–53.

Schneuwly, B., & Rosat, M.-C. (1995). "Ma chambre" ou: comment linéariser l'espace? Etude ontogénétique de textes descriptifs écrits ["My room" or; how to linearize the space? Ontogenetic study of written descriptive texts]. *Bulletin de Linguistique Appliquée, 61,* 83–100.

Schneuwly, B., Rosat, M.-C., & Dolz, J. (1989). Les organisateurs textuels dans quatre types d'écrits. Etude chez des élèves de dix, douze et quatorze ans [The textual organizers in four written texts. Study of students aged ten, twelve and fourteen]. *Langue Française, 81,* 40–58.

Schwinn Lang, C., & Rieben, L. (1992). Evolution et diversité de la production textuelle en situation de classe [Evolution and diversity of the textual production in classroom situation] *Revue Française de Pédagogie, 99,* 25–35.

Sechehaye, A. (1950). *Essai sur la structure logique de la phrase* [Essay on the logical structure of the sentence]. Paris: Champion.

Smith, R., & Frawley, W. J. (1983). Conjunctive cohesion in four English genres. *Text, 3,* 347–373.

Van Dijk, T. A. (1979). Pragmatic connectives. *Journal of Pragmatics, 3,* 447–456.

Chapter 13

Processing Clauses and Their Relationships During Comprehension

David J. Townsend
Montclair State University

How do people acquire knowledge? The variety of answers to this question fall into two broad categories: An associative answer maintains that knowledge comes from associating experiences in the world. A structural answer supposes that knowledge comes from combining small units or ideas in certain ways to form larger memory structures. One difference in the use of these two kinds of knowledge concerns computation. Associative knowledge tends to be elicited without computing intermediate memories, whereas structural knowledge requires the use of smaller units for computing larger structures, often with memories that mediate the smaller units and the larger structures. This chapter shows that acquiring knowledge from text involves an integration of knowledge that is elicited and knowledge that is computed.

We see examples in the use of the two kinds of knowledge in the shortest possible text, a sentence with just two clauses, such as *Kids visit Harry because he raises snakes*. The structural information from this text includes the fact that there are two clauses, *kids visit Harry* and *he raises snakes*. Each of these clauses consists of small units (words and phrases) that have certain structural relationships to one another, for example, verb–object, and each clause has a certain structural relationship to the other. Texts also elicit various kinds of associative information, including memories of events, situations, and words. For example, *visit* may elicit an expectation of volition on the part of the agent *kids*; *because* may elicit an expectation of a cause or reason for children visiting Harry; and *snakes* may elicit memories of earlier fears as well as fascination with these slithery creatures. The knowledge that the comprehender gains from this text is an integration of structural and associative information: Roughly, children visit Harry and the reason why they choose to do so is that he raises snakes and children find these creatures fascinating.

This example also shows that part of the knowledge one gains from text comes from processing the relationships between the clauses of the text. For example, the knowledge that a comprehender obtains from *Kids visit Harry although he raises snakes* differs from that of *Kids visit Harry because he raises snakes*. The use of *although* signals that Harry's raising of snakes did not produce the expected result or outcome. As a result, comprehenders integrate the structures and associations from an *although* sentence in a different way: roughly, children visit Harry and they choose to do so despite that fact that he raises snakes, which scare people, and one would not expect children voluntarily to do things that scare them. The interpretation of these two sentences depends on which aspects of associative knowledge, fascination versus fear, the comprehender integrates with structural information.

Processing the relationships between clauses, therefore, involves integrating structural and associative knowledge. Clauses are fundamental structural units in text, and the way in which comprehenders relate them to one another and to associative memories is part of the basic knowledge that they gain from text.

It is worth emphasizing that interclause processing is merely one example of a more general process of integrating structural and associative information. Integration of structural and associative information may occur at the level of syllables, words, clauses, or sentences. Consider the familiar sentence *Colorless green ideas sleep furiously*. The structural information in this sentence includes the fact that *green* and *ideas* are related as modifier and head of a noun phrase. When processing this sentence, comprehenders also draw on the associative information that *green* refers to a certain physical property and *ideas* refers to nonphysical mental states. The sentence is odd because integrating the structural and associative information leads to the contradiction that the structural relation between *green* and *ideas* attributes a physical property to a nonphysical state. Thus, integrating structural and associative information is not restricted to interclause processing.

In this chapter, I review evidence that interclause processing is a focal point for integrating structural and associative information in text comprehension. The chapter begins by summarizing some of the ways in which clauses and their interrelations mediate the integration of structural and associative information. Then I will review how connectives with different meanings serve as traffic signals for directing resources to associative versus structural information and show that interclause relationships in sentence processing affect comprehension in longer texts as well. The chapter concludes with a discussion of how interclause processing influences the formation of new associative knowledge about words.

THE ROLES OF CLAUSES
IN TEXT COMPREHENSION

Clauses have three major roles in text comprehension: They are basic structural units, they can mediate the integration of new information and already known information, and their interrelationships contribute to semantic coherence.

Structural and Semantic Units

The *clause* is a structural unit that contains smaller parts that are related to one another syntactically. It is the unit of expression for a complete semantic idea or proposition. Clauses need not contain the entire set of phrases that corre-spond to a proposition. For example, the phrase *mixing drinks* in *mixing drinks is an art* is a kind of degraded clause that corresponds to "somebody mixes drinks."

Clauses also may have certain kinds of structural relations to one another. For example, one clause may be the main clause of a sentence and the other structurally subordinate to it, as in *Kids visit Harry because he raises snakes*, or clauses may be structurally coordinate, as in *Sam died and he went to heaven*. Words like *because, and, although, that, which*, and so on may mark the beginning of a clause, but sometimes they occur within clauses and sometimes they do not occur at all.

Given and New Information

Subordinate clauses often contain presupposed or given information that the comprehender already knows, while main clauses often contain asserted or new information that the comprehender does not yet know. For example, in *Sarah knows that class starts at 9:00 a.m. sharp*, the given information is that class starts at 9:00 a.m. sharp, and the new information is that Sarah knows it. Because subordinate clauses often begin with one of a small set of subordinating words, comprehenders can use these markers to determine what information is given, and, hence, may be retrieved from memory. The given information may be available from memory of the earlier parts of a text or it may be available from comprehenders' experiences prior to the text.

Integrating the new information of a sentence with information that already is known is an important part of text comprehension (Haviland & Clark, 1974).

Anaphoric devices such as definite articles, pronouns, synonyms, and so on can signal already known information. These devices enable comprehenders to develop coherency in a text by showing how the new information that is asserted in a sentence should be organized with previously mentioned entities. For example in the text *A '54 Chevy roared around the corner. The old jalopy slammed into a telephone pole*, the phrase *the old jalopy* refers back to *a '54 Chevy*, and, thus, comprehenders should store the new information *slammed into a telephone pole* with *a '54 Chevy*. The signaling function of subordinating words for given information is similar to that of anaphoric devices. One difference between the two is that subordinating words often signal already-known propositions rather than already-known referents.

Semantic Coherence

Coherence in a text requires more than a set of clauses that overlap in their referents and propositions. Johnson-Laird (1988) made this point with the following text:

> Furtively he dragged a package out of the reeds towards him. Out of curiosity, he opened the package and hid it beneath the bank in safety. He struggled with a youth who killed him. Then they stretched out indolently on the bank. (p. 344)

The noun phrases of this text overlap a great deal; for example, there are three references to a package, and six references to the protagonist. Despite frequent references to the same entities, we do not consider the text to be coherent.

Coherence also depends on determining how the clauses and sentences of a text are related to one another semantically. One way comprehenders can relate the sentences of a text is to construct a mental model that is based on memories of similar events and situations (Schank & Abelson, 1977). For example, a story of a birthday party may activate memories of what events typically occur at birthday parties and the order in which they typically occur. Thus, the mental model may contain asserted or implied events as they unfolded for the protagonist or for someone else. The lack of coherence of Johnson-Laird's passage, however, is not due to difficulty in establishing the temporal order of events, but rather in establishing a causal chain, in which each event is both the result of an earlier event and the cause of a later event (Trabasso & van den Broek, 1985). Johnson-Laird's passage breaks the causal chain when the protagonist is killed and then stretches out indolently on the bank.

Clausal and sentential connectives show how the events of a text fit into a causal chain. Table 13.1 lists several examples of markers that signal semantic relations between clauses (Townsend, 1983). These connectives often signal both causal and temporal meanings (McCabe & Peterson, 1985). Events that are joined with temporal connectives like *then* may be causally related because causes precede or coincide with their effects. Conversely, causal connectives like *because* imply temporal relations because causes cannot occur later than their effects. The connectives in Table 13.1 differ in how explicitly they signal causes, ranging from explicitly stating a causal event (*because*), to stating an earlier or simultaneous event that is potentially a cause (*after*), to stating a later event that is potentially an effect (*before*), to explicitly stating an effect (*so*), to explicitly denying an expected causal relation (*although*).

Connectives that deny an expected causal relation are called adversatives. *Although* indicates that, although the information in the subordinate clause should be stored in memory as an event that did occur, the occurrence of this event did not cause the event that one would have expected. To integrate the meaning of an *although* sentence into a coherent representation of text, the

TABLE 13.1
Causal-Temporal Meanings of Connectives

Causal Event:
because, if, for, since
He was angry because the chair was ruined.

Earlier Event:
since, after, previously, beforehand
She ran into the den after hearing a loud noise.

Simultaneous Event:
as, when, while, and, meanwhile, simultaneously
When the chair tilted over, beer spilled on it.

Later Event:
before, until, and, afterward, subsequently, then
Claudia opened a can of beer before going into the den.

Effect:
so, and, consequently, therefore
Sam was thirsty so he opened a can of beer.

Denial of Expected Causal Role:
although, while, despite
Although the new chair was ruined, he wasn't angry.

Unexpected Effect:
but, whereas, however, nevertheless, yet
The new chair was ruined, but he wasn't angry.

comprehender must determine what causal relation was expected but did not occur. For example, in *Although Sally called up her aunt each night...*, the speaker may have expected that Sally's calling up her aunt each night would cause any one of a number of events.comprehenders can infer which causal relation was expected from information in the main clause of the sentence. If the sentence continues *...her telephone bill was low*, it becomes clear that the speaker's expected causal relation is that Sally's calling her aunt each night causes her telephone bill to be high. If instead it continues as *she still submitted her manuscript on time*, the anticipated but denied causal relation is that Sally's calling her aunt each night causes her to neglect other duties such as completing a writing assignment. Or if the sentence continues as *...she did not get a divorce*, the anticipated but denied causal relation is that Sally's calling her aunt nightly might have caused her divorce.

Comprehenders also may obtain information about the expected causal relation that an *although* sentence denies from associations to earlier statements in a text. For example, in *The kids arrived for Tommy's birthday party. They played Pin the Tail on the Donkey. They sang Happy Birthday as Tommy's mom carried in the cake. Although Tommy blew as hard as he could...* the earlier parts of the text elicit expectations of certain events that are causally related: Blowing very hard causes all of the candles burning on the birthday cake to go out. This expectation arises because of stored memories of birthday parties, cakes, and candles. Thus, integrating the structure of clauses and the information that is associated to events that were stated earlier in a text contributes to semantic coherence.

SENTENCE PROCESSING

Comprehenders have limited resources for processing certain kinds of information (Just & Carpenter, 1992; Townsend & Bever, 1991). Because connectives differ in their requirements for establishing semantic coherence, they induce comprehenders to direct resources in different ways. The development of comprehension skills involves learning how to direct these resources to different kinds of information. In a clause-picture matching task, Townsend and Ravelo (1980) found that times to determine a match depended at different points in development on the structural versus temporal role of the clause. Three-year olds responded fastest to pictures of main clause events, whereas 4-year olds responded fastest to pictures of earlier events. The resource-directing functions of connectives can be summarized as follows:

- CAUSAL: Store the events as cause–effect and focus resources on the causal chain.

- TEMPORAL: Store the events as temporally ordered and potentially cause–effect and divide resources between the temporal chain and structural properties to determine whether a causal inference is warranted.
- ADVERSATIVE: (a) Store the main clause event with the stated "cause" as an exception to the expected cause–effect relation and focus resources on this causal chain, and (b) If there is no unique expected cause-effect relation, focus resources on structural analysis of the main clause in order to infer one.

Causal connectives indicate that the stated events fit directly into the causal chain of a text. If the sequence of these events in the text corresponds to this causal chain, these connectives will direct resources to the more conceptual representation of text. For example, the sequence of events in *Because Harry raises snakes, kids visit him* corresponds to the cause–effect order, so comprehenders can direct resources immediately toward the conceptual interpretation. *Kids visit Harry because he raises snakes* does not correspond to the cause–effect ordering, and comprehenders, therefore, must retain more structural information until the events can be reorganized into a causal chain.

Temporal connectives potentially can be related causally. If the clauses appear in a way that corresponds to temporal order, these connectives direct resources to conceptual information, but not as strongly as causal connectives, because some resources also are directed to structural properties to determine whether they warrant a causal relation. *Adversative connectives* signal that an anticipated cause–effect relation did not occur. If the expected causal relation is available, these connectives direct resources to conceptual information. If not, they direct resources to structural information to infer the causal relation the speaker had expected.

Immediate Memory

Townsend and Bever (1978) showed that connectives influence comprehenders' access to different kinds of memories. They presented two different probe tasks near the ends of subordinate clauses that were introduced by one of several connectives. One probe task depended on structural information, whereas the other depended on associative information. The materials included:

1. a. If Pete calls up his aunt each...*up*
   b. If Pete calls his aunt up each...*up*
   c. If Pete calls up his aunt each...*using the phone*

2. a. Though Pete calls up his aunt each...*up*
   b. Though Pete calls his aunt up each...*up*
   c. Though Pete calls up his aunt each...*using the phone*

For the (a) and (b) examples, subjects said whether *up* had appeared in the sentence fragment. This task requires attention to the words of the clause. Because the target *up* appears in different positions within the clause in (a) and (b), any difference in reaction times for (a) versus (b) indicates relative attention to the location of words within clauses. For the (c) example, subjects said whether *using the phone* is associated with any part of the sentence fragment. This task requires attention to information that is associated with words and phrases in the clause. In this case, *using the phone* and *calls up* are associated.

Townsend and Bever (1978) found that response times differed more for Example 2a and Example 2b than for Example 1a and Example 1b. This result suggested that *though* directs resources toward structural information. However, response times were faster for Example 1c than for Example 2c. This suggested that if directs resources toward associative information.

Townsend and Bever (1978) also found that the causal explicitness of connectives influenced the salience of structural versus associative information. As causal explicitness increased from *though* to *while* to *when* to *since* to *if*, response times on the associative task became faster. This result suggests that causal explicitness increased accessibility to associative information. However, response time differences between the (a) and (b) versions in the structural task decreased with the causal explicitness. Structural and associative information apparently can compete for limited resources, and comprehenders can divide these resources between different kinds of information.

Attention

Townsend, Hoover, and Bever (1984) confirmed that connectives influence how comprehenders allocate attention during sentence comprehension. Subjects first read a cue word or phrase and then listened to sentences like Example 3 and Example 4.

3. a. *young people:* If Harry keeps snakes on the farm kids visit every day.
   b. *young people:* Though Harry keeps snakes on the farm kids visit every day.
4. a. *kig:* If Harry keeps snakes on the farm kig visit every day.
   b. *kig:* Though Harry keeps snakes on the farm kig visit every day.

The subjects' task was to monitor for one of two targets. If the subjects received *young people* as a cue, they were to monitor for a word that was associated semantically to this phrase. If they received a nonsense syllable like *kig* as a cue, they were to monitor for a syllable that matched it. Response times for semantic associates were faster for *if* than for *though*. This result suggests that the availability of a causal chain, signaled by *if*, directs attention more to semantic associations. Response times for nonsense words, however, were faster for *though* than for *if*. This result suggests that the demand for determining the expected causal relation that is required by *though* directs attention to structural units (syllables). Because these differences between connectives occur in online monitoring tasks, they depend on online processing activities.

Integration

Townsend (1983) used a naming task to show that processing interclause relations influences the availability of different kinds of information for later integration. Subjects listened to fragments of sentences that began with *if* or *though* and ended with an ambiguous phrase like *landing planes*. After hearing the last word of the ambiguous phrase, subjects saw either *is* or *are* on a screen. The subjects' task was to read aloud this target word and indicate whether or not it was an appropriate continuation for the sentence fragment. Townsend (1983) measured the time that subjects took to name this target word.

The structural and associative information in the material between the connective and the ambiguous phrase either supported or did not support the target. The structural information in this material refers to whether or not the initial clause of the sentence fragment contained an instance of *is* or *are*, whereas the associative information refers to how the entire initial clause of the sentence fragment biases comprehenders toward singular versus plural target verbs (Tyler & Marslen-Wilson, 1977). Thus, the sentence fragment *If the pilot is required to attend flight school, landing planes...* structurally supports an *is* target because *is* occurs in the fragment. Both *If the pilot is required to attend flight school, landing planes...* and *If the pilots are required to attend flight school, landing planes...* associatively support a singular target verb like *is*, since pretesting showed that subjects more often complete these sentence fragments with a singular verb. Table 13.2 shows examples of materials that were biased associatively toward plural targets as well.

Structural biases had significant effects on naming times only when *though* introduced the fragment. For *though* fragments, response times were faster when the verb in the initial clause matched the target, but for *if* fragments, initial clause verb had no effect. This shows that connectives can increase or decrease the availability of structural information for later integration.

Semantic associations had no overall effect on naming times and did not interact with connective. The failure to find that *if* significantly increased availability of semantic associations was surprising. This led Townsend and Bever (1982) to examine the interaction between structural and associative processing by comparing the effects of target verbs of different number. The structure of a phrase like *landing planes* is ambiguous when it appears in isolation or in a sentence like *Landing planes can be dangerous*. One interpretation of *landing planes* corresponds to a gerund structure like *mixing drinks*, in which *drink* is the object of the verb *mixing*. The other interpretation of *landing planes* corresponds to an adjectival structure like *diving submarines*, in which *diving* is a modifier of the head noun *submarines*. The verb *is* in *Landing planes is easy* signals that the ambiguous phrase has a gerund structure, whereas *are* in *Landing planes are hazardous* signals that it has an adjectival structure. The gerund and adjectival structures differ in how closely they correspond to complete clauses. The gerund structure is more complete than the adjectival because it presents the final phrase (Verb–Object) of the most common English sentence form, Subject–Verb–Object.

Townsend and Bever (1982) found that when semantic association to the initial clause supported the gerund interpretation of the ambiguous phrase, naming times were faster for *is* than for *are*, providing that *if* introduced the initial clause. Naming times did not differ for *is* versus *are* targets when the semantic association was biased toward the adjectival interpretation, whether *if* or *though* introduced the initial clause. These results suggest that comprehenders computed both the gerund and adjectival structures at the point of hearing *landing planes*. The fact that the target affects naming time only when semantic associations support the gerund structure suggests that more complete structures are units of integrating the structural interpretation of *landing planes* and

TABLE 13.2
Associative and Structural Biases on Target Words

Singular Associative Bias:	
Singular Structural Bias:	If the pilots are required to attend flight school
Plural Structural Bias:	If the pilot is required to attend flight school
Plural Associative Bias:	
Singular Structural Bias:	If the airline's ground crew is on the runway, landing planes…
Plural Structural Bias:	If ground crews are very often on the runway, landing planes…

associative information from the initial clause. This associative information is most available when *if* introduces the initial clause.

These studies have shown that interclause relations influence comprehenders' attention to different kinds of information when listening to isolated sentences. Comprehenders attend to structural units such as syllables, words, and their position within a sentence during an adversative clause, but they attend to associations to words and events during a clause that fits directly into a causal chain. Thus, interclause relationships influence how comprehenders direct resources to structural versus associative information.

TEXT PROCESSING

Texts usually consist of more than one sentence. What effect does this have on processing clauses and their interrelationships? One possibility is that the knowledge that comprehenders gain from the earlier sentences in a text makes it unnecessary to identify clauses and the structure within them. Another possibility is that the earlier sentences of text can make available the background information that comprehenders need for placing events into a coherent representation of text. This background information may reduce the need for determining the relationships between clauses. For example, if the earlier sentences in a text provide information about anticipated causal relations, we might expect that comprehenders will integrate events immediately into a coherent representation of text whether the events serve a causal or adversative role. Does a larger text eliminate structural processing, or does it reduce the need for processing interclause relations?

Structural Processing of Clauses

We tested the hypothesis that text eliminates the processing of clauses by varying systematically the associative support for a clause (Townsend & Bever, 1989). The notion of scripts provided the framework for these tests. Scripts are memories that contain knowledge of the typical events that occur in ordinary situations, such as eating in a restaurant, visiting a doctor, and/or getting a flat tire while driving (Schank & Abelson, 1977). The early sentences in a text can activate these memories and influence subsequent memory for sentences and inferences (Singer, 1990). The question is whether these memories eliminate the structural processing of clauses. The fact that comprehenders retain better the structural details of sentences with weaker support from a script suggests that structural processing within clauses still occurs in larger texts (Bower,

Black, & Turner, 1979; Singer, 1990; Townsend, Carrithers, & Bever, 1987). Nevertheless, such results can be interpreted to show that strong support from a script renders structural processing irrelevant.

In a series of studies, we embedded a critical sentence in a passage that strongly or weakly supported the sentence (Townsend & Bever, 1989). There was strong support for the critical sentence when it stated an event that was central to the underlying script and weak support when it was peripheral. Some examples appear in Table 13.3.

We might expect that the second passage in Table 13.3 activates prior knowledge of what events typically occur when one has a flat tire. For example, one way of dealing with this situation is to replace the flat tire, and, to do that, one first has to remove it from the car. We might also expect that this passage activates particular lexical associations that are related to these events, such as *trunk, jack, wrench, remove, flat, tire,* and so on (Sharkey & Mitchell, 1985). Does the activation of these semantic and lexical associations eliminate structural processing?

In one study, subjects read texts line-by-line in a self-paced reading task. The lines randomly ended either at a clause boundary or just before the final word of a clause. A major variable was whether the critical sentence, *Jones took off the flat tire,* appeared entirely on one line, as in Example 5:

5. ...damaged and a fender was smashed in.
    Jones took off the flat tire.
    Then she installed the...

or as all but the last word of the sentence, as in Example 6:

6. ...damaged and a fender was smashed in.
    Jones took off the flat
    tire. Then she installed the...

TABLE 13.3
Passages with Weak versus Strong Associative Support for an Event

---

Weak Associative Support:

Jones found a wreck by the road. She found nothing suspicious inside the car. She examined the damage outside the car. The windshield was shattered. She noticed that one wheel was damaged and a fender was smashed in. *Jones took off the flat tire.* Then she installed the spare tire.

Strong Associative Support:

While driving her car, Jones heard a loud bang and a flapping sound. She stopped the car and set the brake. She took the jack, a wrench, and the spare from the trunk. She loosened the bolts on the wheel. She jacked up the car. *Jones took off the flat tire.* Then she installed the spare tire.

The critical data were times to read the line containing the complete target clause, *Jones took off the flat tire*, compared to a line containing all but the last word of the target clause, *Jones took off the flat*. To facilitate comparison, reading times were adjusted for number of words in the line. When the target clause appeared entirely on one line (Example 5), target line reading times were faster for passages with strong associative support than for passages with weak associative support. When the target clause was not entirely on one line (Example 6), target line reading times did not differ for passages with strong versus weak associative support for the target event. Since associative support had an effect on reading only complete clauses, it apparently does not eliminate structural processing prior to the end of a clause.

Intersentence Relations

Does the appearance of a sentence in a longer text affect the processing of interclause relations? Townsend (1983) provided several demonstrations that comprehenders process causal–temporal relations in text. For example, in a self-paced sentence reading task, subjects read texts such as Examples 7–8a or Examples 7–8b:

7. Harry began raising snakes on his farm.
8. a. Therefore, kids visited the farm everyday.
   b. However, kids visited the farm everyday.

A sentential connective from one of several points on the causal- temporal continuum of connectives introduced the target sentence (see Table 13.1). For example, *therefore* signals that the event in the second sentence is a conclusion that follows from the event in the first sentence, but *however* signals that the event in the second sentence occurred even though the event in the first sentence would have led one to expect some other event (Halliday & Hasan, 1976). The results showed that reading times for the target sentence depended on the causal-temporal meanings of the connectives. For example, reading times were faster for *therefore* sentences than for *however* sentences. Sentences that fit directly into a causal chain require less processing time than do sentences that require modification of a causal chain.

Interclause Relations

Self-paced reading times do not tell us whether causal connectives actually direct resources to semantic associations. In a second study using script-based stories (Townsend & Bever, 1989), found that *although* elicits greater attention to associative information than does *because*. Subjects listened to passages like those in Table 13.3. In this study, the clause containing the target event was introduced by either *because* or *although*. On certain trials, however, subjects heard all but the last word of the target clause, as in *Although Jones took off the flat*... At this point, the subjects heard a tone, then a phrase like *removing a tire*. Their task was to say whether or not the phrase was similar in meaning to what came before. As in the previous script-based study, it was expected that the passage about having a blowout while driving (Table 13.3) would elicit associations such as the idea of removing a tire, sequences of events such as "take off flat—install spare," or perhaps specific lexical associations such as *removing* and *tire*.

For *because* sentences, associative support had no effect on response times to *removing a tire*, but for *although* sentences, response times were significantly faster for the passage with strong associative support. These results suggest that supportive contexts increase attention to associative information only during adversative clauses, not during causal clauses. Apparently, a supportive text like the blowout passage makes available an expected sequence like "take off flat — install spare," and this sequence draws attention to the causal chain. The same expected sequence is available when *because* introduces the target event, but it is less effective, since *because* shifts attention toward the causal chain regardless of the context. Thus, background information from a text does not eliminate processing interclause relations, though it may modify this processing by making available information that is useful for establishing coherence.

LEARNING NEW WORDS

I began by pointing out that text comprehension is an example of knowledge acquisition, and I have suggested that knowledge acquisition generally consists of an integration of structural and associative information. This claim about text comprehension was supported by showing that the interclause relations that are cued by connectives influence the processing and memory of clauses in isolated sentences and in texts. In this section I show that the processing of interclause relations influences knowledge of unfamiliar words that appear in text. This extends the principle that processing interclause relations is a point of interaction between associative and structural processing.

People learn words primarily as a part of processing language in natural contexts (e.g., Van Daalen-Kapteijns & Elshout-Mohr, 1981; Nagy, Herman, & Anderson, 1985). Natural contexts provide many clues to the meanings of unfamiliar words. Sternberg and Powell (1983) suggested that several variables can mediate the use of these contextual clues to words and their meanings.

Recent research suggests that processing interclause relations is one factor that influences the acquisition of lexical knowledge.

Structural processing can contribute to the meanings we associate with words. For example, if an unfamiliar word appears in a clause after a noun that is known to be animate and before a noun that is known to be inanimate, one infers that the word is a transitive verb. This knowledge about the unfamiliar word depends on establishing a structural relation between words in the clause. Knowledge about unfamiliar words also may come from direct association. For example, part of our knowledge of adjectives like *dry* includes a specific antonym (*wet*). Our knowledge of other adjectives like *arid*, however, does not include a specific lexical association (Gross, Fischer, & Miller, 1989). Charles and Miller (1989) suggest that knowledge of antonyms like *dry* versus *wet* includes specific lexical associations because *dry* and *wet* appear more frequently within the same sentence, compared to more conceptual antonyms like *arid* and *humid*. If Charles and Miller (1989) are correct, this type of knowledge depends on forming an association between words that occur together, not on determining a structural relation between words.

Memory for New Words

Connectives affect memory for unfamiliar words that appear in text. In Townsend (1989), subjects read passages like those in Table 13.3, except that the word *flat* was replaced by a rare word that is conceptually related to it (e.g., *dehiscent*). This rare word appeared in the clause that was strongly or weakly supported by the preceding sentences in the text; the target clause was introduced by either *although* or *because*. After reading several passages like these, subjects received a word recognition test in which they had to indicate whether or not each of several test words appeared in any of the passages. When a rare target word had appeared in an *although* clause, strong associative support reduced response times for recognizing the target. When the target had appeared in a *because* clause, however, the level of associative support had no effect on target recognition times. Once again, the activation of an expected causal relation from the preceding sentences of the text had a greater effect on processing adversative clauses. In this case, the processing of interclause relations mediated simple recognition memory for unfamiliar words that appear in text.

Form Versus Meaning

Because of their different requirements for coherence, connectives also could affect what kinds of information comprehenders retain about unfamiliar words.

In Lehman (1990), subjects read two-sentence passages in a self-paced reading task. Either *because* or *although* introduced the second sentence which contained a rare medical term, as in *Children with measles will usually stay home from school. Although the girl had morbilli, she did not stay home from school.* After reading several passages like these, subjects were given two memory tests. The first test examined their memory for the orthographic form of the rare target word (e.g., *morbilli*). This test consisted of presenting, in random order, the target and two orthographically similar distractors (e.g., *morbilli, morbilous, morbility*), and asking the subjects which word had appeared in one of the passages. For the orthographic test, performance was better when the target word appeared in an *although* clause than when it appeared in a *because* clause. Comprehenders focused attention more on the orthographic form of rare lexical items when they read adversative clauses than when they read causal clauses.

The second memory test examined subjects' memory for the synonym that had appeared in the context sentence (e.g., *measles*). In this test, subjects were asked to select the best synonym for each target word from four items (e.g., *morbilli, measles, death, mumps, disease*). For the synonym test, performance was better when the target word had appeared in a *because* clause than when it had appeared in an *although* clause. It appears that comprehenders established an association between the rare target word and familiar words that appeared outside the sentence when it occurred in a causal clause. Thus, processing of interclause relations influences which kinds of information comprehenders retain about unfamiliar words that appear in text: adversatives lead to retention of structural aspects of words, while causals lead to retention of words that may be semantically associated.

CONCLUSION

Text comprehension involves an integration of linguistic structures and already known associative information. A fundamental structure in text is the clause. Associative information includes memories of words, events, and sequences of events. Structural information tends to require computation of intermediate memories whereas associative information tends to be activated directly. However, comprehenders can direct attentional resources toward the structural information in text or toward information that the text elicits by association. Because of the information they require to establish semantic coherence in a text, connectives induce comprehenders to direct these resources toward structural versus associative information. When there is little linguistic context, adversatives direct attention toward structural properties, whereas causals direct attention toward semantic associations. Two factors modify the effects of connectives. One factor is the availability of background information. Background information such as an expected causal relation can aid in developing a coherent text representation, particularly for adversative clauses, and, therefore, draws attention to associative meaning. A second factor that can modify the effects of connectives is the presence of an unfamiliar word. Unfamiliar words can negate the effects of context; they shift attention toward structural properties when they appear in adversatives but toward potential semantic associates when they appear in causals. Thus, text comprehension involves the interaction of structural and associative knowledge.

ACKNOWLEDGMENT

Preparation of this chapter was supported by a Distinguished Scholar Award from Montclair State University.

REFERENCES

Bower, G., Black, J., & Turner, T. (1979). Scripts in memory for text. *Cognitive Psychology, 11*, 177–220.

Charles, W., & Miller, G. (1989). Contexts of antonymous adjectives. *Applied Psycholinguistics, 10*, 357–375.

Gross, D., Fischer, U., & Miller, G. (1989). The organization of adjectival meanings. *Journal of Memory and Language, 28*, 92–106.

Halliday, M. A. K. & Hasan, R. (1976). *Cohesion in English.* London: Longman.

Haviland, S., & Clark, H. H. (1974). What's new? Acquiring new information as a process in comprehension. *Journal of Verbal Learning and Verbal Behavior, 13*, 512–521.

Johnson-Laird, P. N. (1988). *The computer and the mind.* Cambridge, MA: Harvard University Press.

Just, M. A., & Carpenter, P. A. (1992). A capacity theory of comprehension: Indivudual differences in working memory. *Psychological Review, 99*, 122–149.

Lehman, M. (1990). The effect of format, context, and connective on reading and understanding of medical terms by skilled and average readers. Unpublished master's thesis, Montclair State University, Upper Montclair, New Jersey.

McCabe, A., & Peterson, C. (1985). A naturalistic study of the production of causal connectives by children. *Journal of Child Language, 12*, 145–159.

Nagy, W. E., Herman, P. A., & Anderson, R. C. (1985). Learning words from context. *Reading Research Quarterly, 20*, 233–253.

Schank, R. C., & Abelson, R. (1977). *Scripts, plans, goals, and understanding.* Hillsdale, NJ: Lawrence Erlbaum Associates.

Sharkey, N. E., & Mitchell, D. C. (1985). Word recognition in a functional context: The use of scripts in reading. *Journal of Memory and Language, 24*, 253–270.

Singer, M. (1990). *Psychology of language: An introduction to sentence and discourse processes.* Hillsdale, NJ: Lawrence Erlbaum Associates.

Sternberg, R. J., & Powell, J. S. (1983). Comprehending verbal information. *American Psychologist*, 38, 878–893.

Townsend, D. J. (1983). Thematic processing in sentences and texts. *Cognition*, 13, 223–261.

Townsend, D. J. (1989). Discourse Processing Strategies of Skilled and Average Readers: Some Implications for Learning from Discourse. Psychonomic Society. November, Atlanta.

Townsend, D. J., & Bever, T. G. (1978). Inter-clause relations and clausal processing. *Journal of Verbal Learning and Verbal Behavior*, 17, 509–521.

Townsend, D. J., & Bever, T. G. (1982). Natural units of representation interact during sentence comprehension. *Journal of Verbal Learning and Verbal Behavior*, 21, 688–703.

Townsend, D. J., & Bever, T. G. (1989). Expertise and constraints on sentence processing. In *Proceedings of the Eleventh Annual Conference of the Cognitive Science Society* (p. 582–589). Hillsdale, NJ: Lawrence Erlbaum Associates.

Townsend, D. J., & Bever, T. G. (1991). The use of higher level constraints in monitoring for a change in speaker demonstrates functionally distinct levels of representation during discourse comprehension. *Language and Cognitive Processes*, 6, 49– 77.

Townsend, D. J., Carrithers, C., & Bever, T. G. (1987). Listening and reading processes in college- and middle school-age readers. In R. Horowitz & J. L. Samuels (Eds.), *Comprehending oral and written language*. (p. 217–242). New York: Academic Press.

Townsend, D. J., Hoover, M., & Bever, T. G. (1984, April). The Use of Monitoring Tasks for Investigating the Organization of Speech Comprehension Processes. Paper presented at the Eastern Psychological Association, Philadelphia, PA.

Townsend, D. J., & Ravelo, N. (1980). The development of complex sentence processing strategies. *Journal of Experimental Child Psychology*, 29, 60–73.

Trabasso, T., & van den Broek, P. (1985). Causal thinking and the representation of narrative events. *Journal of Memory and Language*, 24, 612–630.

Tyler, L. K., & Marslen-Wilson, W. (1977). The on-line effects of semantic context on syntactic processing. *Journal of Verbal Learning and Verbal Behavior*, 16, 683–692.

Van Daalen-Kapteijns, M. M., & Elshout-Mohr, M. (1981). The acquisition of word meanings as a cognitive learning process. *Journal of Verbal Learning and Verbal Behavior*, 20, 386–399.

Author Index

A

Abdi, H., 166–169, 171, 177, 181, 188, 197
Abelson, R. P., 162, 178, 268, 275, 281
Adam, J. M., 247, 249, 262
Adams, M., 114, 118
Akmajian, A., 53, 71
Aksu-Koç, A., 228, 241
Ammon, M., 237, 241
Anderson, A., 11, 19
Anderson, J. R., 79, 91
Anderson, R. C., 278, 281
Antinucci, F., 229, 241
Antoine, G., 246, 262
Antos, S. J., 59, 73
Applebee, A. N., 24, 46
Auchlin, A., 57, 73
Austin, J. L., 55, 71

B

Baillet, S. D., 14, 21, 79, 92
Bain, D., 204, 216, 245, 248, 262
Bally, C., 246, 262
Bamberg, M., 27, 29, 33, 46, 202, 216, 229, 235, 241
Banfield, A., 113, 118
Barbault, M. C., 57, 71
Barr, R., 151, 152
Bartlett, E. J., 27, 46
Bates, E., 3, 19, 227, 234, 235, 239, 241, 242
Baudet-Briquet, N., 68, 72
Baum, L. F., 96, 101, 105–109, 118
Beattie, G. W., 186, 196
Bebout, L. J., 143, 152
Becker, A., 185, 186, 199
Beeman, M., 4, 20
Bennett-Kastor, T. L., 27, 46
Bereiter, C., 188, 189, 196, 211, 217
Berman, R. A., 230, 241
Bern, H., 79, 91
Bert-Erboul, A., 65, 71
Bessonat, D., 182, 183, 194, 196
Bestgen, Y., 158, 159, 169, 175, 176, 177, 178, 183, 187, 196, 204–207, 209, 210, 211, 214–216, 216, 217

Bever, T. G., 56, 73, 78, 93, 237, 243, 270–272, 274–277, 282
Biasci, C., 247, 262
Bingham, G., 14, 21, 79, 92
Black, J. B., 12, 19, 79, 91, 276, 281
Blank, M., 122, 136
Bloom, L., 26, 27, 46, 56, 71, 99, 118, 121–123, 125, 126, 128, 132, 136, 137, 142, 143, 152, 153, 162, 177, 229, 214
Bolliger, C. M., 4, 12, 21
Bond, S. J., 185, 186, 196
Bonnotte, I., 229, 242
Botvin, G., 24, 25, 46
Bourcier, D., 247, 262
Bower, G. H., 12, 19, 215, 216, 217, 275, 281
Bracewell, R. J., 187, 188, 194, 198
Braddock, R., 185, 186, 196
Bradshaw, G. L., 79, 91
Braine, M. D. S., 55, 71
Bransford, J. D., 84, 92
Braunwald, S. R., 122–126, 136, 162, 177
Bray, R., 215, 216
Brent, S. B., 143, 153
Brewer, W. F., 25, 46
Brislin, R. W., 123, 136
Britton, B. K., 183, 184, 196
Bronckart, J. P., 157, 177, 204, 216, 229, 241, 245, 246, 248, 249, 251, 262, 263
Brown, G., 182, 183, 196
Brown, P., 14, 21, 79, 92, 188, 189, 193, 196
Bruder, G., 97, 119
Brunot, F., 246, 262
Bruthiaux, P., 160, 177
Bruxelles, S., 247, 262
Buczowska, E., 229, 243
Burtis, P. J., 188, 189, 196
Butterworth, B., 205, 216
Byrne, R. M. J., 55, 72
Byrnes, J. P., 121, 125, 131–133, 136

C

Caccamise, D. J., 188, 197
Cain, K., 4, 10, 21
Capatides, J., 121, 126, 132, 136

Subject Index